BLACK FOREST

CUISINE

THE CLASSIC BLENDING
of EUROPEAN FLAVORS

BLACK FOREST
CUISINE
THE CLASSIC BLENDING
of EUROPEAN FLAVORS

BY WALTER STAIB

with Jennifer Lindner McGlinn

RUNNING PRESS
PHILADELPHIA · LONDON

© 2006 by Walter Staib
Photographs © 2006 by William Deering
All rights reserved under the Pan-American and
International Copyright Conventions

Printed in China

*This book may not be reproduced in whole or in part, in any form
or by any means, electronic or mechanical, including photocopy-
ing, recording, or by any information storage and retrieval system
now known or hereafter invented, without written permission
from the publisher.*

9   8   7   6   5   4   3   2   1
Digit on the right indicates the number of this printing

Library of Congress Control Number: 2006920649

ISBN-13: 978-0-7624-2135-0
ISBN-10: 0-7624-2135-5

Cover and interior design by Frances J. Soo Ping Chow
Edited by Diana C. von Glahn
Food styling by Walter Staib
Typography: Bembo Titling, ITC Berkeley, Congress,
Copperplate, Mrs Saint-Delafield, and Voluta Script

This book may be ordered by mail from the publisher.
Please include $2.50 for postage and handling.
But try your bookstore first!

Running Press Book Publishers
125 South Twenty-Second Street
Philadelphia, Pennsylvania 19103-4399

Visit us on the web!
www.runningpresscooks.com
www.runningpress.com
www.blackforestcuisine.com

Table of Contents

First, I would like to thank my grandmother, Karoline Breuninger; my mother, Herta Staib; my uncle and aunt, Walter and Ruth Eberle; and my uncle, Karl Hintze, from whom I learned my true and lifelong passion for the culinary arts, and who taught me many of the recipes in this book.

My sincere thanks to my wife and business partner, Gloria, for supporting this and every other project I've ever undertaken, and for understanding most how much this book means to me. Your love and encouragement have been a constant source of strength and inspiration, for which I am eternally grateful.

Many, many thanks go to my Director of Marketing and Special Projects, Paul Bauer, who stewarded this project from inception to publishing, rewriting and refining recipes, compiling the manuscript, arranging the photography, handling the edits, etc. He is the "brains" of my operation and, as always, handled this project with aplomb.

Jennifer Lindner did such a great job as writer of the *City Tavern Baking & Dessert Cookbook* that I couldn't imagine asking anyone else to help with *Black Forest Cuisine*. Jennifer spent countless hours documenting and crafting all of the stories I remembered from this special period in my life. She is a very talented writer and has made an enormous contribution to this book. Through her writing she has helped me realize my lifelong dream of paying a special tribute to my homeland.

I owe a great debt of gratitude to Diana von Glahn, our editor, who was such an enthusiastic supporter of this project, and who lobbied to make this such a spectacular book. Also, special thanks to Frances Soo Ping Chow for making my vision come to life through her stunning design work!

Bill Deering is, without a doubt, the most talented photographer I know, and it was such a pleasure to work with him again!

Many thanks go to my Chef de Cuisine, Bill Sederman, and my Pastry Chef, John Burkart, who assisted with recipe testing, styling and how-to photography.

A special thanks goes to my brother, Peter, for his assistance with my rusty German.

A very heartfelt thanks goes to Dr. Tim Ryan, president of our nation's foremost culinary school, Culinary Institute of America, and to Franz Mitterer, publisher and founder of *Art Culinaire*, for their gracious Forewords.

I couldn't have done this without any of you!

FOREWORDS

MORE THAN A COOKBOOK

CHEF WALTER STAIB IS PROBABLY BEST KNOWN FOR HIS PASSIONATE RE-MASTERY OF EIGHTEENTH-CENTURY AMERICAN CUISINE, FEATURED ON THE MENU AT PHILADELPHIA'S CITY TAVERN. IN *BLACK Forest Cuisine*, this devoted student of history and cuisine takes us on a journey that looks back to his own childhood and formative culinary years in Germany's Black Forest.

Up until now, many of us might have held only a vague vision of the Black Forest—a region renowned for its dark, seemingly magical, woods; folk traditions; and, of course, rich namesake cake. In *Black Forest Cuisine*, Chef Staib's stories and recipes broaden our view of his homeland as he shares with us the many colorful experiences and memories that shaped his youth. His journey takes us to a variety of venues, each presenting traditional dishes in a manner unique to the region. We visit kitchens and tables in the home, café, Gasthaus, and Hotel, and finish with menus representative of celebratory holiday feasts.

The recipes Chef Staib shares with us convey the Black Forest's rich personality—one formed over the centuries as diverse peoples and influences left their flavorful marks on the culture. From Russian Eggs to Gingerbread; Vol-au-Vent with Veal Ragoût to Cream Puffs; Schlachtplatte to Spätzle; Herring à la Bonne Femme to Rice Pudding with Meringue; and Beignets to Wassail, Chef Staib shows us just how broad and varied Black Forest cuisine really is. **EACH RECIPE HAS A SPECIAL PLACE IN HIS MEMORY AND A PERSONAL STORY, REMINDING US THAT FOOD SHAPES AND DEFINES WHO WE ARE.** *Black Forest Cuisine* is, in fact, as much a memoir as it is a cookbook. As we learn about the region's cuisine, we also learn much about life in post-WWII Germany; about the importance community played in daily activities; and, in the midst of it all, about the making of a chef.

As a former chef-instructor and now president of the Culinary Institute of America, I have witnessed thousands of students journey toward their dreams of one day becoming successful chefs. They train hard, acquire new skills, gain discipline, and learn to utilize their own talents so they might one day achieve the goals they so desire. All of this is important and vital for success in such a competitive industry. Yet, I hope for them something more as well—something more deeply rooted and profound.

Not all of us are as fortunate as Chef Staib to have experienced such an early and sustained connectedness to food and cooking. Perhaps its rarity is what makes it all the more inspiring. It is the intense passion he displays throughout his childhood and apprenticeship that, I think more than anything else, is vital for young cooks to develop as early as possible and maintain as they go forward. A teacher cannot necessarily teach passion, but he or she can convey its meaningful importance to students. Throughout these pages, Chef Staib does just this.

I am hopeful that all who read the recipes and stories that follow will become better acquainted with the Black Forest and its cuisine. Even more, though, I hope that they gain renewed appreciation for the role that food and cooking play in our everyday lives.

DR. TIM RYAN, PRESIDENT
THE CULINARY INSTITUTE OF AMERICA

VIELEN DANK, Chef Staib

IWAS BORN AND RAISED NEAR BREGENZ, AUSTRIA, CLOSE TO THE BODENSEE—A RELATIVELY SMALL BODY OF WATER SHARED BY GERMANY, AUSTRIA, AND SWITZERLAND. BECAUSE OF OUR PROXIMITY TO THIS UNIFYING LAKE AND TO the southern border of the Black Forest, my family had the good fortune to eat, drink, and live in much the same manner as Chef Walter Staib and his family.

Growing, cooking, and preserving a variety of foods in accordance with the seasons was hardly considered trendy in the Germany and Austria of our youth. Modern innovations—such as international shipping, the availability of hydroponic produce, and industrial-strength refrigeration—were as yet unavailable, so we relied on traditional Old World ways of life. It didn't occur to me until I left Austria that I had been fortunate to eat fresh local products: meat from the butcher; cheese from the cheese maker; bread from the baker; and sweets from the *pâtisserie*. My mother worked in the home, preserving fruits and vegetables, maintaining the garden and root cellar, and preparing three hearty daily meals for the family. Our lives were naturally simple and seasonal.

When I left Austria in the 1970s to pursue a career as a chef in the United States, I never realized how much I would miss the foods and foodways of my native country. At that time, Austrian restaurants in America were practically nonexistent, and German restaurants presented a hopelessly diluted selection of heavy, greasy fare that failed to reflect the unique regional characteristics of such a large and diverse country. Now, some thirty years later, although German and Austrian cuisines enjoy slightly higher profiles in restaurants throughout the United States, they are still largely misunderstood. I am hopeful that Chef Staib's *Black Forest Cuisine* will enlighten and educate readers about this most special region of Germany.

On a personal level, the reminiscences and recipes Chef Staib shares have returned me to my family's table. They have elicited warm memories of such dishes as roast pork, *knödel*, and sauerkraut, which my mother prepared in the same manner as Chef Staib's mother. On a broader scale, I believe that Chef Staib's ode to the Schwarzwald offers readers yet unfamiliar with the region the opportunity to understand its unique and colorful foods and traditions.

Vielen Dank, Chef Staib, for giving us a glimpse into the Black Forest with the passion and generosity of spirit that are so inherent to your beautiful homeland.

FRANZ MITTERER
PUBLISHER/FOUNDER, ART CULINAIRE

A WORD from CHEF STAIB

EVER SINCE I BECAME CHEF/PROPRIETOR OF PHILADELPHIA'S HISTORIC CITY TAVERN RESTAURANT, I HAVE WAITED FOR THE OPPORTUNITY TO PAY TRIBUTE TO MY NATIVE BLACK FOREST IN GERMANY. ALTHOUGH I have authored two cookbooks on colonial American cuisine, *City Tavern Cookbook* and *City Tavern Baking & Dessert Cookbook*, my desire to write about this fabled region has persisted. In the book before you, my dream of memorializing the way of life and food I experienced as a child and as a young culinary apprentice has finally come true. The pages that follow represent years of joyful food memories, and I happily share them with you.

The food and culture of the Black Forest remain mysterious, even to those who are familiar with German traditions. **THIS SOUTHWEST REGION—BORDERED BY SWITZERLAND TO THE SOUTH AND FRANCE TO THE WEST—IS INDEED PART OF GERMANY, BUT ITS UNIQUE TERRAIN AND HISTORICALLY DIVERSE POPULATION GIVE IT A PERSONALITY ALL ITS OWN. THE REGION'S CUISINE OF COURSE REFLECTS THIS.** To speak of German food as a single category not only denies its regional differences, but is also simply incorrect. Over the centuries, the Black Forest has developed its own culinary traditions and characteristics, and I have tried my best to represent many of them in the recipes I have chosen for this book.

Understanding how the Black Forest came to be so different from the rest of Germany requires a brief history recap. When Catholic King Louis XIV revoked the Edict of Nantes in 1685, the protestant Huguenots found themselves the subjects of a religious witch-hunt and fled France. Huguenots escaping Burgundy settled just across the French border in protestant-friendly Alsace-Lorraine, Switzerland, and the Black Forest region of Germany. These immigrants carried with them well-established French traditions of hospitality and gastronomy, little

My Maternal Grandparents Gasthaus zum Buckenberg

known in Germany at the time. The region quickly became infused with them, and this food- and-family-centered *joie de vivre* transformed into a *Freude zu leben* that has contributed to the area's uniqueness ever since.

MY MATERNAL GRANDFATHER DESCENDED FROM THE EARLY HUGUE-NOTS WHO IMMIGRATED TO THE BLACK FOREST. HE WAS A TRUE BON VIVANT AND EPICURE. HIS ENTIRE FAMILY, IN FACT, HAD A REPUTATION FOR GREAT CULINARY PROWESS AND CONVIVIAL HOSPITALITY. Growing up in this family of chefs and restaurateurs, I knew early on that my life would somehow revolve around food. Out of a long line of relatives, brothers, sisters, cousins, and nephews, my family always believed I was the one who would commit to a culinary career. They were right.

Even as a child, I displayed a passion for food and cooking. At the age of four, I started spending most of my free time in the kitchen at my aunt and uncle's establishment, *Gasthaus zum Buckenberg*. My uncle worked mostly in the butcher shop, while my aunt spent most of her time cooking and organizing daily menus. I loved working with both of them.

My parents recognized my enthusiasm for the culinary arts. Thanks to their vision and persistence, I had the opportunity to apprentice in a superior establishment, the Hotel Post in Nagold, which was established in 1773. This elegant hotel was renowned for its cuisine and many high-profile patrons, including Napoleon Bonaparte. By the time I began my three-year apprenticeship there, I had already acquired ten years of cooking experience at the *Gasthaus zum Buckenberg*. I was familiar with the routines of a professional kitchen and was armed with much more culinary knowledge and savvy than most of my classmates. My uncle had even taught me how to butcher meat and make sausages—advanced skills for a 14-year-old apprentice. Needless to say, within weeks of arriving at the Hotel Post, I had set myself apart from the other culinary students. Many of the recipes I learned to prepare in these early years have become some of my most cherished, and I have included them here.

My apprenticeship at the Hotel Post

By the time I finished my apprenticeship at the Hotel Post, I had achieved the status of a young professional chef. The military-like system in which I trained had taught me much, but I knew I still needed more experience in order to advance in the culinary field. I decided, therefore, to travel to Bad Wildbad and work at the Sommerberg Hotel. It was there that I became skilled in preparing the elegant cuisine for which the Black Forest is so well known.

As I moved on, working in other restaurants in Switzerland, Italy, and France, I realized that my culinary training in the Black Forest had prepared me well to become a competitive and well-respected young chef. One of my greatest experiences took place in Gstaad, Switzerland. There, the Aga Khan's restaurant, The Chessery, recruited me for the *chef de grille* position. (This chef, always outgoing and multi-lingual, is stationed in the dining room to prepare dishes in view of the guests, often tableside on a guéridon.) The work was challenging and helped me to hone my skills. I admit it was also exciting to work at such a swanky establishment—one recognized by many at the time as *the playground of the rich and famous.*

While in Switzerland, I took advantage of many other culinary opportunities as well. I worked for the Vatican at the Casa Berno in Ascona; I was *chef de cuisine* at Beau Rivage in Neuchâtel; and I worked at the Hotel Belvedere in Interlacken, from which I was recruited to cook in the United States. I agreed to work for only one year in America, fully intending to return to my hometown of Pforzheim and take the reins of the family restaurant, *Gasthaus zum Buckenberg*. Ultimately, however, my culinary journey was to take me in a different direction.

Once in the United States, I worked at Chicago's luxurious Mid-America Club and then as executive chef at the Hyatt Regency in Atlanta. A few years later, I moved to Brazil to consult on the development of several five-star resorts there. In the late 1970s and 1980s, I worked for a number of

*Chef de grille
at the Chessery
Chef Staib
at City Tavern*

prominent hotel corporations and traveled to restaurants throughout the world. These many experiences led me to start my own company, Concepts by Staib, Ltd., in 1989, and my travels continued to such places as Russia, Thailand, and the Caribbean. These were exciting years, filled with new challenges and inspiring events. Still, memories of the Black Forest continued to inspire me everyday, and I gratefully relied on the skills and repertoire I had developed during my years as a young apprentice.

In 1994, when I took over the historic City Tavern in Philadelphia, I discovered that life in eighteenth-century America paralleled traditional Black Forest culture in more ways than I ever could have imagined. When Germans began settling in Pennsylvania in 1680, they arrived with cooking techniques and recipes that they applied to the climate and foodstuffs of the New World. They maintained time-honored methods of preparing food, such as storing, preserving, and butchering local produce and meat, and even continued to follow many Old World recipes. When I was growing up in the Black Forest, we were, in many ways, still practicing the traditional cookery our ancestors transplanted to America two hundred years earlier.

Hospitality truly flourished during the post-World War II years of my early childhood, and it is this period I have tried to capture in *Black Forest Cuisine*. The flavorful recipes that follow are easy to prepare at home. Nearly all of the ingredients are available at local markets, and for those that are a bit more unique, I have provided a list of reliable sources. I encourage you to try these dishes so you may experience for yourself the uniqueness and magic of the Black Forest.

Guten Appetit!

WELCOME TO
THE BLACK FOREST

by Jennifer Lindner McGlinn

"FAREWELL, YE WORLD,
YOUR CONVERSATION IRKS ME."

IN JOHANN JACOB CHRISTOFFEL VON GRIMMELSHAUSEN'S RENOWNED SEVENTEENTH-CENTURY ROMANCE NOVEL, *DER ABENTEURLICHE SIMPLI-CISSIMUS*, THE PROTAGONIST, SIMPLICISSIMUS, SPEAKS THIS SENTIMENT upon withdrawing from the world to live as a hermit. Grimmelshausen, who wrote the novel while living in the Black Forest, also found elements of his "modern" society and changing world distracting and troublesome. Undoubtedly, many of us today can find everyday life to be loud, complicated, and downright irksome. As a result, we look to faraway places and traditions of the past to quiet, soothe, and lift our spirits. We are doing just that as we return to the Grimmelshausen's homeland in *Black Forest Cuisine*.

The following chapters reveal a region that has, in many ways, remained much the same for hundreds of years. These pages, however, focus on neither Simplicissimus' seventeenth century nor the present, but, rather, on a brief span of time during the mid-1900s. These post-World War II years define Chef Walter Staib's Black Forest as a period when hospitality and culinary skill were highly prized and respected. During this time, Old World traditions remained largely intact, and daily life was filled with real events and characters that might have inspired the fanciful fairy tales and folklore of earlier centuries.

The Black Forest lies in the southwest of Germany, bordered by Switzerland to the south and France to the west. The region has been populated for more than 2000 years, settled by Celts in the fifth century B.C. and later inhabited by the Romans 400 years later. The Romans first coined the term *silva nigra* (black forest) due to the region's dense forested areas. Naturally occurring warm springs enticed them to build formal baths, which still exist today and are celebrated at elegant spas in cities like Baden-Baden, Bad Dürrheim, Bad Wildbad, and Hinterzarten. Germanic tribes largely replaced Roman communities in 1000 A.D., clearing land and building monasteries and towns. Growth continued throughout the centuries as dynasties developed and disintegrated and territories coalesced and scattered. The years following World War II saw more change. Two major regions joined to create a single state, giving the *Schwarzwald* the formal name of Baden-Württemberg.

Although part of Germany, the Black Forest has developed a character all its own over the centuries. In this small corner of the country, German traditions mingle with those of France, Alsace, Switzerland, Italy, Austria, and even Hungary and Poland. As in many areas of Europe, the people of the Black Forest have always been a hearty bunch who enjoys physical activity. The region is renowned for its skiing, biking, and, of course, hiking. It is still common, in fact, for folks to spend a full Saturday or Sunday on foot pursuing a special pastry or the *plat du jour* in a café far from home.

Chef Staib's Black Forest focuses mostly in the northern part of the region. He grew up in Pforzheim, a mere twenty-five minute drive from the Black Forest's northernmost city of Karlsruhe and only forty-five minutes from Strasbourg in Alsace. The Romans founded the city at the point where the Nagold, the Enz, and the Würm Rivers intersect, giving easy access to the region. Recognizing this, they were the first to name the city *portus* (gateway). The name has endured, and Pforzheim is still referred to today as the "gateway of the Black Forest."

Like most Black Forest cities, Pforzheim is recognized for its unique trades and special areas of interest. **IT IS KNOWN AS THE GOLD CITY DUE TO ITS PROSPEROUS JEWELRY AND WRISTWATCH INDUSTRIES, AND HAS LONG BEEN RECOGNIZED AS THE LEADER OF GERMAN CLOCK MAKING. THE CUCKOO CLOCK IS, OF COURSE, THE MOST FAMOUS OF BLACK FOREST CLOCKS.** Clock making requires long hours of focused time as well as an abundance of wood, and eighteenth- and nineteenth-century Black Forest families certainly had lots of both during the long, cold, housebound winters.

The twists and turns of the Nagoldtal lead south from Pforzheim to the town of Nagold. It was there that at just fourteen years of age, Chef Staib began

Thermal Bath
Cuckoo Clock

17

his culinary apprenticeship at the acclaimed Hotel Post. Unlike his hometown, which sustained much wartime damage, Nagold remains much the same as it did when it was established 750 years ago. The Nagold River, half-timber houses, elliptical street plan, and various Romanesque and medieval sites lend historic richness to the elegant and prestigious hotels and restaurants that continue to thrive in the area.

Following the Enz River southwest from Pforzheim, you arrive at the spa town of Bad Wildbad, where aristocrats have vacationed since the early 1900s to enjoy the thermal baths. It was there, among miles of hiking paths on Sommerberg mountain, mountain marshes, and incomparable views, that Chef Staib continued his esteemed culinary training.

The Pforzheim, Nagold, and Bad Wildbad of Chef Staib's youth are representative of mid-twentieth-century Black Forest towns. Although the war made life throughout the region more challenging, family, community, and Old World traditions continued to shape and give meaning to everyday routines.

At that time, daily life in the Black Forest was filled with events and characters that, for most of us today, only exist in magical fairy tales and enchanting folklore. There was the man who went from house to house with a cart slicing cabbage for sauerkraut, and another who made special home deliveries of frozen cod. There was the neighborhood lady who traveled through town selling eggs from her basket, and the man who sold homemade tisanes (herbal teas) door to door. Another man made frequent stops at each house to sharpen scissors and knives, while yet another delivered vegetable oil from a huge vat. Chef Staib's Black Forest is one where frozen leeks and Brussels sprouts were harvested with bare fingers in the winter; where families hiked for hours through the dense woods for a much-anticipated slice of cake at a café; where freshly-made sausages hung from bedroom rafters to cure; and where a King and Queen of Asparagus were crowned each spring.

Some of these traditions and ways of life continue still, but certainly not to the extent that they did sixty years or centuries ago. *Black Forest Cuisine* is a mere glimpse back in time to a region that is still rich in tradition despite inevitable cultural and social changes. As Simplicissimus lamented, modern life can indeed be irksome. Rather than becoming reclusive, though, stepping back in time and place can often be refreshing and enlightening. I hope you find this the case as you read on.

—JLM

The
HOME
TABLE

~ා

THERE WAS SOMETHING VERY SPECIAL ABOUT GROWING UP IN THE BLACK FOREST DURING THE AFTERMATH OF WORLD WAR II. AS A BOY IN PFORZHEIM, GERMANY, MY HOME AND FAMILY WERE THE CENter of my universe. We lived in a close-knit community and our home reflected this. It was a crowded, busy, and wonderful place, with my parents, siblings, grandparents, and cousins all living under one roof. Like almost every other family who lived in the Black Forest in those days, we raised livestock, kept numerous large gardens, and tended to our orchards. We lived in Old-World fashion, at once intensely self-reliant and also intimately linked with our community.

Times have changed so much that it is difficult to convey how significant the preparation and enjoyment of food were to families like ours. Convenience stores and supermarkets were nonexistent. We relied on our local butcher for sausages and other specialty meats and purchased bread from local bakeries, but we mostly ate the meat and poultry we raised and the fruit and vegetables we grew. During the warm months, we enjoyed a wide variety of fresh produce, while in the colder months, we feasted on the fruits and vegetables my mother and grandmother preserved. When the milk bottles were poured dry, we had to work to refill them. Our goats assisted us with this, and we only hoped that when we were ready, they were, too.

For those unaccustomed to rural living, this way of life might sound quite difficult and taxing. Although it was demanding, it was also wonderful. In this environment, where we had to constantly work to nourish ourselves, the table was the embodiment of success, of the benefits of hard labor, and of community coming together to celebrate bounty and blessings. It also represented the order and discipline required to make it so. Unlike today when we run out for a sandwich for lunch or pick up a ready-made dinner to toss in the microwave, my mother planned nearly every meal in advance. This was as much in keeping with her personality as it was a necessity of circumstance. She needed time to organize ingredients and prepare a variety of wholesome dishes for our large family. When the summer garden was filled with tomatoes and the herbs were flourishing, for example, we would feast on tomato and basil salad many times during the week. If she made a huge pot of split pea soup, she might also have bought some frankfurters from the butcher to toss in as a special treat. When preparing my beloved Maultaschen (meat-stuffed ravioli), she would make a huge pile and serve the tender morsels sautéed, in soup, or cold throughout the week. If there were apples going soft and shriveled in the root cellar, we could pretty much bet an apple strudel was in our future. My mother's cooking was organized, orderly, and practical, and she relied on the preparedness of her pantry as well as on the availability of fresh, seasonal ingredients to ensure that it remained so.

During the week, food at home was ample but simple. For breakfast, we might have had a simple boiled egg and a bit of bread and preserves. Lunch and supper dishes were pretty much interchangeable, although supper was usually the lightest meal of the day. My mother often prepared basic dishes like quiche and, even though it was expensive, she sometimes treated us by adding Black Forest Ham. She always kept herring on hand, as well as cold cuts, pota-toes, and the ingredients for spätzle, which she could make at a moment's notice. Of course, sauerkraut was a staple, too. We prepared it ourselves from cabbage we grew, leaving it to ferment in large vats in the cellar alongside the root vegetables and apples stored there. We ate lots of soups, stews, ragoûts, and casseroles throughout the year as well, many prepared with fresh chicken, rabbit, lamb, and pork from our farm. These warming dishes were made even more sub-stantial with rolls, pretzels, or rye or pumpernickel bread we bought daily from the local bakery. In the Black Forest, most bread is baked in gigantic loaves and sold in large pieces. Like every family, we stored our bread in a breadbox and used the bread slicer that sat beside it to slice pieces as needed.

MANY CENTURIES-OLD FOLKWAYS PERSIST IN THE BLACK FOREST AND A KITCHEN WITCH IS ONE OF THE MOST POPULAR. EVEN IN MODERN HOMES, SHE IS SEEN HANGING IN THE KITCHEN STRADDLING HER BROOM AS IF IN FLIGHT. LIKE HEX SIGNS ON PENNSYLVANIA GERMAN BARNS, SAINT FRANCIS OF ASSISI STATUES IN GARDENS, AND GRAPEVINE WREATHS IN WINE CELLARS, THE KITCHEN WITCH IS A TALISMAN WHOSE POPULARITY HAS CONTINUED FOR GENERA-TIONS. SOMETIMES PLACED OVER THE STOVE, IN A KITCHEN DOOR-WAY, OR NEAR THE KITCHEN TABLE, SHE IS BELIEVED TO CONFER GOOD LUCK ON THE COOK. KITCHEN WITCHES WERE ORIGINALLY CRAFTED AT HOME OUT OF STRAW, TWIGS, AND BITS OF MATERIAL. NOW THEY ARE SOLD COMMERCIALLY AND ARE AVAILABLE IN A VARIETY OF SHAPES, SIZES, AND COSTUMES. REGARDLESS OF HER APPEARANCE, HOWEVER, THE KITCHEN WITCH IS BELIEVED TO ASSIST THE COOK IN PREPARING SUCCESSFUL, FLAVORFUL DISHES AND IN MAINTAINING THE CLOSENESS OF THE FAMILY.

Lunches and dinners were as often sweet as they were savory. We loved cream of wheat, sometimes enjoying it hot and creamy like polenta, and other times cooled, cut, fried, and served with syrup or preserves. *Berliner* (doughnuts) also made sweet lunches, and my mother made

them often. My mother was, and still is, a wonderful baker, so the cookie jar was usually full and we always had cake or pie for dessert. Unlike in America, where we visit bakeries for whole cakes and large pastries, folks in the Black Forest visit *Konditorei* (pastry shops) and cafés for special plated confections. Like most women of her day, my mother baked every week, relying on ingredients she kept in the pantry and using any fresh or preserved fruit she had on hand.

If weekday meals were simple, Sunday dinners were something else again. What productions! The dishes we enjoyed were still fairly basic, but the table was downright overflowing with them. The first person to awaken on Sunday walked to the bakery for fresh bread. My mother spent most of the morning preparing the big mid-day meal, which she completed and served after church. Roasts or slow-cooked braised meats, vegetable dishes, and salads were among the delicacies we enjoyed, and in great abundance. Visitors often stopped by as well, so the table was always prepared *just in case*. Of course, desserts were bountiful, too. Never did I experience a Sunday without a cake, or two, or three! A typical Sunday might have included a cheesecake, a fruit tart, and a kugelhopf. My mother would bake a variety of things, set them aside in the coldest room in the house, and serve them with whipped cream for dessert or as snacks for guests.

Every Sunday was a celebration, and the eau de vie (*Schnaps*) and hard cider flowed perhaps even more freely than they did during the week. The Black Forest is renowned for its many varieties of eau de vie, crystal clear brandies distilled from the juice of the region's abundant fruit. We made our own eaux de vie from the bushels of mirabelle plums, pears, and berries that we picked from our orchards. My mother used much of the fruit for preserves, in desserts and the like, but there was always such a great quantity of fruit that we able to prepare various eaux de vie each year. We relied on our neighbor several houses down to assist us with the task, as he had a large still and made a business of transforming the fruit folks took to him into bottles of clear fire. Hard cider made us equally happy. Every year we prepared it ourselves from the apples we picked in the orchards. First we pressed the fruit, then set barrels of the juice in the cellar. There, over a period of weeks, it fermented in the company of the root vegetables and sauerkraut, its sweet personality slowly relenting to its conversion into potent alcohol.

Looking back now on the post-war years that shaped my childhood, I have great respect and admiration for my family who found the resources to feed our bodies and spirits with abundant nourishment. These were lean, challenging times in many respects, but as a boy I believed all was well with the world. We all worked together to keep house and tend to the garden, orchards, and livestock and we learned to take pride in our responsibilities. Whether I was charged with picking frozen Brussels sprouts from the winter garden, my fingers numbed to the bone, or turning fruit in the root cellar to keep it from spoiling, or basting a roast, I was happy that my mother trusted me enough to assign me such important tasks. Granted, the end results were sometimes less successful than planned. One time, I cheated and exchanged the big bowl to be filled with digit-freezing Brussels sprouts for a smaller one so I wouldn't have to pick so many. I'm sure I didn't always turn every apple in the root cellar. And at least once I did let a very important stuffed veal I was in charge of basting burn to a crisp. I learned from all of these experiences, though. Mostly I came to respect my parents' hard work and authority. Time after time, my flawed, youth-driven attempts at detours proved they really did know best.

AMONG THE MANY FOODS AND BEVERAGES FOR WHICH THE BLACK FOREST IS RENOWNED, THE CLEAR, COLORLESS LIQUOR KNOWN AS **SCHNAPS** IS ONE OF THE MOST HIGHLY CELEBRATED. LITERALLY TRANSLATED AS "MOUTHFUL," THIS DRINK IS REALLY NO DIFFERENT FROM **EAU DE VIE**—A CLEAR, DRY, AND POTENT BRANDY OR SPIRIT DISTILLED FROM FERMENTED FRUIT. IT IS NOT TO BE CONFUSED, HOWEVER, WITH AMERICAN SCHNAPPS, WHICH IS DISTILLED FROM GRAINS OR POTATOES. THESE VARIETIES ARE QUITE DIFFERENT FROM GERMAN SCHNAPS, AS THEY CAN BE SWEET OR DRY AND ARE OFTEN FLAVORED WITH HERBS OR SPICES.

THE PRODUCTION OF SCHNAPS RELIES ON THE ABUNDANCE OF FRUIT AVAILABLE IN THE BLACK FOREST. VIRTUALLY ANY FRUIT, INCLUDING CHERRIES, PEACHES, BERRIES, AND PLUMS, ARE SUITABLE FOR MAKING SCHNAPS, AND VARIOUS TOWNS ARE RENOWNED FOR PARTICULAR TYPES. BAD WILBAD, FOR EXAMPLE, IS WELL KNOWN FOR ITS CHERRY SCHNAPS, OR KIRSCHWASSER. ALL VARIETIES OF SCHNAPS, THOSE MADE FROM A SINGLE FRUIT AS WELL AS **OBSTLER** (MIXED FRUIT SCHNAPS), ARE PRODUCED IN **SCHNAPSBRENNEREI** (DISTILLERIES) AROUND THE REGION. THE FRUIT IS FIRST PICKED, PITTED OR STONED IF NECESSARY, AND SET IN LARGE BARRELS TO FERMENT. AFTER FERMENTING FOR SEVERAL WEEKS, THE FRUIT AND JUICES ARE TAKEN TO LOCAL DISTILLERIES, WHERE THEY ARE DISTILLED AND BOTTLED OR POURED INTO JUGS.

SCHNAPS IS PRODUCED ON LARGE AND SMALL SCALES IN THE BLACK FOREST. IT IS TYPICAL FOR FAMILIES TO ENGAGE IN THE PROCESS TOGETHER, PICKING THE FRUIT, SETTING IT TO FERMENT, AND TAKING IT TO THE DISTILLERY. THE GOVERNMENT PERMITS EACH FAMILY TO PRODUCE A CERTAIN AMOUNT OF SCHNAPS EACH YEAR TAX FREE, AND IT IS ENJOYED IN THE HOME AS A **DIGESTIF**, USED FOR MEDICINAL PURPOSES, AND ADDED TO CONFECTIONS AND BAKED GOODS.

At an early age, I came to understand that cooking is an admirable craft and that carefully and lovingly prepared food deserves appreciation. In my family, written recipes passed from generation to generation are prized possessions. To this day, women in the Black Forest still cook from recipe books kept by their mothers and their mothers' mothers. Sure, we improvised here and there, but I suspect that for these women following recipes was, and still is, a way of remaining connected not only to family members but also to respected methods and techniques.

Food shapes our history in both the preparation and eating of it. All of the chapters in this book demonstrate this. Yet, this chapter in particular, devoted entirely to home cooking and my memories of it, is a testament to the people, the events, and the food that influenced me so profoundly that I chose to devote my life to passionately, joyfully, nourishing others.

Russian Eggs

RUßISCHE EIER

I F I HAD TO CHOOSE THE MOST POPULAR DISH IN THE BLACK FOREST, THIS MIGHT BE THE ONE. IT IS SERVED THROUGHOUT THE REGION IN HOMES AS WELL AS IN ALL TYPES OF RESTAURANTS. EASY TO PREPARE ANY TIME OF YEAR, RUßISCHE EIER ARE USUALLY SERVED UNADORNED OR WITH A LITTLE PARSLEY AT HOME. IN CAFÉS AND RESTAURANTS, WHERE THE DISH IS MOST OFTEN SPRUCED UP, COOKS TAKE GREAT CARE TO FINELY CUT THE VEGETABLES INTO PERFECT TINY CUBES CALLED BRUNOISE, AND THE EGGS ARE SERVED WITH DELIGHTFUL LITTLE SPOONFULS OF CAVIAR, AS I HAVE SUGGESTED HERE. ENJOY THESE EGGS ANY TIME OF DAY AS WE STILL DO IN THE BLACK FOREST. THEY ARE LOVELY AS SNACKS, OR FOR LUNCH OR DINNER AS PART OF A SALAD OR COLD BUFFET.

1. Whisk together the mayonnaise, mustard, Worcestershire sauce, salt, pepper, and cayenne pepper in a medium bowl to make a dressing.

2. Combine the carrots, celery root, potatoes, and peas in a large bowl. Reserve 1 cup of the dressing for serving and gently toss the vegetables with the remaining dressing.

3. To serve, place several leaves of lettuce on each plate and spoon the vegetables overtop. Slice the eggs in half lengthwise and arrange two halves on top of each plate of vegetables. Spoon the remaining dressing neatly over the top and garnish, spooning a dollop of caviar on top of each egg half and garnish with parsley.

In this recipe, carrots, celery root, and potato are all cut to the size of fresh peas

Serves 8

2½ cups Mayonnaise (page 314)

1 teaspoon powdered mustard

1 teaspoon Worcestershire sauce

1 teaspoon salt

1 teaspoon freshly ground white pepper

¼ teaspoon ground cayenne pepper

1 cup finely cubed carrots, cooked and cooled

1 cup finely cubed celery root, cooked and cooled

1 medium potato, peeled, cut into small cubes, cooked, and cooled (about 1 cup)

1 cup fresh peas, cooked and cooled

2 heads Bibb lettuce, cored and leaves separated

8 hard-cooked eggs, cooled and peeled (see Chef's Note)

Salmon or sturgeon caviar, for garnish

Chopped fresh curly-leaf parsley, for garnish

CHEF'S NOTE: To make no-fail hard-cooked eggs, place the eggs in a small saucepan and cover with cold water. Bring the water to a boil, remove from the heat, cover, and let sit for 10 to 12 minutes. (In the Black Forest, we traditionally add 1 tablespoon of white vinegar along with the water to help seal the eggs in case some crack during cooking.) Drain the eggs and set under cold running water to cool.

Stuffed Tomatoes

GEFÜLLTE TOMATEN

1. Slice the tops off of the tomatoes and scoop out the seeds and membranes, leaving enough flesh on the sides to keep the shells firm. Set the tomatoes in a dish, cover with plastic wrap, and refrigerate for 1 hour.

2. Stir together the mustard and vinegar in a small bowl and slowly drizzle in the olive oil, whisking constantly. Stir in the red onion, pickles, and chives and season the dressing with salt and pepper.

3. Combine the bologna and cheese in a medium bowl and pour the dressing overtop, tossing gently to coat.

4. Spoon the dressed sausage and cheese filling into the tomatoes. Place each tomato on a plate and garnish with a handful of lettuce.

WHEN MY FAMILY'S RICH GREEN GARDEN BECAME COLORFULLY SPECKLED WITH TOMATOES DURING THE SUMMER, WE KNEW IT WOULDN'T BE LONG BEFORE STUFFED TOMATOES APPEARED ON OUR DINING TABLE. QUICK TO PREPARE AND FILLED WITH FRESH INGREDIENTS, WE GENERALLY ENJOYED THEM FOR A SIMPLE LUNCH OR AS PART OF A COLD BUFFET WHEN MY FAMILY ENTERTAINED AT DINNER. SET ON TOP OF MY FAVORITE POTATO SALAD (PAGE 123), THERE IS NO BETTER SUMMER MEAL.

Serves 8

8 large ripe tomatoes

2 teaspoons Dijon mustard

½ cup red wine vinegar

¼ cup olive oil

1 red onion, peeled and finely chopped

2 dill pickles, sliced into thin strips
  about 2 inches long and ⅛-inch wide

2 tablespoons chopped fresh chives

Salt

Freshly ground black pepper

1 pound bologna, sliced into thin strips
  about 2 inches long and ⅛-inch wide

8 ounces Swiss cheese, sliced into thin strips
  about 2 inches long and ⅛-inch wide

Bibb Lettuce, for garnish

Lentil Soup

LINSEN SUPPE

1. At least 8 hours before serving the soup, pour the lentils into a colander and rinse thoroughly, removing any stones or hard bits. Remove the lentils to a large bowl, add water until the lentils are covered by about 1 inch, and set aside at room temperature for 8 hours or overnight. The next day, or when ready to prepare the soup, drain and rinse the lentils and set aside.

2. Heat the vegetable oil in a large saucepan over medium-high heat. Add the onions and sauté until slightly softened, about 1½ minutes. Add the carrots and sauté until slightly softened, about 2 minutes more. Add the garlic and continue to sauté until tender but not brown, about 1 more minute.

3. Add the lentils, stock, bay leaf, and thyme. Bring to a boil over high heat, reduce the heat to medium, and simmer for about 1 hour, or until the lentils have become soft and the consistency of purée.

4. Remove the bay leaf and thyme sprig, season with salt and pepper and serve the soup in a tureen or in individual soup bowls.

HEARTY, SATISFYING, AND FLAVORFUL, LENTILS ARE A STAPLE THROUGHOUT THE BLACK FOREST. NEARLY ANY VARIETY OF LENTILS WILL WORK WELL IN THIS SOUP, ALTHOUGH I SUGGEST YOU RESERVE FRENCH LENTILS FOR SALADS AND OTHER MORE DELICATE PREPARATIONS.

ENJOY THIS DISH SERVED SIMPLY, AS WE DID DURING THE COLD MONTHS, OR ADD SOME SPÄTZLE AND SAUSAGE, SUCH AS FRANKFURTERS, FOR A HEARTIER SOUP MORE TYPICALLY FOUND IN RESTAURANTS. REFRIGERATE LEFTOVERS IN AIRTIGHT CONTAINERS FOR UP TO ONE WEEK. THIS SOUP CAN ALSO BE FROZEN, BUT THE VEGETABLES HAVE A TENDENCY TO BECOME MUSHY WHEN REHEATED.

Serves 8 to 10

½ cup lentils

¼ cup vegetable oil

2 medium yellow onions, peeled and finely chopped

2 large carrots, peeled and finely chopped

2 cloves garlic, peeled and finely chopped

2½ quarts Chicken Stock (page 308)

1 dried bay leaf

1 sprig fresh thyme

Salt

Freshly ground black pepper

Cabbage Soup

WEIßKOHL SUPPE

THIS HEARTY SOUP COMES TOGETHER QUICKLY AND IS PERFECT FOR
COOL WEATHER LUNCHES OR LIGHT DINNERS. TAKE THE TROUBLE
TO FIND YUKON GOLD POTATOES FOR THIS DISH IF POSSIBLE. THEY
ARE QUITE SIMILAR TO THE GERMAN YELLOW POTATOES WE USE IN THE
BLACK FOREST AND THEY MARRY MARVELOUSLY WITH MARJORAM, ONE OF
THE REGION'S MOST POPULAR HERBS.

OMIT THE BACON AND SAUSAGE FOR A VEGETARIAN SOUP, OR ADD
SOME HUNGARIAN PAPRIKA FOR COLOR AND A BIT OF SWEET SPICINESS.

---

1. Melt the butter in a 6-quart saucepan over medium heat, add the bacon, and sauté until lightly browned, about 3 minutes. Add the onion, sautéing for about 2 minutes more, and toss in the garlic, sautéing until translucent, about another 2 minutes. Stir in the cabbage, continuing to sauté until any liquid it releases has evaporated, about 5 minutes. Incorporate the potatoes and sauté for 2 more minutes.

2. Pour in the stock, reduce the heat to medium low, and simmer for about 10 to 15 minutes, until the potatoes are tender. (Do not allow the soup to boil, or the potatoes will begin to break down.)

3. Stir in the knockwurst or kielbasa and marjoram, season with salt and pepper, and simmer for about 5 minutes, until the sausage is heated.

4. Serve the soup in a tureen or in soup bowls and garnish with herb croutons.

Serves 8

1 tablespoon unsalted butter

1 slice bacon, finely chopped

1 large Spanish onion, peeled and finely chopped

1 tablespoon finely chopped garlic

1 medium green cabbage, cored and chopped
(about 12 cups loosely packed)

About ¾ pound Yukon gold potatoes,
peeled and cubed (about 3 cups)

2 quarts Chicken Stock (page 308)

1 cup cubed knockwurst or kielbasa

1 teaspoon chopped fresh marjoram

Salt

Freshly ground white pepper

Herb Croutons (page 31), for garnish

Split Pea Soup

ERBSEN SUPPE

1. At least 8 hours or the day before serving the soup, pour the split peas into a colander and rinse thoroughly, removing any stones or hard bits. Remove the peas to a large bowl, add water until the peas are covered by about 1 inch, and set aside at room temperature for 8 hours or overnight. The next day, or when ready to prepare the soup, drain and rinse the peas and set aside.

2. Place the potatoes in a medium saucepan and pour in lightly salted cold water to cover by about 1 inch. Bring to a boil over high heat and cook until tender, about 10 minutes. Drain the potatoes and set aside.

3. Melt the butter in a large saucepan over medium heat, add the bacon, and sauté until lightly browned, about 3 minutes. Toss in the onion and garlic and sauté until golden brown, about 3 minutes more.

4. Stir in the split peas and stock and bring to a boil over high heat. Reduce the heat to medium and simmer for about 1½ hours.

5. Pour the soup through a strainer into a large bowl, pressing with a spoon or spatula to purée the vegetables and force them through the strainer. Discard the bacon and return the puréed soup to the saucepan.

6. Stir in the potatoes and cream, season with salt and pepper, and serve in a tureen or in bowls garnished with fried leeks.

A TUREEN OF THIS THICK, WARMING SOUP WAS ALWAYS A WELCOME ADDITION TO OUR FAMILY MEAL, ESPECIALLY WHEN THE WEATHER TURNED COLD. SERVED UNADORNED AND ACCOMPANIED BY HEARTY BREAD, IT WAS JUST RIGHT FOR A SIMPLE LUNCH OR DINNER. IF YOU WISH, HOWEVER, DRESS THE SOUP UP A BIT BY ADDING WHOLE OR CUT-UP FRANKFURTERS OR PIECES OF PORK OSSO BUCO (BRAISED PORK SHANK). SERVE IT IN INDIVIDUAL BOWLS GARNISHED WITH FRIED LEEKS, AS I HAVE SUGGESTED HERE, FOR AN EVEN SNAZZIER PRESENTATION.

FRIED LEEKS ARE A PERFECT ACCOMPANIMENT TO THIS DISH, THEIR CRISP SALTINESS CONTRASTING DELICIOUSLY WITH THE SMOOTH PURÉE. WHEN I WAS A BOY, FRESH LEEKS WERE AVAILABLE TO US THROUGHOUT THE WINTER; WE LEFT THEM IN THE GARDEN WHERE THEY REMAINED FROZEN AND PROTECTED AND SIMPLY HARVESTED THEM AS NEEDED. DIGGING THEM UP WAS A COLD BUSINESS, BUT WELL WORTH THE EFFORT.

BEGIN PREPARING THE SOUP AT LEAST EIGHT HOURS OR THE DAY BEFORE SERVING SO THAT THE PEAS HAVE TIME TO SOAK.

REFRIGERATE LEFTOVERS IN AIRTIGHT CONTAINERS FOR UP TO ONE WEEK. THIS SOUP CAN ALSO BE FROZEN, BUT THE VEGETABLES HAVE A TENDENCY TO BECOME MUSHY WHEN REHEATED.

Serves 10 to 12

1 pound yellow or green split peas

2 pounds red-skinned potatoes (about 6 medium), peeled and cubed

4 tablespoons unsalted butter

8 ounces lean bacon (about 9 slices), finely chopped

1 large white onion, peeled and finely chopped

2 cloves garlic, peeled and finely chopped

3 quarts Chicken Stock (page 308)

1 cup heavy cream

Salt

Freshly ground black pepper

Fried Leeks, for garnish (recipe follows) (optional)

Fried Leeks

AUSGEBACKENER LAUCH

2 cups vegetable oil, for frying

1 medium leek, trimmed, sliced in half lengthwise,
   and rinsed well

Salt

1. Heat the oil in a wide saucepan over medium heat to 350°F., or until it appears to shimmer on the surface.

2. Slice the halved leek into strips as finely as possible (about $\frac{1}{16}$-inch thick) and thoroughly pat dry between paper towels.

3. Carefully drop the leek strips in the oil and fry until golden brown. (Watch carefully as they burn easily.)

4. Remove the leeks with a slotted spoon or wire mesh skimmer to a paper towel-lined baking sheet, sprinkle with salt, and set aside to cool.

Slice the halved leek into strips as finely as possible

Herb Croutons

KRÄUTER CROUTONS

Makes 2 cups

4 tablespoons unsalted butter

2 medium shallots, peeled and chopped

3 cloves garlic, peeled and chopped

$\frac{1}{4}$ cup olive oil

$\frac{1}{2}$ cup chopped fresh basil

3 tablespoons chopped fresh parsley

1 sprig fresh thyme, stemmed and chopped

1 tablespoon grated Parmesan cheese

1 baguette (with or without the crusts), cut into $\frac{1}{2}$-inch cubes

1. Preheat the oven to 350°F.

2. Melt the butter in a small saucepan over medium heat, add the shallots and garlic, and sauté until golden, about $1\frac{1}{2}$ minutes.

3. Combine the oil, herbs, cheese, and sautéed shallots and garlic in a medium bowl, add the bread cubes, and toss until well coated.

4. Spread the bread cubes in a single layer on a baking sheet and bake until golden brown and crisp, about 10 to 15 minutes. Cool completely and store in an airtight container.

Green Bean & Mushroom Salad

GRÜNE BOHNEN & CHAMPIGNON SALAT

Serves 8 to 10

MY FAMILY OFTEN ENJOYED THIS SIMPLE SALAD ON WARM SUMMER DAYS WHEN OUR GARDEN WAS FILLED WITH FRESH GREEN BEANS. IT IS A DELICIOUS ADDITION TO A SIMPLE DINNER, BUT IT IS ALSO EASILY TRANSFORMED INTO A FULL MEAL BY TOSSING IN SOME THINLY SLICED BOLOGNA OR HAM. FOR AN EVEN DRESSIER SALAD OR MAIN DISH, YOU MIGHT WANT TO FOLLOW THE EXAMPLE OF SOME BLACK FOREST RESTAURANTS AND USE HARICOTS VERTS (THIN GREEN BEANS) RATHER THAN STRING BEANS FROM THE GARDEN OR FARMERS' MARKET.

- 2½ pounds fresh green beans, trimmed
- 6 tablespoons walnut oil or olive oil
- 3 tablespoons red wine vinegar or balsamic vinegar
- 2 teaspoons Dijon mustard
- About 1 pound white button mushrooms, sliced (about 5½ cups)
- 3 medium shallots, peeled and chopped
- Salt
- Freshly ground black pepper

1. Bring a large saucepan of salted water to a boil over high heat. Toss in the green beans and cook for 3 to 5 minutes, until the beans are just tender but still firm. Drain and place them in a large bowl.

2. Whisk together the oil, vinegar, and mustard in a small bowl until the dressing is blended.

3. Add the mushrooms and shallots to the bowl of green beans and pour the dressing overtop. Season with salt and pepper, tossing gently to coat, and serve at room temperature.

Spicy Cabbage Slaw

WÜRZIGER WEIßKOHL SALAT

1. Toss the cabbage and salt in a large bowl. Cover with plastic wrap and refrigerate for about 1½ hours, until the cabbage has released its water. Remove the cabbage to a colander and thoroughly rinse and drain it, pressing lightly to remove any additional water.

2. Return the cabbage to the large bowl and stir in the green bell peppers and red pepper flakes.

3. Heat a small sauté pan over medium heat, add the bacon, and sauté until lightly browned and crisp, stirring occasionally, about 3 minutes. Leaving the drippings in the pan, scoop out the bacon and spread onto paper towels to drain.

4. Return the sauté pan with the drippings to medium heat, toss in the scallion, and sauté until golden brown.

5. Add the vinegar to the pan, stirring with a wooden spoon to loosen any browned bits from the bottom. Remove from the heat.

6. In a small bowl, stir together the parsley, mustard, cayenne pepper, and sugar. Whisk in the hot vinegar and drippings and slowly drizzle in the olive oil, whisking the dressing constantly.

7. Toss together the cabbage and warm dressing, season with salt and pepper, and serve sprinkled with the crisp bacon pieces.

CABBAGE IS FEATURED IN NUMEROUS BLACK FOREST DISHES BECAUSE IT IS PLENTIFUL, VERSATILE, STORES WELL, AND IS EASILY COMBINED WITH A VARIETY OF INGREDIENTS. TYPICAL OF MANY FAMILIES IN THE BLACK FOREST, WE HARVESTED OUR CABBAGE FROM THE GARDEN AND STORED IT IN THE CELLAR FOR USE DURING THE FALL AND WINTER MONTHS.

THIS WARM, VIBRANT, AND SLIGHTLY SPICY SLAW IS LOVELY SERVED AS SUGGESTED HERE, BUT YOU COULD MAKE IT A BIT RICHER BY USING FATBACK (UNSMOKED, UNSALTED PORK FAT) IN PLACE OF, OR IN ADDITION TO, LEAN BACON. IF YOU PREFER AN EVEN SPICIER DISH, FEEL FREE TO ADD MORE CAYENNE PEPPER, TOO, AS MANY IN THE BLACK FOREST WOULD DO.

Serves 8

½ medium green cabbage, finely shredded
  (about 4 cups)

1 tablespoon salt

2 medium green bell peppers, stemmed, seeded,
  and finely chopped (about 1½ cups)

½ teaspoon dried red pepper flakes

1½ slices lean bacon, chopped

1 scallion, trimmed and finely chopped

2 tablespoons red wine vinegar

1 tablespoon chopped fresh parsley

1½ teaspoons whole-grain mustard

½ teaspoon ground cayenne pepper

¼ teaspoon sugar

¼ cup olive oil

Salt

Freshly ground black pepper

Tomato & Basil Salad

TOMATEN & BASILIKUM SALAT

TOMATOES ARE ABUNDANT IN THE BLACK FOREST DURING THE SUMMER. WHEN I WAS A BOY, EVERY FAMILY GREW TOMATOES OF NUMEROUS COLORS AND SIZES, INCLUDING HEIRLOOM VARIETIES, IN THEIR HOME GARDENS. THESE DAYS, EVEN CITY APARTMENT DWELLERS CARRY ON THE BLACK FOREST GARDENING TRADITION, BRIGHTENING AND ADORNING THEIR BALCONIES WITH FLOURISHING TOMATO PLANTS.

THIS RECIPE WAS INSPIRED BY THE MANY WONDERFUL TOMATO SALADS I ENJOYED GROWING UP, AS WELL AS BY THE MORE TYPICALLY ITALIAN INGREDIENTS THAT FREQUENTLY CROSSED THE BORDER TO FLAVOR OUR REGIONAL CUISINE. ADMITTEDLY, GARLIC WOULD HAVE BEEN AN UNUSUAL ADDITION TO TRADITIONAL BLACK FOREST TOMATO SALADS, BUT MY BURGUNDIAN GRANDFATHER ENJOYED IT IN THIS DISH AND TAUGHT US TO DO SO AS WELL, SO I'VE INCLUDED IT HERE. TOGETHER, THE RED ONION AND GARLIC MAKE THE SALAD A BIT SPICY, AND SUMMER BASIL LENDS TO IT A WONDERFUL PERFUME AND HERBAL FRESHNESS.

Serves 4

4 vine-ripened or heirloom tomatoes, cored and sliced into thin wedges

1 small red onion, peeled and finely chopped

About $\frac{1}{3}$ cup fresh basil leaves, thinly sliced into strips about 2 inches long and $\frac{1}{8}$-inch wide

1 small clove garlic, peeled and finely chopped

$\frac{1}{2}$ cup red wine or balsamic vinegar

$\frac{1}{2}$ cup olive oil, sunflower oil, or walnut oil

Salt

Freshly ground black pepper

1 head Bibb lettuce, cored and leaves separated

Fresh basil leaves, for garnish

1. Combine the tomatoes, onion, basil, and garlic in a large bowl, toss with the vinegar and oil to coat, and season with salt and pepper.

2. Arrange about 2 lettuce leaves on each serving plate (try to form them into a "bowl"), spoon some of the tomato salad into the leaves, and garnish with basil.

Marinated Herring
with Caraway Potatoes

ROLLMOPS HERING MIT KÜMMELKARTOFFELN

1. Place the potatoes and caraway seeds in a large saucepan, pour in water just to cover, and lightly season with salt. Bring to a boil and cook until the potatoes are just tender, about 15 minutes. Drain the potatoes and set aside to keep warm momentarily.

2. Stir together the sour cream and chives in a small serving bowl.

3. To serve, place the potatoes in a large serving bowl and arrange the herring on a platter. Serve the chive sour cream and slices of bread on the side.

EVERY SELF-RESPECTING GERMAN HOUSEHOLD KEEPS A JAR OF MARINATED HERRING IN THE REFRIGERATOR. EVEN THOUGH I HAVE LIVED IN THE UNITED STATES FOR MOST OF MY ADULT LIFE, I HAVE, AT ANY GIVEN MOMENT, AT LEAST ONE JAR IN MY HOME REFRIGERATOR, USUALLY SOMEWHERE BETWEEN THE MULTIPLE JARS OF MUSTARD AND DILL PICKLES.

IN THE BLACK FOREST, HERRING IS A DELICIOUS ADDITION TO AN INFORMAL AND LIGHT SUMMER MEAL. THIS RECIPE COMBINES OUR BELOVED MARINATED HERRING WITH OTHER REGIONAL FAVORITES, INCLUDING YELLOW POTATOES, CARAWAY SEEDS, AND SOUR CREAM.

ROLLMOPSE ARE HERRING FILLETS WRAPPED AROUND PICKLE AND ONION SLICES AND MARINATED IN WHITE WINE AND SPICED VINEGAR. YOU SHOULD BE ABLE TO FIND THEM IN MOST DELICATESSENS, BUT, IF YOU WISH, YOU CAN EASILY SUBSTITUTE THE BITE-SIZE PICKLED HERRING MARINATED IN WHITE WINE THAT IS AVAILABLE IN THE REFRIGERATED SECTION OF EVERY SUPERMARKET.

Serves 4

1½ pounds small Yukon gold potatoes

1 teaspoon caraway seeds

Salt

½ cup sour cream

2 tablespoons finely chopped fresh chives

8 herring fillets (*Rollmopse*),
    or 1 (18-ounce) jar pickled herring, drained

Slices of pumpernickel or dark rye bread, for serving

Meatloaf

HACKBRATEN

MEATLOAF IS COMFORT FOOD AT ITS BEST. REGARDLESS OF ITS ACCENT OR DIALECT, THIS DISH SPEAKS IN ONE UNIFYING LANGUAGE, DECLARING THAT OFTEN THE MOST MEMORABLE MEALS ARE PREPARED WITHOUT FUSS AND WITH THE FRESHEST, MOST BASIC OF INGREDIENTS.

IN THE BLACK FOREST, MEATLOAF APPEARS ON RESTAURANT MENUS AS A DAILY SPECIAL AS OFTEN AS IT DOES ON FAMILY TABLES. IT IS DELICIOUS SERVED HOT WITH A SIMPLE MUSTARD-CREAM SAUCE, AS I HAVE SUGGESTED HERE, OR SERVED COLD WITH A BIT OF MUSTARD ON THE SIDE. I LIKE THE FLAVOR AND TEXTURAL COMBINATION OF PORK AND BEEF, BUT FEEL FREE TO VARY THE RECIPE WITH VEAL OR TURKEY AS WELL.

---

1. Preheat the oven to 350°F.

2. To make the meatloaf, melt the butter in a small sauté pan over medium heat, add the onion, and sauté until softened and any liquid it releases has evaporated, about 2 minutes. Set aside to cool completely.

3. Combine the onion, pork, beef, eggs, egg yolks, scallions, bread, parsley, and marjoram in a large bowl, season with salt and pepper, and mix thoroughly but gently with clean hands. On a greased baking sheet, form the mixture into a 9 x 5 x 3-inch loaf and bake for 45 to 55 minutes, or until a wooden skewer inserted in the center comes out clean.

4. Remove from meatloaf from the oven and set on a rack to cool slightly, about 5 to 7 minutes.

5. To make the sauce, stir together the demi-glace, mustard, and sour cream in a medium saucepan and bring to a gentle simmer over medium-low heat, stirring frequently.

6. Turn the meatloaf out of the pan and serve sliced with sauce.

Serves 6

MEATLOAF:

2 tablespoons unsalted butter

1 yellow onion, peeled and finely chopped

1 pound ground pork

1 pound ground beef

4 eggs

2 egg yolks

2 scallions, trimmed and finely chopped

1 cup soaked bread (*see Chef's Note*, page 47)

2 tablespoons chopped fresh parsley

1 teaspoon dried marjoram

Salt

Freshly ground black pepper

SAUCE:

2 cups Demi-Glace (page 312) or prepared brown sauce

2 teaspoons Dijon mustard

3 tablespoons sour cream

Baked Cod
with Spinach

GEBACKENER KABELJAU MIT SPINAT

1. Preheat the oven to 375°F.

2. Coat a large ovenproof sauté or shallow saucepan with 1 teaspoon of the butter, sprinkle the onions in the dish, and arrange the fillets on top. Season with salt and white pepper, place another tablespoon of butter on each fillet, and set 1 bay leaf on top of the butter. Bake for about 10 minutes, or until the fish turns an opaque white.

3. Remove the fish from the pan, discard the bay leaves, and set aside, loosely covered with foil to keep warm, while finishing the sauce.

4. Place the pan with the butter and fish juices over medium-high heat, stir in the wine, and bring to a boil. Add the cream, reduce the heat to medium low, and simmer, stirring frequently, until the sauce thickens enough to coat the back of a spoon, about 5 minutes.

5. Add the spinach to the sauce and bring to a boil over medium heat, stirring until the leaves are just wilted. Season with additional salt and white pepper, as needed.

6. To serve, arrange the fillets on a platter, spoon the sauce overtop, and serve the rice pilaf on the side in a serving bowl.

WHEN I WAS GROWING UP, THERE WAS LITTLE COMMERCE BETWEEN THE NORTHERN SEAPORTS AND THE BLACK FOREST, MAKING FRESH SALTWATER FISH RATHER SCARCE. COD, HOWEVER, WAS AVAILABLE TO US SKINNED, FROZEN, AND PACKAGED. UNLIKE TODAY, WHEN WE ARE SURE TO FIND VIRTUALLY ANY FISH FRESH OR FROZEN IN THE SUPERMARKET, WE PURCHASED OUR COD FROM A MAN WHO SOLD THIS FROZEN COD, KNOWN AS **KABELJAU**, DOOR-TO-DOOR FROM HIS FREEZER TRUCK.

COD REMAINS POPULAR IN THE BLACK FOREST TO THIS DAY. IT IS PARTICULARLY ENJOYED IN CATHOLIC HOMES ON FRIDAYS, WHEN MANY STILL REFRAIN FROM MEAT. ALTHOUGH WE WEREN'T CATHOLIC, MY FAMILY LOOKED FORWARD TO THIS DISH. MY MOTHER LIKED IT BECAUSE IT WAS EASY AND QUICK TO PREPARE, AND I LOVED IT BECAUSE IT WAS CREAMY, FLAVORFUL, AND THE COD WAS ALWAYS FREE OF PESKY BONES.

Serves 8

3 tablespoons unsalted butter

2 tablespoons finely chopped onion

8 cod fillets (8 to 10 ounces each)

Salt

Freshly ground white pepper

8 dried bay leaves

½ cup white wine, such as Sauvignon Blanc

1 cup heavy cream

1 cup packed fresh spinach

Rice Pilaf (page 261), for serving

Puszta Stew

PUßTA GULASCH EINTOPF

1. Heat the oil in a large stockpot over medium heat, toss in the bacon, and sauté until lightly browned, stirring occasionally, about 5 minutes.

2. Season the pork slices with salt and pepper, place them in the stockpot with the bacon, and sauté until golden brown, about 5 to 10 minutes.

3. Add the onions, sautéing until translucent, about 5 minutes. Stir in the garlic, add the peppers, and sauté for an additional 5 to 8 minutes.

4. Increase the heat to high, incorporate the tomato paste, and add the paprika, stirring frequently to prevent it from burning. Sprinkle in the flour, mixing until thoroughly incorporated, and remove the pan from the heat.

5. Pour in the red wine and stock, add the red pepper flakes, and bring to a boil over medium heat, stirring frequently. Drop in the potatoes, reduce the heat to low, and simmer until the potatoes are just tender, about 20 minutes.

6. Adjust the seasoning with salt and pepper and serve in a tureen or in individual soup bowls.

Serves 15 to 20

1 cup vegetable oil

3 pounds bacon, cut into pieces about 2 inches square

5 pounds pork tenderloin,
    sliced very thinly into medallions

Salt

Freshly ground black pepper

5 large onions, peeled and coarsely chopped
    (about 7½ cups)

½ cup coarsely chopped garlic

5 red bell peppers, stemmed, seeded,
    and cut into pieces about 2 inches square

5 green bell peppers, stemmed, seeded,
    and cut into pieces about 2 inches square

1 (18-ounce) can tomato paste

1 cup Hungarian paprika

1½ cups all-purpose flour

1 (750-ml) bottle full-bodied red wine, such as Burgundy

2 quarts Beef Stock (page 310)

¼ cup dried red pepper flakes, or to taste

2 pounds Yukon gold potatoes,
    peeled and cut into 1½-inch cubes

CHEF'S NOTE: I suggest using pork tenderloin here as it cooks quickly and easily. You can certainly substitute thinly sliced pieces of pork loin, but they will require a longer cooking time and more attention to prevent them from burning. Regardless of the meat you choose, be sure to keep a close eye on this stew and stir it frequently so that the paprika doesn't burn, as well. To make the dish even heartier, stir in some cooked pasta, such as orzo, elbow macaroni, or fusilli. For even more heat and spiciness, add some cayenne pepper in addition to, or in place of, the red pepper flakes.

THIS STEW PAYS TRIBUTE TO THE MANY HUNGARIANS FROM THE PUSZTA PLAINS WHO ARRIVED IN THE BLACK FOREST AFTER WORLD WAR II. ALTHOUGH SPICES LIKE HUNGARIAN PAPRIKA, DRIED RED PEPPER FLAKES, AND CAYENNE PEPPER MIGHT NOT BE TYPICALLY ASSOCIATED WITH BLACK FOREST CUISINE, THEY HAVE, IN FACT, COME TO HOLD PROMINENT PLACES IN THE REGION'S SPICE CABINETS OVER THE PAST SIXTY YEARS OR SO.

PUSZTA STEW EXEMPLIFIES THE TRADITIONAL ONE-POT (EINTOPF) MEAL THAT I ENJOYED AS A CHILD. AS IN MOST FAMILIES, MY MOTHER USUALLY SERVED IT LATE IN THE EVENING AFTER A NIGHT OF PLAYING CARDS OR HOSTING A CELEBRATION WITH FRIENDS. ON THOSE OCCASIONS, SHE WOULD PRESENT THIS STEW PIPING HOT IN A TUREEN ACCOMPANIED BY SOME WARM ROLLS, PRETZELS, OR FRENCH BREAD.

THIS RECIPE MAKES A LOT OF STEW, SO PLAN TO SERVE IT FOR A CROWD, MUCH AS MY FAMILY DID WHEN I WAS A BOY. REFRIGERATE LEFTOVERS IN AIRTIGHT CONTAINERS FOR UP TO ONE WEEK. THIS STEW CAN ALSO BE FROZEN, BUT THE VEGETABLES HAVE A TENDENCY TO BECOME MUSHY WHEN REHEATED.

Roast Pork

GEBRATENER SCHWEINERÜCKEN

1. The day before serving the roast, place the pork in a large casserole and add the onions, garlic, bay leaf, thyme, and red wine. Cover with plastic wrap and set in the refrigerator to marinate overnight, turning occasionally in the marinade.

2. The next day, preheat the oven to 375°F.

3. To roast the pork, remove it from the marinade and set it in another large casserole or roasting pan, reserving the marinade. Coat the pork with mustard, season with salt and pepper, and roast for about 1½ hours. When the pork is nicely browned and nearly done, toss the carrots, onions, and celery root into the casserole and roast for another 30 minutes, or until a meat thermometer inserted in the pork registers 155°F.

4. Meanwhile, pour the reserved marinade into a small saucepan and bring to a boil over high heat. Reduce the heat to medium high and simmer until it has reduced to ¼ cup, about 10 minutes. Remove from the heat, discard the bay leaf and thyme sprig, and set aside.

5. Transfer the finished pork to a serving platter and set aside to rest for 15 minutes (the internal temperature will rise about five degrees during this time).

6. To finish the dish, pour the fat out of the roasting pan and discard it. Set the pan over medium heat and add the red wine to deglaze, stirring with a wooden spoon to loosen any browned bits on the bottom of the pan. Stir in the reduced marinade and simmer until reduced by half, about 10 minutes. Add the mushrooms, demi-glace, and cream and reduce the heat to medium low. Simmer until the mushrooms are softened, then season with salt and pepper.

7. To serve, slice the pork and arrange the slices on a serving platter. Garnish with scallions and serve the sauce in a gravy boat on the side.

LIKE MANY FAMILIES, WE ENJOYED A LARGE, RELAXING MEAL ON SUNDAYS. ROASTS WERE PERFECT FOR THESE OCCASIONS. MY MOTHER WOULD MARINATE THE MEAT THE NIGHT BEFORE AND TOSS IT IN THE OVEN TO ROAST THE NEXT MORNING WHILE WE WENT OFF TO CHURCH. THIS IS A SIMPLE BUT DELICIOUS DISH THAT WE OFTEN ENJOYED WITH SPÄTZLE, A VEGETABLE, OR A GREEN SALAD.

Serves 8 to 10

MARINATING THE PORK:

1 boneless pork loin (6 to 8 pounds)

7 medium yellow onions, peeled and sliced

8 cloves garlic, peeled and chopped

1 dried bay leaf

1 sprig fresh thyme

2 cups full-bodied red wine, such as Burgundy

ROASTING AND FINISHING THE PORK:

3 tablespoons Dijon mustard

Salt

Freshly ground black pepper

1 cup chopped carrots

1 cup chopped onion

1 cup chopped celery root

2 cups full-bodied red wine, such as Burgundy

7½ cups sliced mushrooms (about 1½ pounds)

2 cups Demi-Glace (page 312)
   or prepared brown sauce

1 cup heavy cream

Sliced scallions (green parts only), for garnish

43

Pork Goulash & Sauerkraut Casserole

SZEGEDINER SCHWEINEGULASCH

1. Preheat oven to 350°F.

2. Heat the oil or melt the butter in a large shallow casserole or oven-proof saucepan over medium heat, add the garlic, and sauté until golden brown, about 2 minutes. Toss in the onions and sauté just until translucent, about 2 minutes more.

3. Season the pork with salt and pepper, place in the casserole, and cook over high heat, stirring constantly with a wooden spoon until any liquid it releases has evaporated.

4. Stir in 2 cups of the water to deglaze, stirring with a wooden spoon to loosen any browned bits on the bottom of the pan, and simmer until the pan is nearly dry.

5. Stir in the tomato paste, the remaining 1 cup of water, and paprika. Add the sauerkraut, stirring to pull the strands apart, and incorporate it into the other ingredients. Pour in the wine (and additional water if the casserole is too thick) and bring to a boil. Remove from the heat, cover, and set in the oven to cook for 45 minutes, or until the pork is tender.

6. Remove the casserole from the oven, season with red pepper and additional salt and pepper if necessary, and fold in the sour cream.

THIS CASSEROLE FLAVORFULLY REPRESENTS THE MERGING OF HUNGARIAN AND GERMAN CUISINES, SO TYPICAL OF BLACK FOREST COOKERY. ANOTHER POPULAR ONE-POT (EINTOPF) MEAL, IT IS PUNGENT AND SPICY AS WELL AS CREAMY AND COMFORTING. ADD AS MUCH OR AS LITTLE RED PEPPER AS YOU WISH, BUT DON'T SKIMP ON THE AMOUNT OR TYPE OF PAPRIKA I HAVE SUGGESTED. HUNGARIAN PAPRIKA IS SWEET AND FULL-FLAVORED AND CONTRIBUTES A UNIQUE CHARACTER TO THIS CASSEROLE THAT NO OTHER VARIETY CAN REPLICATE. MY MOTHER ALWAYS SERVED THIS WITH SMASHED POTATOES (PAGE 156) OR BUTTERED EGG NOODLES (PAGE 158) ON THE SIDE.

THIS RECIPE SERVES A LOT OF PEOPLE, BUT IF YOU WISH TO MAKE A SMALLER AMOUNT SIMPLY DIVIDE THE INGREDIENTS IN HALF.

Serves 12 to 14

1 cup vegetable oil,
 or ½ pound (2 sticks) unsalted butter

1 cup coarsely chopped garlic

6 pounds white onions, peeled and coarsely chopped

4 pounds pork (preferably boneless pork shoulder),
 cut into 2- to 2½-inch cubes

Salt

Freshly ground black pepper

3 cups water

1½ cups tomato paste

¾ cup Hungarian paprika

4 pounds prepared sauerkraut (bagged or canned)

2 cups dry white wine, such as Sauvignon Blanc

2 teaspoons dried red pepper flakes, or to taste

1 cup sour cream

This comforting and substantial dish originally hails from Königsberg, a town in northern Germany near Berlin, but is prepared all over the country in restaurants and home kitchens alike.

Often served with rice pilaf, I have chosen here to pair it simply with white rice, which I think nicely complements the creamy but slightly briny and piquant flavor of the caper sauce.

Meatballs in Caper Sauce

KÖNIGSBERGER KLOPSE

1. Melt 2 tablespoons of the butter in a small sauté pan over medium heat, add the finely chopped onion, and sauté until softened and any liquid it releases has evaporated, about 2 minutes. Set aside to cool completely.

2. Combine the cooked and cooled onion with the pork, beef, eggs, egg yolks, scallions, soaked bread, and parsley in a large bowl, season with salt and pepper, and mix thoroughly but gently with clean hands. Using slightly damp hands, shape the mixture into meatballs, about the size of golf balls (or larger if preferred).

3. Bring the stock to a boil in a large saucepan over high heat, reduce the heat to low, and maintain the stock at a simmer. Drop the meatballs gently into the stock and cook until they are completely cooked, about 7 to 10 minutes. (They will float to the top when done, but if you're still not certain, remove a meatball and cut it open.) Remove the meatballs with a wire mesh skimmer or slotted spoon and set aside momentarily. (If you wish, the stock and meatballs may be refrigerated at this point and the dish finished later.)

4. Bring the stock again to a boil over high heat and boil until reduced by half (to about 4 cups). Strain through a fine mesh strainer and set aside.

5. Melt the remaining 3 tablespoons of butter in a large sauté pan over medium heat, add the coarsely chopped onion, and sauté until softened and translucent. Add the garlic and sauté for another minute until softened. Sprinkle in the flour, stirring to incorporate (making a roux). Cook for about 1 minute, and remove from the heat.

6. Whisk the reduced stock into the roux, making sure the sauce is free of lumps. Bring to a boil over high heat, reduce the heat to medium, and simmer until the sauce is thick enough to coat the back of a spoon. Season with white pepper and additional salt if necessary, strain through a fine mesh strainer, and return the sauce to the sauté pan.

7. Place the meatballs in the sauce, stir in the cream, capers and brine, and parsley, and simmer over low heat for about 10 minutes.

8. Serve the meatballs over a platter of white rice.

Serves 6

5 tablespoons unsalted butter

2 yellow onions, 1 peeled and finely chopped,
    1 peeled and coarsely chopped

1 pound ground pork

1 pound ground beef

4 eggs

2 egg yolks

2 scallions, trimmed and finely chopped

1 cup soaked bread (*see Chef's Note*)

2 tablespoons chopped fresh parsley

Salt

Freshly ground black pepper

2 quarts Chicken Stock (page 308)

1 clove garlic, peeled and coarsely chopped

4 tablespoons all-purpose flour

Freshly ground white pepper

1 cup heavy cream

4 tablespoons pickled petit nonpareil (very small) capers,
    plus about 1 tablespoon of the brine

3 tablespoons finely chopped fresh parsley

Steamed white rice, for serving

CHEF'S NOTE: Soak about 3 cups of bread in about 3/4 cup of water until they have absorbed most of the liquid. Squeeze the pieces to remove as much water as possible. You should have 1 cup of soaked bread after squeezing out the water.

47

Pan-Seared Beef & Pork Patties

FLEISCHKÜCHLE

1. Melt 2 tablespoons of the butter in a small sauté pan over medium heat. Add the onion and sauté until softened and any liquid it releases has evaporated, about 2 minutes. Remove from the heat and set aside to cool completely.

2. Combine the cooled onion, beef, pork, eggs, egg yolks, scallions, bread, parsley, and marjoram in a large bowl, season with salt and pepper, and mix thoroughly but gently with clean hands. Shape the mixture into patties about 3 inches in diameter and $1/2$ inch thick (about 4 ounces each). Dredge in the bread crumbs, coating generously, and set aside momentarily.

3. Heat the oil and melt the remaining 4 tablespoons of butter in a large sauté pan over high heat. Carefully arrange the patties in the pan and cook for about 4 minutes on each side, until they are golden brown and completely cooked, but still juicy.

4. Meanwhile, melt the 4 tablespoons butter in a large sauté pan over medium heat, toss in the sliced onions, and season with salt and pepper. Sauté until softened, reduce the heat to medium low, and continue to cook slowly, stirring frequently, until they are lightly browned and caramelized, about 5 minutes.

4. Serve the patties on individual plates with potato and tomato salads.

THESE PATTIES MAKE FOR A DELICIOUS AND EASY MEAL. THE INGREDIENTS CAN BE MIXED HOURS BEFORE SERVING AND SET ASIDE IN THE REFRIGERATOR SO THAT, AT DINNER TIME, ALL YOU NEED TO DO IS SHAPE, BREAD, AND COOK THEM. MY MOTHER USED TO PREPARE FLEISCHKÜCHLE FOR DINNER AT LEAST ONCE A WEEK AND OFTEN SERVED THEM WITH SEVERAL ROOM TEMPERATURE SALADS, INCLUDING POTATO SALAD, TOMATO SALAD, AND CUCUMBER SALAD.

THIS RECIPE ALSO LENDS ITSELF TO OTHER FLAVORFUL DISHES. INSTEAD OF SHAPING IT INTO PATTIES, USE IT TO STUFF PEPPERS OR CABBAGE.

Serves 6 to 8

6 tablespoons unsalted butter

1 yellow onion, peeled and finely chopped

1 pound ground beef

1 pound ground pork

4 eggs

2 egg yolks

2 scallions, trimmed and finely chopped

1 cup soaked bread (*see Chef's Note*, page 47)

2 tablespoons chopped fresh parsley

1 teaspoon dried marjoram

Salt

Freshly ground black pepper

2 cups dry bread crumbs

$1/4$ cup vegetable oil

4 tablespoons ($1/2$ stick) unsalted butter

3 large yellow onions, peeled and sliced

Potato Salad (page 123), for serving

Tomato & Basil Salad (page 35), for serving

Knockwurst with Potato Salad

KNACKWURST MIT KARTOFFELSALAT

WE OFTEN ENJOYED THIS DISH AT HOME AND CONSIDERED IT AN OLD STAND-BY. WE ALWAYS HAD POTATOES ON HAND, AND MY MOTHER COULD SEND ME AT A MOMENT'S NOTICE TO THE BUTCHER'S SHOP, SO SHE WAS ABLE PUT THIS DISH TOGETHER QUICKLY FOR AN EARLY SUPPER. EVEN WHEN ENJOYING SIMPLE DISHES LIKE THIS ONE, MY FAMILY ENJOYED DINNER TOGETHER AT A PROPERLY SET TABLE. MY MOTHER ALWAYS TOOK THE TIME TO ARRANGE THE TABLE LINENS AND FLATWARE AND TO FILL BOWLS WITH ACCOMPANIMENTS SUCH AS PICKLES, MUSTARD, AND ROLLS. WE NEVER RUSHED OUR MEALS, BUT, INSTEAD, TOOK ADVANTAGE OF THE TIME WE HAD TOGETHER AROUND THE TABLE.

---

1. Place the potatoes in a large saucepan, pour in water just to cover, and season lightly with salt. Bring to a boil and cook the potatoes until they are just tender, about 20 minutes. Drain the potatoes, cool slightly, peel, and cut into slices about ¼ inch thick.

2. Gently stir together the potatoes, onion, vinegar, and oil in a medium bowl. Season with salt and pepper and incorporate the bouillon a little at a time until the salad is moist but not too wet. (You might not need all of the bouillon.)

3. Bring a large saucepan of salted water to a boil and reduce the heat to low. Add the sausages and simmer until they are just heated, about 5 minutes. (Boiling the sausages will cause them to burst.)

4. To serve, place potato salad in a serving bowl and garnish with chives. Arrange two sausages on each plate and serve with mustard on the side.

Serves 6

12 medium Yukon gold potatoes

Salt

1 large yellow onion, peeled and finely chopped

¼ cup red wine vinegar

¼ cup vegetable oil

Freshly ground white pepper

2 cups Beef Bouillon (page 309)

12 sausages (in natural casings and about 4 ounces each), such as knockwurst, frankfurters, or kielbasa

Chopped fresh chives, for garnish

Dijon or whole-grain mustard, for serving

Spätzle &
Potato Stew

VERHEIRATETE

WHEN I WAS GROWING UP, THIS COMFORTING AND DELICIOUS STEW WAS VERY POPULAR IN OUR HOUSE. LIKE MANY OF THE DISHES WE ENJOYED, MY MOTHER RELIED ON STAPLES SHE ALWAYS HAD ON HAND AND SHE WAS ALSO ABLE TO MAKE USE OF A VARIETY OF LEFTOVERS.

I CALL FOR BEEF BOUILLON IN THIS RECIPE, BUT MY MOTHER WOULD USUALLY USE THE BROTH FROM A PIECE OF BOILED MEAT SHE SERVED FOR LUNCH OR DINNER THE DAY BEFORE. WHILE THE POTATOES WERE COOKING, SHE QUICKLY PREPARED FRESH SPÄTZLE AND TOSSED IN LEFTOVER BOILED OR ROASTED MEAT OR WHATEVER SAUSAGES OR HAM WAS IN THE REFRIGERATOR. WITH THE ADDITION OF SOME QUICKLY CARAMELIZED ONIONS AND FRESH HERBS, MY MOTHER SERVED A GORGEOUS TUREEN OF STEW FIT FOR FAMILY AND FRIENDS.

Serves 8 to 10

4 tablespoons unsalted butter

1 clove garlic, peeled and chopped

2 medium yellow onions, 1 peeled and chopped,
    1 peeled and sliced

1 leek (white part only), trimmed and chopped

1½ pounds small Yukon gold potatoes,
    cut into quarters

2 quarts Beef Bouillon or Chicken Stock
    (pages 309 and 308)

½ teaspoon dried marjoram

Salt

Freshly ground black pepper

2 cups chopped ham, sausage, or roasted meat

1½ pounds (about 12 cups) Spätzle (page 161)

About ½ cup chopped fresh parsley

2 tablespoons chopped fresh chives

⅛ teaspoon freshly ground nutmeg

---

1. Melt 2 tablespoons of the butter in a large casserole or saucepan over medium heat, add the garlic, chopped onion, and leek, and sauté until translucent, about 1½ minutes.

2. Stir in the potatoes, beef bouillon or chicken stock, and marjoram and season with salt and pepper, simmering until the potatoes are just tender, about 15 minutes.

3. Stir the ham (or other meat), spätzle, parsley, chives, and nutmeg into the potatoes and continue to simmer for another 5 to 8 minutes.

4. Meanwhile, melt the remaining 2 tablespoons of butter in a small sauté pan over medium-high heat, add the sliced onion, and sauté until well caramelized and browned (but not burnt), about 7 minutes.

5. Pour the stew into a soup tureen and spoon the caramelized onion overtop to serve.

Braised Beef

GESCHMORTER RINDERBRATEN

1. Preheat the oven to 350°F.

2. Stir together the oil, salt, and pepper in a small bowl.

3. Rub the seasoned oil over the beef, set in a casserole or roasting pan, and roast for about 1 hour.

4. Add the red wine to deglaze, stirring with a wooden spoon to loosen any browned bits on the bottom of the pan. Stir in the garlic, carrots, onion, celery root, and demi-glace, cover the casserole, and braise in the oven for 30 to 45 minutes more, basting frequently.

5. Remove the roast to a serving platter. If the sauce is too thick, stir in some additional red wine. Serve the sauce on the side in a gravy boat, strained or with the vegetables.

CHEF'S NOTE: For an even more intensely flavored dish, marinate the beef overnight in the Marinade for Beef (page 309).

THIS DISH IS COMFORT FOOD AT ITS MOST BASIC. WE OFTEN ENJOYED IT FOR SUNDAY DINNER, BUT IT IS SO PAINLESS TO PREPARE THAT IT'S GREAT ANY NIGHT OF THE WEEK.

BRAISING PRODUCES TENDER, MELT-IN-YOUR-MOUTH MEAT THAT PAIRS WONDERFULLY WITH ALL SORTS OF SIDE DISHES. WE PARTICULARLY LIKED CHANTERELLE MUSHROOMS, EITHER SAUTÉED AND SERVED AS A VEGETABLE OR ADDED TO THE SAUCE. THEY GROW ABUNDANTLY IN THE BLACK FOREST, AND MY PARENTS OFTEN SPENT AFTERNOONS PICKING THEM FRESH FROM THE WOODS. POTATO DUMPLINGS, BRAISED RED CABBAGE, OR BRUSSELS SPROUTS FREQUENTLY APPEARED ON THE TABLE AS WELL TO ROUND OUT THE MEAL.

Serves 6

¼ cup vegetable oil

2 teaspoons salt

1 teaspoon freshly ground black pepper

6 pounds boneless beef chuck

2 cups full-bodied red wine, such as Burgundy

2 cloves garlic, peeled and chopped

1 cup chopped carrots

1 cup chopped onion

1 cup chopped celery root

6 cups Demi-Glace (page 312)
   or prepared brown sauce

Beef & Spätzle Stew

GAISBURGER MARSCH

1. Place the short ribs in a large casserole or saucepan and cover with water. Season with salt and pepper, toss in the bouquet garni, and bring to a boil, skimming off any foam that surfaces. Reduce the heat to medium low and simmer until the meat begins to shrink away and easily separate from the bones, about 45 minutes. Remove the meat, setting aside to cool, and strain the stock, discarding the bones and bouquet garni. Slice the cooked and cooled meat into 1½-inch cubes.

2. Melt 2 tablespoons of the butter in another large saucepan over medium heat, add the 2 chopped onions, carrots, celery root, and leek, and sauté until softened and translucent. Add the marrowbones, cubed meat, strained stock, potatoes, bay leaves, and parsley, season with salt and pepper, and simmer the stew just until the potatoes are tender, about 20 minutes, skimming any foam that rises to the surface.

3. Meanwhile, melt the remaining 2 tablespoons of butter in a small sauté pan over medium-high heat, add the sliced onion, and sauté until well caramelized and browned (but not burnt), about 2 to 3 minutes. Remove from the heat and set aside momentarily.

4. Stir the spätzle and nutmeg into the stew and remove from the heat.

5. To serve, set a marrowbone in the center of a soup bowl, ladle some of the stew overtop, and garnish, arranging about 3 chives in the marrowbone and sprinkling the stew with chopped chives.

54

THIS STEW WAS NAMED FOR GAISBURG, A SMALL NEIGHBORHOOD IN STUTTGART IN SOUTHWEST GERMANY. DURING WWI, AS SOLDIERS TRAVELED DOWN THE STREETS OF THIS TOWN, LOCALS WOULD GIVE THEM WHATEVER FOOD AND INGREDIENTS THEY HAD, FILLING THE COOKING POTS THE SOLDIERS CARRIED WITH THEM. JUST AS THEIR POTS ENDED UP WITH A LITTLE BIT OF EVERYTHING, SO DID OUR STEW DEVELOP, AS WE ADDED A BIT OF WHATEVER WE HAD ON HAND DURING SUCH FRUGAL TIMES.

THIS DISH IS SERVED AS A DAILY SPECIAL IN RESTAURANTS AS OFTEN AS IT IS PREPARED AT HOME. MY FAMILY OFTEN ENJOYED THIS STEW FOR LUNCH OR SUPPER, ESPECIALLY ON THE WEEKENDS. A FLAVORFUL COMBINATION OF BEEF, MARROWBONES, VEGETABLES, AND SPÄTZLE, IT WAS PARTICULARLY WONDERFUL DURING THE COLD FALL AND WINTER MONTHS WHEN WE CRAVED SOMETHING HOT AND SUBSTANTIAL. THIS STEW IS EASY TO PREPARE, BUT TAKES TIME. PLAN TO SPEND ABOUT TWO HOURS FROM START TO FINISH.

Serves 8

8 beef short ribs (about 1 pound each),
    rinsed several times in cold water

3 to 4 quarts water

Salt

Freshly ground black pepper

1 Bouquet Garni (*see Chef's Note*, page 80)

4 tablespoons unsalted butter

3 medium yellow onions, 2 peeled and chopped,
    1 peeled and thinly sliced

2 cups chopped carrots

2 cups chopped celery root

1 leek (white part only), trimmed and chopped

8 small beef marrowbones,
    rinsed several times in cold water

1½ pounds Yukon gold potatoes, cut into quarters

2 dried bay leaves

1 bunch fresh parsley, chopped

1½ pounds (about 12 cups) Spätzle (page 161)

⅛ teaspoon freshly grated nutmeg

Chopped and whole fresh chives, for garnish

Lentils & Kielbasa

LINSEN & WURST

1. Pour the lentils into a colander and rinse thoroughly, removing any stones or hard bits.

2. Remove the lentils to a large saucepan and add water until the lentils are covered by about 2 inches. Pierce the whole onion with the bay leaf and cloves, add to the lentils, and bring to a simmer over medium-low heat. Reduce the heat to low, partially cover the pan, and simmer until the lentils are tender, about 1 hour.

3. Heat the oil in a medium sauté pan over medium-low heat, add the chopped onion, and sauté until lightly browned. Stir in the flour to form a smooth paste (roux) and cook, stirring frequently, until golden brown, about 10 minutes.

4. When the lentils are tender, discard the onion, stir in the tomato paste, horseradish, mustard, carrot, celery root, and roux, and season with salt and pepper. Bring to a boil over medium heat, reduce the heat, and simmer until thickened, about 15 minutes. (If the lentils are too thick, stir in a bit of chicken stock or water.)

5. Season with additional salt and pepper if necessary and stir in the vinegar.

6. Serve the lentils in a large serving dish, topped with ham, Canadian bacon or kielbasa, and garnish with parsley. Serve the spätzle in a separate bowl on the side.

HERE IS ANOTHER VERSION OF THE MANY LENTIL DISHES WE PREPARED AT HOME. ADDING MUSTARD, HORSERADISH, AND VINEGAR MAKES THESE LENTILS SUPREMELY TYPICAL OF THE BLACK FOREST, AND A GARNISH OF BACON AND SAUSAGE STRENGTHENS THE REGIONAL DIALECT OF THIS DISH EVEN FURTHER. I ESPECIALLY LIKE THESE LENTILS SERVED WITH SPÄTZLE (PAGE 161) TO ROUND OUT THE MEAL.

CHOOSE ANY VARIETY OF LENTILS YOU LIKE FOR THIS DISH, SAVE FOR THE FRENCH LENTILS, WHICH ARE BEST SUITED TO SALADS AND MORE DELICATE PREPARATIONS.

Serves 8

1 pound lentils

2 small onions, 1 peeled and whole,
    1 peeled and chopped

1 small dried bay leaf

2 whole cloves

¼ cup vegetable oil

¼ cup all-purpose flour

1½ tablespoons tomato paste

1½ tablespoons freshly grated horseradish

2 teaspoons Dijon mustard

1 medium carrot, peeled and finely chopped

¼ cup finely chopped celery root

Salt

Freshly ground black pepper

¼ cup red wine vinegar

1 pound ham or Canadian bacon, cubed,
    for serving (optional)

1 large cooked kielbasa or other sausage,
    for serving (optional)

Chopped fresh parsley, for garnish

Black Forest Home Fries

SCHWARZWÄLDER BRATKARTOFFEL

1. Place the potatoes in a large saucepan, pour in water just to cover, and season lightly with salt. Bring to a boil and cook the potatoes until they are just tender, about 20 to 25 minutes. Drain the potatoes, cool slightly, and cut into slices about ¼ inch thick.

2. Heat a large cast iron skillet or heavy-bottomed sauté pan over medium-high heat, add the bacon, and sauté until crisp. Remove the bacon with a slotted spoon to paper towels to drain, reserving about 3 tablespoons of rendered fat in the pan.

3. Heat the reserved fat over medium heat, add the garlic and onion, and sauté until golden brown. (If you wish to add meat to the dish, toss it in at this point.)

4. Toss in the bacon, potatoes, and marjoram and season with salt and pepper. Cook the home fries, stirring frequently, until well browned and the potatoes come together to form one big cake.

5. Serve the home fries on a large platter.

AS SIMPLE AS THESE HOME FRIES ARE, THEY CONTAIN ALL THE ELEMENTS OF A DELICIOUS AND SATISFYING BLACK FOREST MEAL. THE FEW INGREDIENTS CALLED FOR HERE ARE STILL TYPICALLY FOUND IN EVERY KITCHEN IN THE REGION, AND THE DISH COMES TOGETHER IN NO TIME.

RATHER THAN COOK POTATOES JUST FOR HOME FRIES, MY MOTHER RELIED ON LEFTOVER BOILED POTATOES FROM THE PREVIOUS DAY'S LUNCH OR DINNER. IN ADDITION TO THE BACON, SHE MIGHT HAVE TOSSED IN HAM, PIECES OF ROAST FROM THE NIGHT BEFORE OR MUSHROOMS. TO MAKE A COMPLETE MEAL, SHE OFTEN ADDED EGGS (SEE THE VARIATION BELOW), MAKING A FRITTATA OF SORTS, AND FINISHED IT IN THE OVEN.

SERVE THESE HOME FRIES FOR BRUNCH OR AS PART OF A SATISFYING LUNCH. TOSS IN SOME MEAT OR VEGETABLES, GARNISH THE DISH WITH CHOPPED CHIVES, AND SERVE IT WITH A GLASS OF DRY WHITE WINE FOR A QUICK BUT ELEGANT SUPPER.

Serves 6

2 pounds Yukon gold potatoes, peeled

Salt

1 pound bacon, cut into strips about 2 inches long and ⅛ inch wide

2 cloves garlic, peeled and chopped

1 medium yellow onion, peeled and finely chopped

½ teaspoon dried marjoram

Freshly ground black pepper

VARIATION: Make this a full meal by adding eggs. After browning the potatoes, fold about 8 to 10 lightly beaten eggs into the home fries and place in a 350°F. oven until the eggs are just cooked, about 5 minutes.

Baked Bucatini
with Cheese

KÄSEMAKKARONI

1. Preheat the oven to 375°F. and butter a 2-quart ovenproof casserole dish.

2. Bring a large saucepan of lightly salted water to a boil and toss in the bucatini. Boil until just slightly firm (al dente), drain in a colander (do not rinse), and set aside momentarily.

3. Melt the butter in a large saucepan over medium heat, stir in the flour to form a smooth paste (roux), and cook for about 1 minute. Pour in the milk, whisking constantly, and bring to a boil. Remove from the heat, season with salt and pepper, and add the nutmeg and thyme. Stir in the cheese a bit at a time until incorporated and smooth.

4. Add the bucatini to the cheese sauce, stirring gently to coat, and pour into the prepared casserole dish. Sprinkle the top evenly with Parmesan cheese and bake for 10 minutes. Remove the casserole from the oven and place under the broiler until bubbly and golden brown. (Watch carefully to prevent the top from burning.)

5. Sprinkle with paprika and serve hot.

My mother often prepared this dish at home during the week. It is really just a version of macaroni and cheese, and my family enjoyed it often because it was inexpensive, came together without fuss, and made use of the leftover cheese we often served on weekends. It was also great during especially busy weeknights; once baked, it could stand in a warm oven for a bit until we were ready to eat. Warming, creamy, and delicious, my mother served Käsemakkaroni for lunch and supper accompanied by a simple green salad or tomato salad.

I suggest using bucatini here because I find that the long, hollow strands, slightly thicker than spaghetti, hold the cheese sauce well and create a firm casserole. Virtually any shape pasta will do, however.

Serves 4 to 6

2 pounds 100% semolina bucatini

3 tablespoons unsalted butter

3 tablespoons all-purpose flour

1½ cups milk

Salt

Freshly ground white pepper

⅛ teaspoon freshly grated nutmeg

⅛ teaspoon dried thyme

1 pound semisoft and/or semifirm cheese, such as Swiss, Gruyère, or Gouda, grated or finely chopped

½ cup grated Parmesan cheese

Hungarian paprika, for garnish

Apple Strudel

APFELSTRUDEL

STRUDEL IS POPULAR IN MUCH OF CENTRAL EUROPE, INCLUDING AUSTRIA AND GERMANY. REALLY ANY FRUIT CAN BE USED FOR THE FILLING, ALTHOUGH APPLES ARE TRADITIONAL FAVORITES.

THE BLACK FOREST IS RICH WITH APPLE ORCHARDS, AND, LIKE MANY FAMILIES, WE STORED APPLES IN OUR CELLAR, BEING CAREFUL TO KEEP EACH VARIETY SEPARATE SO IT DIDN'T QUICKLY SPOIL THE OTHERS. DESPITE ALL OF THIS WORK, HOWEVER, APPLES SIMPLY DON'T KEEP WELL, AND THOSE WE PICKED IN THE FALL WERE NEARLY SHRIVELED BY JANUARY. NEVER FEARFUL OF A LITTLE WRINKLING, NOR WILLING TO WASTE A BIT OF FOOD, WE ENJOYED THESE APPLES, NONETHELESS. THEY STILL HAD GREAT FLAVOR AND WERE JUST RIGHT FOR STRUDEL FILLING, WHERE THEY WERE ENCASED IN, AND COMPLEMENTED BY, DELICATE PASTRY.

STRUDEL IS A BIT TIME CONSUMING TO PREPARE, BUT IT IS WELL WORTH THE EFFORT. TAKE YOUR TIME WHEN WORKING WITH THE DOUGH. ALTHOUGH IT SEEMS INCREDIBLE, IT WILL IN FACT STRETCH TO NEAR PAPER THINNESS IF YOU JUST HAVE PATIENCE. BE SURE TO PLAN AHEAD, THOUGH, AND WORK ON A TABLE MEASURING AT LEAST 3 FEET BY 4 FEET TO GIVE YOURSELF ROOM TO ACCOMPLISH THE TASK. IF, HOWEVER, YOU FIND YOU DON'T WANT TO BOTHER WITH ALL OF THIS WORK, THERE IS NO HARM IN MAKING LIFE A BIT EASIER AND USING STORE-BOUGHT PUFF PASTRY FOR THE JOB.

Serves 10 to 12

APPLE FILLING:

½ cup plus 2 tablespoons sugar

3 tablespoons cake flour

2 teaspoons ground cinnamon

⅛ teaspoon freshly grated nutmeg

6 Granny Smith apples, peeled, cored, and cut into 2-inch cubes

½ cup golden raisins

STRUDEL DOUGH:

4 tablespoons (½ stick) unsalted butter, melted and cooled to room temperature

3 large egg yolks

2 tablespoons white vinegar

½ teaspoon salt

½ cup water

1¼ cups high-gluten or bread flour

ASSEMBLY:

½ pound (2 sticks) unsalted butter, melted

4 cups bread crumbs

3 large eggs

1 tablespoon water

⅛ teaspoon salt

Confectioners' sugar, for dusting

Ice cream, for serving (optional)

CHEF'S NOTE: If you wish to substitute puff pastry for the strudel dough, use about 3 pounds of prepared puff pastry and roll it carefully until it is about ⅛ inch thick.

1. To make the apple filling, stir together the sugar, flour, cinnamon, and nutmeg in a small bowl. Place the apples and raisins in a large bowl, sprinkle the sugar mixture overtop, and toss until well combined. Set the filling aside at room temperature or in the refrigerator while you prepare the dough.

2. To make the strudel dough, combine the butter, egg yolks, vinegar, salt, and water in the bowl of an electric mixer fitted with the dough hook attachment and mix on medium speed until combined. Reduce the mixing speed to low and gradually add the flour, mixing until the dough comes together. Increase the speed to medium and mix until the dough pulls away from, and begins to slap against, the sides of the bowl, about 8 minutes. (When the dough is fully and properly developed, it will stretch 3 to 4 inches without breaking.)

3. Coat a large bowl with cooking spray, transfer the dough to the bowl, and spray the dough with additional spray. Cover with plastic wrap, making sure the wrap directly touches and completely covers the dough, and set aside to relax in a warm place for at least 1 hour.

4. Preheat the oven to 425°F. and line a large baking sheet with parchment paper.

5. Drape a clean linen tablecloth or sheet over the work surface, lightly dust with flour, and set the relaxed dough in the center. Dust the top of the dough with additional flour and roll until it covers about three-quarters of the surface. At this point, the dough should measure about 2 ft. 4 in. by 3 ft. 2 in.

6. Lightly flour the backs of your hands, carefully place them under the center of the dough, and, working out toward the edges, stretch the dough until it is transparent and measures a little more than 3 x 4 feet.

7. To assemble the strudel, working lengthwise, brush two-thirds of the dough with melted butter and sprinkle the remaining one-third of the dough with bread crumbs. Carefully spread the apple filling evenly over the bread crumbs in a strip about 3 inches wide and 2 inches high. Cover the filling with the edge of the dough and begin rolling into a log shape, lifting the clean linen tablecloth or sheet to facilitate the rolling. Continue lifting and rolling to form the strudel and fold the ends under it to seal in the bread crumbs and filling.

8. Carefully transfer the strudel to the prepared baking sheet, curving one or both ends to fit it on the sheet. Whisk together the eggs, water, and salt in a small bowl to make an egg wash and brush over the strudel. Prick the surface of the strudel all over with a fork. (This will allow steam to escape as it bakes.) Bake for 20 minutes, or until golden brown. Set the strudel aside to cool slightly on the baking sheet.

9. Place the strudel on a serving platter, dust with confectioners' sugar, and serve slices with ice cream.

Apple Pancakes

APFELKÜCHLE

1. Stir together the flour, sugar, baking powder, salt, and $\frac{1}{8}$ teaspoon of the nutmeg in a large bowl and slowly pour in the milk, whisking until smooth. Whisk in the eggs and the egg yolks one at a time, add the rum, and set the batter aside to chill in the refrigerator for at least 1 hour or overnight.

2. The next day or when you are ready to assemble the pancakes, toss together the sugar, cinnamon, and remaining $\frac{1}{8}$ teaspoon of nutmeg in a small bowl. Heat a 6-inch omelet or crêpe pan over medium heat, coat it lightly with vegetable spray, and add 1 tablespoon of the melted butter, moving the pan around to coat the bottom. Add a scant handful of apples and about 2 heaping tablespoons of walnuts. Sprinkle with about 1 heaping tablespoon of the spiced sugar and sauté, stirring, until the apples are tender but still firm, about 1 minute.

3. Using a 3-ounce ladle, pour the pancake batter into the center of the hot pan, tilting the pan to spread the batter evenly. Increase the heat to medium high and cook the pancake until bubbles begin to form, about 45 seconds. Loosen the edges of the pancake with a spatula, flip it, and lightly brown the second side, about 45 seconds more. Remove the pancake to a plate to keep warm and continue the assembly process to make a total of about 12 pancakes.

4. Serve the pancakes with chantilly cream and cinnamon.

CHEF'S NOTE: Be sure to make the pancake batter at least 1 hour or the night before serving the pancakes.

Makes 1 dozen pancakes

PANCAKE BATTER:

$1\frac{1}{3}$ cups all-purpose flour

2 tablespoons sugar

1 teaspoon baking powder

$\frac{1}{2}$ teaspoon salt

$\frac{1}{4}$ teaspoon freshly grated nutmeg

1 cup whole milk

6 large eggs

6 large egg yolks

3 tablespoons light rum

ASSEMBLY:

1 cup granulated sugar

$\frac{1}{2}$ teaspoon ground cinnamon

$\frac{1}{4}$ pound plus 4 tablespoons ($1\frac{1}{2}$ sticks) unsalted butter, melted

4 apples, peeled, cored, and cut into thin slices

2 cups walnuts, roughly chopped

Chantilly Cream (recipe follows), for serving

Ground cinnamon, for garnish

Chantilly Cream

SCHLAGSAHNE

Makes 4 cups

2 cups heavy cream, chilled

$\frac{1}{2}$ cup confectioners' sugar, sifted

Pour the cream into the bowl of an electric mixer fitted with the whisk attachment and whip on medium-high speed until it just begins to thicken. Add the sugar and whip to soft peaks. Refrigerate until ready to serve.

THESE PANCAKES ARE EASY TO MAKE AND DELICIOUSLY SATISFYING. MY FAMILY PARTICULARLY ENJOYED THEM DURING THE FALL MONTHS WHEN THE AIR WAS CRISP AND THE APPLES WERE ABUNDANT AND FRESH. THE CHANTILLY CREAM IS A BIT OF A FANCY TOUCH, BUT ITS CREAMY SWEETNESS IS A WELCOME COMPLEMENT TO THE WARM PANCAKES.

Gingerbread

INGWERBROT

1. Preheat the oven to 350°F. and butter and flour one 10-inch round cake pan.

2. In the bowl of an electric mixer fitted with a paddle attachment, beat together the brown sugar and eggs on medium-high speed until light and smooth, about 8 minutes.

3. Meanwhile, sift together the bread flour, baking powder, baking soda, cinnamon, ginger, cardamom, cloves, and salt in a medium bowl.

4. Reduce the mixing speed of the sugar and eggs to medium low and add the dry ingredients, about half at a time, until the batter just comes together.

5. Stir together the butter and milk in a medium bowl and gradually pour into the beating batter, stopping occasionally to scrape down the sides of the bowl.

6. Pour the batter into the prepared pan and bake for 45 minutes, or until golden brown and a toothpick inserted in the center comes out clean. (Do not open the oven until 45 minutes have passed or the gingerbread will fall.)

7. Remove the gingerbread from the oven, set on a rack to cool in the pan for 10 minutes, and turn out onto a rack to cool completely.

8. Slice the gingerbread and serve with chantilly cream.

In the Black Forest, every family serves gingerbread around Christmas and the New Year. Many wonderful variations have been passed down through generations, although we believe the best gingerbread is baked in Nürnberg in southwestern Germany. The city has been selling their prized cake in tins for years and shipping it throughout the country. Even my mother, who is a skilled baker and prepared her own gingerbread every holiday season, now purchases Nürnberg's tinned version.

My mother's opinions notwithstanding, I suspect once you try this recipe you will never again be satisfied with store-bought or boxed gingerbread. The aroma of this freshly baked cake is intoxicating, and its delicate spiciness is seductively satisfying.

Makes one 10-inch cake

2½ cups dark brown sugar

3 large eggs

1⅓ cups bread flour

1 tablespoon baking powder

½ teaspoon baking soda

2 tablespoons ground cinnamon

1 teaspoon ground ginger

1 teaspoon ground cardamom

½ teaspoon ground cloves

½ teaspoon salt

¼ pound plus 4 tablespoons (1½ sticks) unsalted butter, melted

¾ cup whole milk, at room temperature

Chantilly Cream (page 64), for serving (optional)

Lebkuchen

CLOSELY RELATED TO GERMANY'S BELOVED GINGERBREAD, LEB-KUCHEN HAS A SPICIER CHARACTER AND MORE INTENSE PERSON-ALITY THAN ITS SOFTER, MORE DELICATE COUSIN. THE ADDITION OF COCOA POWDER AND CANDIED FRUIT GIVES THE CAKE ITS UNIQUE FLAVOR AND TRADITIONALLY CHEWY DENSENESS. LIKE GINGERBREAD, LEBKUCHEN IS MOST OFTEN PREPARED DURING THE CHRISTMAS SEASON, AND, BECAUSE OF ITS DENSE STRUCTURE AND PROPENSITY FOR BECOMING DRY AND HARD QUITE QUICKLY, IT IS ALSO A FAVORITE CHOICE FOR DECO-RATING GINGERBREAD HOUSES.

THIS RECIPE COMES TOGETHER QUICKLY, BUT JUST BE SURE TO PLAN AHEAD AND BEGIN PREPARATIONS AT LEAST EIGHT HOURS OR ONE DAY BEFORE YOU WISH TO SERVE THE FINISHED CAKE.

---

1. At least 8 hours or the day before serving the lebkuchen, butter a 9 x 13-inch baking pan and dust with flour.

2. Whisk together the honey, brown sugar, egg yolks, and orange juice in a medium bowl.

3. Sift together the all-purpose flour, bread flour, cocoa powder, baking soda, cinnamon, allspice, and cardamom three times into a large bowl. (Although it seems tedious, the multiple sifting will ultimately lighten the cake.)

4. Stir the sifted dry ingredients into the egg mixture and add the almonds and candied fruits, stirring until just incorporated.

5. Transfer the batter to the prepared baking pan, spreading it out evenly. Cover the pan with plastic wrap and chill in the refrigerator for at least 8 hours or overnight.

6. The next day, or when ready to finish the cake, preheat the oven to 350°F.

7. Bake the chilled batter for 15 minutes, or until a toothpick inserted in the center comes out clean. Set it on a rack to cool for at least 30 minutes before cutting and serving.

Makes one 9 x 13-inch cake

1 cup honey

¾ cup light brown sugar

3 large egg yolks

1 tablespoon orange juice

2 cups all-purpose flour

½ cup plus 1 tablespoon bread flour

3 tablespoons unsweetened
    Dutch processed cocoa powder

½ teaspoon baking soda

1 teaspoon ground cinnamon

1 teaspoon ground allspice

½ teaspoon ground cardamom

⅓ cup sliced almonds, toasted and cooled
    (*see Chef's Note,* page 165)

2 tablespoons roughly chopped Candied Orange Peel
    (page 316)

2 tablespoons roughly chopped Candied Lemon Peel
    (page 316)

2 tablespoons roughly chopped Candied Ginger
    (page 317)

Kugelhopf

GUGELHUPF

1. Butter and flour one 4-cup Bundt or kugelhopf pan.

2. To make the sponge, stir together the yeast and milk in a large bowl. Incorporate the flour, stirring until smooth. Cover with a kitchen towel and set aside in a warm area until the sponge has tripled in volume, about 30 minutes.

3. To make the dough, place the flour, sugar, eggs, salt, and risen sponge in the bowl of an electric mixer fitted with the paddle attachment. Mix on low speed until combined, about 2 minutes. Add the butter about 2 tablespoons at a time and continue mixing until the dough is smooth, about 3 minutes. Add the raisins and mix until incorporated.

4. Scrape the dough into the prepared pan, cover with a kitchen towel, and set aside in a warm area until nearly doubled in volume, about 1 hour.

5. Preheat the oven to 450°F.

6. Place the kugelhopf in the oven and immediately reduce the temperature to 375°F. Bake until golden and a skewer inserted in the center comes out clean, about 20 minutes. Set the kugelhopf on a wire rack to cool completely in the pan before turning out of the pan and serving.

7. Dust with confectioners' sugar and serve.

THIS RICH, SLIGHTLY SWEET BREAD IS FOUND THROUGHOUT POLAND, AUSTRIA, ALSACE, AND GERMANY. BAKED IN SPECIAL, DECORATIVE KUGELHOPF PANS AND OFTEN DOTTED WITH DRIED FRUIT, CANDIED FRUIT, OR NUTS, THIS BREAD IS AS BEAUTIFUL AND FESTIVE AS IT IS DELICIOUS.

KUGELHOPF IS SERVED IN RESTAURANTS THROUGHOUT THE BLACK FOREST, BUT TO ME IT REPRESENTS THE HOME COOKING OF MY CHILDHOOD. I NEARLY FORGOT TO INCLUDE KUGELHOPF IN THE BOOK, BUT THANKS TO MY MOTHER'S DISCERNING EYE, YOU FIND IT HERE. SHE REMINDED ME THAT KUGELHOPF WAS MY FAVORITE CAKE AS A YOUNG BOY AND THAT SHE BAKED ONE FOR THE FAMILY EVERY WEEK WITHOUT FAIL.

KUGELHOPF WILL STAY FRESH STORED AT ROOM TEMPERATURE FOR ABOUT TWO TO THREE DAYS. EVEN IF IT BEGINS TO GO STALE, THOUGH, SIMPLY ENJOY IT AS WE DID, DUNKED IN HOT CUPS OF TEA OR CAFÉ AU LAIT.

Serves 10 to 12

SPONGE:

2 tablespoons active dry yeast

1 cup plus 2 tablespoons milk, at room temperature

1 cup high-gluten or bread flour

DOUGH:

1¼ cups high-gluten or bread flour

½ cup sugar

3 eggs

1 tablespoon salt

½ pound (2 sticks) unsalted butter, at room temperature

½ cup golden raisins

½ cup dark raisins

Confectioners' sugar, for dusting

Raspberry Tart

LINZERTORTE

1. Preheat the oven to 325°F. and butter a 9 x 1⅜-inch tart pan with a removable bottom.

2. To make the pastry, stir together the flour, almonds, and spices in a large bowl. Combine the butter and sugar in the bowl of an electric mixer fitted with the paddle attachment and beat on medium-high speed until light and fluffy. Add the eggs and vanilla and beat until incorporated, stopping at least once to scrape down the sides of the bowl. Reduce the mixing speed to low and gradually add the flour mixture, mixing just until it forms a soft dough. Wrap the dough in plastic wrap and chill in the refrigerator for at least 30 minutes.

3. Dust the work surface and about half of the chilled pastry dough lightly with flour and roll into a circle about 11 inches in diameter and ¼ inch thick. Ease the pastry into the prepared tart pan, being careful not to stretch it, and gently press it into the sides of the pan. Trim any excess from the edges. Roll the remaining pastry into a 10-inch square about ¼ inch thick and cut into ten 1-inch-wide strips.

4. To assemble the linzertorte, spread the raspberry jam evenly over the bottom pastry and weave the pastry strips diagonally over the jam to create a lattice. Press the ends of the strips into the edges of the bottom crust, trimming any excess as necessary.

5. Bake for 35 to 40 minutes, or until the crust is golden brown, and remove it to a rack to cool completely.

6. Gently remove the sides of the tart pan, place the linzertorte on a serving platter, and serve with chantilly cream or vanilla ice cream.

Makes one 9-inch tart

PASTRY:

4 cups sifted cake flour

2½ cups almonds, toasted and finely ground
   (see Chef's Note, page 165)

1 teaspoon ground cinnamon

½ teaspoon ground allspice

½ teaspoon ground cloves

1 pound (4 sticks) unsalted butter, softened

1½ cups sugar

2 large eggs

1 teaspoon vanilla extract

ASSEMBLY:

1 cup raspberry jam

Chantilly Cream (page 64) or vanilla ice cream,
   for serving

CHEF'S NOTE: This recipe is quite versatile and can also be used to make delicate linzer cookies. Simply cut the dough into rounds and cut out the centers of half of the rounds with a smaller cookie cutter. Spread the full rounds with jam, place the remaining rounds on top, and bake just until golden.

Linzer cookies

Originally hailing from Linz, Austria, linzertorte has been considered an important part of the Black Forest dessert repertoire for generations. Because this is such a simple dessert, the quality of the jam and the pastry are very important. Choose a rich, fruity jam—one that you would be proud to serve on your breakfast table. In addition, when you spread it on the pastry, it is vital to use just the right amount. Don't be skimpy with a thin coating, but don't go crazy either and think the dessert will improve with a thick smear. I realize determining the right thickness is tricky, but I am confident that the amount I have suggested here will work nicely. As for the pastry, Austrians traditionally prepare it with almonds, but we in the Black Forest usually prefer hazelnuts. Like the jam, it is important to roll the dough—especially the lattice—to the proper thickness. If it is too thin, it will burn and fail to give the linzertorte enough substance. If it is too thick, it will rise too much in the oven, almost completely covering the filling, and the finished tart will be all crust and no jam. A perfectly prepared linzertorte will have a delicate, golden lattice top through which you see glistening diamonds of red.

Coconut Cookies

KOKOSNUß GEBÄCK

1. Place the butter in the bowl of an electric mixer fitted with the paddle attachment and begin mixing on medium speed. While mixing, add the sugar in a steady stream and continue mixing until light and fluffy, stopping at least once to scrape down the sides of the bowl. Add the egg and continue to mix until incorporated, again stopping once to scrape down the sides.

2. Gradually incorporate the flour and coconut, mixing just until the dough comes together. (It will be stiff.) Wrap the dough in plastic wrap and refrigerate for 30 minutes.

3. Preheat the oven to 375°F. and lightly butter a baking sheet or line it with parchment paper.

4. Roll the chilled dough into 1-inch balls and arrange them about 1 inch apart on the prepared baking sheet. Bake for about 15 minutes, or until the edges of the cookies are lightly browned. Cool the cookies completely on wire racks and store in an airtight container.

CHEF'S NOTE: Toasting coconut is easy but you need to watch it carefully as it can burn in an instant. Spread the coconut onto a parchment paper-lined baking sheet and toast in a 325°F. oven for several minutes, tossing occasionally so it browns evenly. Remove the toasted coconut immediately from the baking sheet to cool. If it sits on the hot sheet it will continue to toast and become too dark.

THESE COOKIES ARE EASY TO MAKE AND FULL OF SWEET, CHEWY COCONUT. THEY STORE WELL SO YOU CAN KEEP THEM FOR A WHILE.

Makes 3 dozen cookies

10 tablespoons (1¼ sticks) unsalted butter, softened

1 cup sugar

1 large egg

1 cup sifted all-purpose flour

1½ cups shredded unsweetened coconut, toasted (see Chef's Note)

Gingerbread Cookies

INGWER GEBÄCK

1. Sift together the flour, baking soda, and spices into a large bowl.

2. Stir together the cider, molasses, honey, and maple syrup in a medium bowl.

3. Place the butter in the bowl of an electric mixer fitted with the paddle attachment and begin mixing on medium speed. While mixing, add the sugars and ginger and continue mixing until light and fluffy, stopping at least once to scrape down the sides of the bowl.

4. Continuing to mix on medium speed, gradually add the wet ingredients to the butter and sugar, pouring in a thin steady stream and stopping once to scrape down the sides of the bowl.

5. Reduce the mixing speed to low and gradually add the dry ingredients, mixing just until combined. Wrap the dough in plastic wrap and chill in the refrigerator for about 1 hour.

6. Preheat the oven to 375°F. and line baking sheets with parchment paper.

7. Working with about one-quarter of the dough at a time, place it on a lightly floured work surface and roll to ¼ inch thick. Cut into desired shapes, arrange the cookies about 2 inches apart on the baking sheets, and bake until they have lightened in color, about 12 to 15 minutes. Cool the cookies completely on wire racks and store in airtight containers.

LIKE GINGERBREAD AND LEBKUCHEN, GINGERBREAD COOKIES WERE A STAPLE IN OUR HOME, ESPECIALLY AROUND THE HOLIDAYS. CHRISTMAS JUST WOULDN'T HAVE BEEN THE SAME WITHOUT ROLLING OUT THE DOUGH, CUTTING IT INTO FANCIFUL SHAPES, AND FILLING THE HOUSE WITH THE SCENT OF SWEET SPICINESS.

THIS RECIPE RELIES ON THE BOLD, PUNGENT FLAVORS OF A VARIETY OF SPICES AND A HANDFUL OF SWEETENERS, INCLUDING BROWN AND GRANULATED SUGARS, APPLE CIDER, MOLASSES, HONEY, AND MAPLE SYRUP, ALL OF WHICH GIVE THE COOKIES A RICH AND PLEASANTLY BALANCED SWEETNESS.

Makes about 16 cookies
(depending on the size of your cutter)

6¼ cups all-purpose flour

2¼ teaspoons baking soda

1 tablespoon ground ginger

1 teaspoon ground allspice

½ teaspoon ground cloves

½ teaspoon freshly grated nutmeg

½ teaspoon ground cardamom

⅛ teaspoon ground mace

¾ cup apple cider

½ cup dark molasses

¼ cup honey

¼ cup maple syrup

¼ pound (1 stick) unsalted butter

¼ cup dark brown sugar

¼ cup granulated sugar

2 tablespoons chopped fresh ginger

Every kitchen in the Black Forest is outfitted with a welcoming cookie jar, and ours was no exception. My mother was always sure to keep it filled with a variety of confections, not only to satisfy those of us with a sweet tooth, but also for the times when unexpected company popped by for coffee or a visit.

The tray below features coconut, ginger bread, spritz cookies, and spice cookies, all of which are perfect for special occasions, or when you just want to reach in the cookie jar for something sweet.

Spice Cookies

WÜRZ GEBÄCK

1. To make the cookies, sift the flour, spices, and salt into a medium bowl.

2. Place the butter in the bowl of an electric mixer fitted with the paddle attachment and begin mixing on medium speed. While mixing, add the sugar in a steady stream and continue mixing until light and fluffy, stopping at least once to scrape down the sides of the bowl. Add the molasses, egg yolks, and vanilla and continue to mix until incorporated, stopping again at least once to scrape down the sides of the bowl.

3. Reduce the mixing speed to low and gradually incorporate the sifted dry ingredients, mixing until just combined. The dough will be very soft. Scrape it into a plastic container and set in the refrigerator for 30 minutes to 1 hour.

4. Preheat the oven to 350°F. and line baking sheets with parchment paper.

5. Drop teaspoons of the dough about $1\frac{1}{2}$ inches apart onto the baking sheets and bake until golden, about 15 minutes. Set the cookies on a wire rack to cool completely, about another 12 minutes.

6. To make the glaze, whisk together the sugar and lemon juice until smooth and glossy.

7. To finish the cookies, drizzle the glaze over the cooled cookies, allowing them to dry completely before storing in an airtight container.

Makes about 36 cookies

COOKIES:

$2\frac{1}{3}$ cups all-purpose flour

2 teaspoons ground cinnamon

$1\frac{1}{2}$ teaspoons ground ginger

$\frac{1}{4}$ teaspoon freshly grated nutmeg

$\frac{1}{2}$ teaspoon salt

$\frac{1}{2}$ pound (2 sticks) unsalted butter, softened

$\frac{3}{4}$ cup sugar

$\frac{1}{2}$ cup dark molasses

2 large egg yolks

1 teaspoon vanilla extract

LEMON GLAZE:

1 cup confectioners' sugar, sifted

Juice of $\frac{1}{2}$ medium lemon, strained

Spritz Cookies

SPRITZ GEBÄCK

THIS NORTHERN EUROPEAN COOKIE HAS BECOME REPRESENTATIVE OF THE SIMPLE, BUTTERY CONFECTIONS ENJOYED THROUGHOUT GERMANY. THE NAME DERIVES FROM **SPRITZEN**, GERMAN FOR "TO SQUIRT OR SPRAY," AND REFERS TO THE WAY IN WHICH THE DOUGH IS PRESSED THROUGH A COOKIE PRESS TO CREATE A VARIETY OF DECORATIVE SHAPES. THESE COOKIE PRESSES ARE COMMONLY SOLD IN KITCHEN SUPPLY STORES, BUT, IF YOU WISH, SIMPLY FORM THEM BY HAND AS I HAVE SUGGESTED HERE. REGARDLESS OF THEIR SIZE AND SHAPE, THEY ARE SURE TO DISAPPEAR AS QUICKLY IN YOUR HOUSE AS THEY DID IN OURS.

1. Preheat the oven to 350°F. and line baking sheets with parchment paper.

2. Sift the flour, baking powder, and salt into a large bowl.

3. Place the butter in the bowl of an electric mixer fitted with the paddle attachment and begin mixing on medium speed. While mixing, add the sugar in a steady stream and continue mixing until light and fluffy, stopping at least once to scrape down the sides of the bowl. Add the egg yolks and vanilla and continue to mix until incorporated, again stopping at least once to scrape down the sides of the bowl.

4. Reduce the mixing speed to low and gradually incorporate the sifted dry ingredients, mixing until just combined.

5. Roll the dough into 2-inch logs, about the thickness of a finger, and arrange them about 1 inch apart on the baking sheets. Bake until the edges are light golden, about 15 minutes. Set the cookies on wire racks to cool completely and store in an airtight container.

Makes about 2 dozen cookies

5 cups sifted all-purpose flour

4 teaspoons baking powder

1 teaspoon salt

1 pound (4 sticks) unsalted butter, softened

1½ cups sugar

4 large egg yolks

2 teaspoons vanilla extract

CHEF'S NOTE: If you use a cookie press to make these cookies, press the dough directly onto the baking sheets. Your baking time will most likely be reduced, so watch the cookies carefully to prevent over-baking.

CAFÉ ～๑ BITES

IN THE BLACK FOREST, AS IN THE REST OF EUROPE, CAFÉS ARE MORE THAN JUST PLACES TO GRAB A QUICK BITE TO EAT OR A CUP OF COFFEE. THEY DEFINE A WAY OF LIFE THAT IS CHARACTERIZED BY RITUAL, ELEgance, and gracious hospitality.

In my youth, cafés were part of everyday life, and still are today.

Much like the taverns of eighteenth-century America, European cafés developed as community meeting places where folks could relax, socialize, and take refreshment. Today in much of America, where nearly everyone has cars and is accustomed to traveling great distances on a daily basis, the popularity of local taverns and diners has largely waned. In the Black Forest, however, as in much of Europe, cafés remain significant fixtures in towns of all sizes. When I was a boy, few people in my town owned a car, so they walked everywhere, including to church, the butcher's shop, and the cafés. So valued was café life in my day that even the smallest Black Forest village supported several establishments. The community might have been without cars, but they had several varieties of meringues available at nearly any given moment! Our town had more than its fair share of cafés, and, in fact, my Uncle Karl worked for years as head pastry chef in one of the best, the Café Frei in Pforzheim.

Cafés are destination spots of two distinct sorts. On the one hand they serve a local clientele, many of whom visit routinely on weekday afternoons for conversation, coffee, and a snack. They also serve visitors from neighboring towns and villages who take long hikes on the weekends and look forward to stopping for a bite to eat. Some even walk these long distances with a particular café in mind—one that is renowned for its Bienenstich or Black Forest cake, for example.

Weekday and weekend patrons also regard cafés as destination spots for ice cream. Black Forest cafés are renowned for their *spezialitäten Eisbecher* (special ice cream dishes). These frozen

concoctions are much too elegant for paper cups and plastic spoons. Instead, they are presented in elegant silver and glass bowls and served with special long silver spoons. Some of the most popular *Eisbecher* include the *Pfirsich Melba* (Peach Melba), composed of vanilla ice cream, peaches, seedless raspberry sauce, toasted almonds, and whipped cream; the *Coupe Denmark*, prepared with ice cream, hot chocolate sauce, and whipped cream; and the *Schwarzwaldbecher*—an elegant presentation of vanilla ice cream, cherries, kirschwasser, whipped cream, and chocolate.

Whether the café is in your own town or a day's hike away, all cafés serve a variety of food in an elegant and hospitable setting. Unlike in America, where bakeries, dough-

nut shops, and diners are freestanding enterprises, **CAFÉS IN THE BLACK FOREST ARE NEARLY ALWAYS LOCATED BEHIND A KONDITOREI (PASTRY SHOP), WHERE A WIDE ARRAY OF CAKES, COOKIES, MARZIPAN, AND CHOCOLATES ARE ON DISPLAY.** After choosing from among these items, you are seated and served coffee with all of the traditional accoutrements, including a coffee pot and elegant china. For those with less of a sweet tooth or who wish for a more substantial snack, there are savory offerings, too. Every café offers a variety of beers, wines, and creatively prepared sandwiches.

Perhaps cafés have remained popular in the Black Forest and throughout Europe because they not only define a way of eating, but they are also integral to a way of life. Each has a distinct personality characterized by its size, décor, atmosphere, and the people who frequent it. It is noteworthy that, at least in my day, people went to a café to sit, relax, and enjoy a slice of cake or some cookies. Occasionally they took a piece of pastry home, but they did not purchase whole cakes or boxes of con-

Café Pastries

fections there, as we do today in American pastry shops and bakeries. Most women baked and, like my mother, did so quite skillfully and often. For families of the Black Forest, cafés remain an important part of a culture centered around the ritual of communing, eating beautiful, specially prepared Konfekte and savory dishes, and taking time to appreciate the whole elegant affair.

Vols-au-Vent with Veal Ragoût in the Queen's Style

KÖNIGINPASTETCHEN

THIS CLASSIC, ELEGANT DISH CERTAINLY DESERVES ITS ROYAL NAME-SAKE. IT BELONGS TO A LARGE CATEGORY OF SAVORY STUFFED PASTRIES KNOWN AS **GEFÜLLTE BLÄTTERTEIGPASTETCHEN** (FILLED VOL-AU-VENT), WHICH INCLUDES SUCH VARIETIES AS PASTRY FILLED WITH SWEET BREADS, CHICKEN, MUSHROOMS, LOBSTER, AND TRUFFLES. THE RICH, VELVETY VEAL RAGOÛT FEATURED IN KÖNIGINPAS-TETCHEN MARRIES BEAUTIFULLY WITH THE BUTTERY, FLAKY PUFF PASTRY THAT HOLDS IT.

TIME CONSUMING TO PREPARE AND COMPOSED OF SEVERAL PARTS, THIS DISH IS OFTEN SERVED IN CAFÉS AND UPSCALE RESTAURANTS ALIKE, WHERE SKILLED PASTRY CHEFS ARE ON HAND TO CREATE NUMEROUS SWEET AND SAVORY SPECIALTIES. YOU WILL WANT TO BE SURE TO PLAN AHEAD WITH THIS DISH. BEGIN PREPARING THE RAGOÛT AT LEAST ONE DAY BEFORE SERVING SO THAT THE VEAL HAS ENOUGH TIME TO COOK AND THEN COOL COMPLETELY BEFORE YOU FINISH AND ASSEMBLE THE DISH THE FOL-LOWING DAY. TO SAVE SOME TIME, YOU CAN PURCHASE READY-MADE VOLS-AU-VENT IN MOST SUPERMARKETS.

Serves 8

VEAL RAGOÛT:

3 pounds boneless veal shoulder or leg meat

4 cups dry white wine, such as Chardonnay

4 cups water

2 leeks (white part only), trimmed, well rinsed, and chopped

1 rib celery, chopped

1 large yellow onion, peeled and chopped

1 clove garlic, peeled and chopped

1 Bouquet Garni (*see Chef's Note*)

3 tablespoons salt

1½ teaspoons freshly ground white pepper

VOL-AU-VENT:

3 sheets packaged frozen puff pastry, thawed

3 large eggs

1 tablespoon water

⅛ teaspoon salt

TO FINISH THE VEAL RAGOÛT:

½ pound (2 sticks) unsalted butter, at room temperature

About 8 ounces white button mushrooms, cut into ¼-inch pieces

1 cup all-purpose flour

½ cup heavy cream

4 egg yolks, lightly beaten

Juice of 2 large lemons (about ¼ cup), strained

Salt

Freshly ground white pepper

Chopped fresh parsley, for garnish

Lemon wedges, for garnish

CHEF'S NOTE: Bouquets garnis are pouches of spices and herbs, bundled in cheesecloth and tied with kitchen twine. The ingredients can vary greatly, but for this ragoût, bundle the following items in a piece of cheesecloth (about 6 inches square):

4 whole black peppercorns
3 sprigs fresh thyme
2 sprigs fresh parsley
2 medium cloves garlic, peeled
1 medium shallot, peeled and coarsely chopped
1 dried bay leaf

a

b

c

VOL-AU-VENT

Using a 3–inch round cutter, cut the centers from each of these rounds and place one pastry ring on top of each round.

d

e

f

1. One day before serving the veal ragoût, set the veal shoulder or leg meat in a large saucepan or casserole, add the wine and water, and bring to a boil over high heat, skimming any foam that rises to the surface. Add the leeks, celery, onion, garlic, bouquet garni, salt, and pepper and return to a boil. Reduce the heat to medium low and simmer for 1 hour. Remove from the heat and cool to room temperature. Cover and refrigerate overnight.

2. To make the vols-au-vent the next day, roll out one puff pastry sheet to about ⅛ inch thick, dock (prick) it all over using the tines of a fork, and cut the pastry into 8 rounds, using a 4-inch round cutter (images a–b). (Alternatively, turn a 4-inch-diameter bowl upside down on the pastry and cut around the rim using a paring knife.) Arrange the rounds on a parchment paper-lined baking sheet and set aside for the moment in the refrigerator.

3. Roll out a second sheet of puff pastry to about ½ inch thick and cut out 8 more rounds. Using a 3-inch round cutter, cut the centers from each of these rounds to create ½-inch rings (images c–d).

4. Prepare an egg wash by whisking together the eggs, water, and salt in a small bowl. Brush the ⅛-inch-thick, 4-inch rounds with the egg wash and place one pastry ring on top of each round, making certain that the edges are precisely aligned (images e–f). Brush again with egg wash and refrigerate for 30 minutes.

5. Preheat the oven to 425°F.

6. Using a paring knife, make incisions, about ¼ inch apart, around the perimeter of each vol-au-vent, brush again with egg wash, and bake until golden brown, about 20 minutes. Remove from the oven and set aside on a rack to cool. (If storing, wrap the baked vol-au-vent tightly in aluminum foil or seal in an airtight container.)

7. To finish the veal ragoût, melt 2 tablespoons of the butter in a large sauté pan over medium heat, toss in the mushrooms, and sauté until any liquid they release has evaporated, about 3 to 5 minutes. Remove from the heat and set aside momentarily.

8. Lift the veal from the cooled stock and cut it into ¼-inch cubes. Strain the stock into a large bowl through a fine mesh strainer or cheesecloth. Discard the vegetables and bouquet garni and return the stock to the pan. Bring the stock to a boil over high heat and boil for about 15 minutes, or until reduced by half. Reduce the heat to medium low and maintain the stock at a simmer.

9. In a medium bowl, knead together the flour and remaining butter to form a paste (beurre manié). Drizzle about ⅓ cup of the hot stock into the paste, mixing constantly. Stir this thinned paste into the simmering stock and simmer for about 15 minutes, or until the sauce is smooth and velvety.

10. Strain the sauce again through a fine mesh strainer and return it once more to the pan. Bring the sauce to a simmer over medium-low heat (careful to keep it from boiling) and add the cubed veal. Drain the mushrooms of any excess liquid and add them to the sauce.

11. Whisk together the cream and the egg yolks in a medium bowl, gradually fold into the ragoût, and simmer for about 3 minutes (again being careful to keep it from boiling or the egg yolks might curdle). Stir in the lemon juice and season with salt and pepper.

12. To serve, place each vol-au-vent in the center of a plate, fill with ragoût, and garnish with parsley and a lemon wedge.

Mushroom Toast

CHAMPIGNON TOAST

1. Preheat the oven to 350°F.

2. Place the stick of butter in a small bowl and knead in the flour, a bit at a time, to form a smooth paste (beurre manié).

3. Toss together the mushrooms and lemon juice in a small bowl. Melt the remaining 2 tablespoons of butter in a large sauté pan over medium heat, add the shallots, and sauté until translucent and softened (but not colored), about 2 to 3 minutes. Add the mushrooms and sauté until any liquid they release has evaporated, about 4 minutes.

4. Add the brandy and simmer for about 1 minute, setting flame to it (flambéing) if desired. Add the white wine to deglaze, stirring with a wooden spoon to loosen any browned bits on the bottom of the pan. Stir in the cream and bring to a boil over medium-high heat.

5. Stir in the beurre manié a little at a time until incorporated and the sauce thickens. Toss in the parsley, season with salt and pepper, and set aside momentarily.

6. Arrange the baguette slices on a baking sheet and toast in the oven until golden brown, about 5 to 7 minutes.

7. Set 2 slices of bread in the center of each plate and spoon some of the creamed mushrooms overtop. Drizzle with about 2 tablespoons of hollandaise sauce and garnish with parsley.

I LOVE THIS DISH FOR ITS SIMPLICITY AND ELEGANCE. A TESTAMENT TO THE INFLUENCE OF FRENCH CUISINE IN THE REGION, IT APPEARS ON CAFÉ AND RESTAURANT MENUS THROUGHOUT THE BLACK FOREST AND RELIES ON ONLY A HANDFUL OF FRESH, FLAVORFUL INGREDIENTS.

I LIKE SERVING THIS RICH CREAMY MUSHROOM SAUCE ON FIRM, SLIGHTLY CHEWY BAGUETTE SLICES, BUT REALLY THE DISH IS EQUALLY SATISFYING AND DELIGHTFUL WHEN PREPARED WITH TOASTED, GOOD-QUALITY SANDWICH BREAD.

Serves 8

¼ pound (1 stick) plus
  2 tablespoons unsalted butter, softened

¼ cup all-purpose flour

12 white button mushrooms, sliced

Juice of ½ lemon (about 1 tablespoon)

4 shallots, peeled and finely chopped

3 tablespoons brandy

1 cup dry white wine, such as Sauvignon Blanc

2 cups heavy cream

2 tablespoons chopped fresh parsley

Salt

Freshly ground white pepper

1 baguette (or other bread with a crisp crust
  and light chewy interior), cut on the diagonal into 16 slices
  about ¼ inch thick

1 cup Hollandaise Sauce (page 311), for serving

Fresh curly-leaf parsley, for garnish

THIS QUICHE PAYS TRIBUTE TO THE TOWN OF BAD WILDBAD IN THE NORTHERN BLACK FOREST. FAMOUS FOR ITS THERMAL BATHS, THE TOWN IS ALSO CELEBRATED FOR ITS NUMEROUS SMOKE HOUSES AND THE MARVELOUS SMOKED HAMS, SAUSAGES, AND OTHER MEATS PRODUCED BY THE CITY'S INHABITANTS.

CAFÉS SERVE THIS DISH IN A VARIETY OF FORMS. SOMETIMES IT IS THICK, BAKED IN A TART OR PIE PAN, AND OTHER TIMES IT IS QUITE THIN. THIS QUICHE CAN ALSO BE SERVED AT ALMOST ANY TIME OF DAY. IN THE BLACK FOREST, WE ENJOY IT AT ROOM TEMPERATURE OR CHILLED AS A LIGHT LUNCH WITH A GREEN SALAD OR BY ITSELF AS A LATE AFTERNOON SNACK. WITH ALL OF ITS VARIATIONS, THIS MODEST BUT ELEGANT QUICHE AGAIN REPRESENTS THE GREAT INFLUENCE OF FRENCH CUISINE (IN THIS CASE THAT OF THE LORRAINE REGION OF NORTHERN FRANCE) ON THE FOOD OF THE BLACK FOREST.

BE SURE TO CHOOSE A GOOD-QUALITY HAM HERE. I SUGGEST BLACK FOREST HAM, BUT ANY COOKED OR SMOKED HAM WILL DO. YOU COULD EVEN USE BACON OR SAUSAGE FOR THAT MATTER. WHATEVER MEAT YOU CHOOSE, JUST BE SURE IT IS NOT TOO DRY, OR IT WILL BECOME QUITE TOUGH WHEN BAKED IN THE QUICHE.

Quiche with Black Forest Ham

QUICHE WILDBADER ART

1. To make the crust, stir together the flour and salt in a medium bowl. Using a pastry cutter or two knives, cut in the butter and shortening until the mixture resembles coarse meal. Sprinkle the water, 1 tablespoon at a time, over the flour and toss together with a fork until the dough starts to come together. It will be a little sticky or tacky. Form the dough into a disk, wrap in plastic wrap, and chill in the refrigerator for at least 30 minutes.

2. Preheat the oven to 400°F. and coat a 9-inch tart pan (with a removable bottom) with vegetable spray.

3. On a lightly floured surface, roll the chilled dough into a circle about 10 inches in diameter and about 1/4 inch thick. Beginning at one edge of the dough, roll the dough around the rolling pin and unroll it carefully over the tart pan. Ease the dough into the pan, gently pressing it into and against the sides, being careful not to stretch it. Remove any excess dough from the rim of the tart pan. Carefully line the dough with heavy-duty aluminum foil, fill with dried beans or pie weights, and bake for about 15 minutes, or until very light golden. Remove the crust from the oven, carefully lift out the foil and weights, and set aside on a rack to cool. Reduce the oven to 375°F.

4. To make the filling, whisk together the eggs, heavy cream, nutmeg, chives, salt, and pepper in a medium bowl.

5. To assemble the quiche, spread the Gruyère cheese and ham evenly over the bottom of the cooled crust and pour the egg filling overtop. Bake for 25 to 30 minutes, or until a knife inserted in the center comes out clean.

6. Remove the quiche from the oven, place on a rack to set for about 5 minutes, and serve.

Makes one 9-inch quiche

CRUST:

1 1/3 cups all-purpose flour, sifted

1 teaspoon salt

4 tablespoons unsalted butter, chilled and cubed

4 tablespoons vegetable shortening, chilled

4 to 5 tablespoons ice water

FILLING:

6 extra large eggs

2 1/2 cups heavy cream

1/4 teaspoon freshly grated nutmeg

1/4 cup chopped fresh chives

1/2 teaspoon salt

1/4 teaspoon freshly ground black pepper

1 cup grated Gruyère cheese

1 cup finely chopped Black Forest ham

Goulash Soup

GULASCH SUPPE

1. Heat the oil or melt the butter in a large saucepan or stockpot over medium-high heat.

2. Add the garlic and sauté until golden, about 2 to 3 minutes. Toss in the onions and sauté until softened and translucent, about 8 minutes.

3. Season the beef with salt and pepper, place the pieces in the pan, and cook, stirring constantly, until the beef is browned on all sides and the pan is nearly dry.

4. Pour in 1 cup of the wine to deglaze, stirring with a wooden spoon to loosen any browned bits on the bottom of the pan. Raise the heat to high, bring to a boil, and continue to boil until the wine is reduced to the point where the pan is nearly dry again.

5. Stir in the tomato paste, add the remaining $\frac{1}{2}$ cup of red wine, and cook until the pan is nearly dry once more.

6. Reduce the heat to medium low, add the paprika, stock, red pepper flakes, and ground caraway seeds, and simmer for about 30 minutes, stirring frequently to prevent the paprika from burning. If the soup is still too thin after 30 minutes, mix 1 part cornstarch and 2 parts water in a small bowl (start with 1 tablespoon of cornstarch and 2 tablespoons of water), drizzle about half of it into the simmering soup, and cook until it is thickened, adding more if necessary.

7. Season the soup with additional salt and pepper if necessary and stir in the lemon zest just before serving.

8. If desired, place some egg noodles in individual bowls and ladle the soup over the noodles. Garnish with a dollop of sour cream.

Nearly every café in the Black Forest serves this soup, again displaying the influence of Hungarian cuisine in the region. In fact, goulash soup has become so popular that many eateries purchase an excellent ready-made variety, which they confidently serve to their patrons. You will undoubtedly notice the large amount of onions I call for here. This is customary, not only for flavor, but also to give body to the soup, which is traditionally prepared without any flour or cornstarch. I have suggested the latter just in case you find that the soup does need to be thickened a bit before serving. Also traditional to this dish are caraway seeds and lemon zest, so typical of Black Forest cuisine. Be sure to grind the seeds fresh to obtain the most flavor, and add the lemon zest just before serving to add crispness and freshness to this robust soup.

Serves 6 to 8

$\frac{1}{2}$ cup vegetable oil or $\frac{1}{4}$ pound (1 stick) unsalted butter

$\frac{3}{4}$ cup coarsely chopped garlic

$2\frac{1}{2}$ pounds white onions, peeled and coarsely chopped

$1\frac{1}{2}$ pounds beef (preferably beef chuck),
    cut into 1-inch cubes

Salt

Freshly ground black pepper

$1\frac{1}{2}$ cups full-bodied red wine, such as Burgundy

$\frac{3}{4}$ cups tomato paste

$\frac{3}{4}$ cups sweet Hungarian paprika

3 quarts Beef Stock (page 310)

$\frac{3}{4}$ tablespoon dried red pepper flakes, or to taste

$1\frac{1}{4}$ tablespoons freshly ground caraway seeds

Zest of 2 lemons, finely chopped

Cornstarch, as needed

Egg Noodles (page 158), for serving (optional)

Sour cream, for garnish

Open-Faced Sandwich with Black Forest Ham & Eggs

STRAMMER MAX

1. Preheat the oven to 225°F.

2. Whisk together the eggs, parsley, chives, thyme, and nutmeg in a shallow pan and season with salt and pepper.

3. Melt the butter in a large sauté pan or skillet over medium-high heat. Dip each piece of bread in the eggs, coating both sides, and place in the pan, cooking until golden brown on both sides. Arrange the browned bread slices on a baking sheet and set in the oven to keep warm.

4. Remove any browned bread or egg bits from the sauté pan and set over medium heat. Place the ham in the pan and crack the eggs overtop, cooking them sunny-side-up to your desired doneness.

5. Set a slice of warmed bread on each plate, set some ham and 2 eggs on each slice, and garnish with black pepper and chives.

ALTHOUGH THIS OPEN-FACED SANDWICH IS SERVED IN MANY BLACK FOREST CAFÉS, IT IS CONSIDERED SOMEWHAT OF A SPECIALTY ITEM. STRAMMER MAX IS A BIT MORE TIME CONSUMING TO PREPARE THAN SIMPLER COLD SANDWICHES, AS IT IS COOKED TO ORDER AND SERVED WARM. IT ALSO RELIES ON BLACK FOREST HAM, AN INGREDIENT UNCOMMONLY KEPT IN THE CAFÉ REFRIGERATOR, ESPECIALLY IN MY DAY. IN ORDER TO OFFER THIS SANDWICH, A CAFÉ MUST BE LOCATED CLOSE TO A BUTCHER'S SHOP, WHERE A COOK COULD SCURRY ACROSS THE STREET AT A MOMENT'S NOTICE FOR A FEW SLICES OF HAM.

THIS SANDWICH IS REALLY A BLACK FOREST INTERPRETATION OF THE FRENCH CROQUE MADAME. SOME CAFÉS PREPARE AN EVEN FANCIER VERSION, USING FILET MIGNON IN PLACE OF THE HAM AND SERVING FRESHLY GRATED HORSERADISH ON THE SIDE FOR EXTRA KICK.

Serves 4

4 eggs

1 tablespoon chopped fresh parsley

1 tablespoon chopped fresh chives

1 teaspoon stemmed and chopped fresh thyme

1/8 teaspoon freshly grated nutmeg

Salt

Freshly ground black pepper

4 tablespoons unsalted butter

4 thick slices white bread

4 ounces Black Forest ham, thinly sliced

8 eggs

Freshly ground black pepper, for garnish

Chopped fresh chives, for garnish

Camembert Café Frei

ANGEMACHTER CAMEMBERT

For those café visitors who either don't have much of a sweet tooth or simply want a bite of something savory and more substantial, this is the perfect treat. Even if they are quite a ways from a butcher and have little access to cold cuts, every Black Forest café keeps soft cheeses like Camembert on hand. Mashed a bit and mixed with fresh, flavorful ingredients like herbs and spices, these cheeses make delightful spreads, which pair nicely with raw seasonal vegetables and slices of pumpernickel bread.

1. Place the Camembert in a medium bowl and, using a fork, break apart into pieces. Stir the chives, onion, paprika, and caraway seeds into the cheese until well incorporated.

2. To assemble, arrange about 2 lettuce leaves in the center of each plate and spoon one-quarter of the cheese on top. Place 2 slices of bread and 4 radishes around the cheese on each plate and garnish with a sprinkling of paprika and chives.

Serves 4

CHEESE:

4 wedges ripe Camembert cheese
    (about 3½ ounces each), at room temperature
¼ cup chopped fresh chives
1 medium yellow onion, peeled and finely chopped
1 teaspoon Hungarian paprika
1 teaspoon caraway seeds

ASSEMBLY:

1 head Bibb lettuce, cored and leaves separated
8 slices pumpernickel bread
16 red radishes
Hungarian paprika, for garnish
Fresh chives, for garnish

Cream Puffs

WINDBEUTEL

Every café in the Black Forest prepares and serves cream puffs. Some are quite small, the size of silver dollars, and others are as big as apples. Pastry chefs most often dip them in either chocolate or caramel, but, unlike French PÂTISSIERS who fill their cream puffs almost exclusively with pastry cream, Black Forest KONDITERMEISTER (PASTRY CHEFS) will often choose to fill their puffed confections with sweetened whipped cream (see Chantilly Cream recipe, page 64).

Makes 20 Cream Puffs

PÂTE À CHOUX:

½ cup plus 2½ tablespoons bread flour

1 cup whole milk

¼ pound (1 stick) unsalted butter, at room temperature

1 tablespoon sugar

¼ teaspoon salt

⅛ teaspoon freshly grated nutmeg

5 large eggs

1 large egg yolk

CHOCOLATE SAUCE:

1 cup whole milk

8 ounces semisweet chocolate, finely chopped

4 tablespoons unsalted butter, at room temperature

1 cup heavy cream

ASSEMBLY:

6 cups Pastry Cream (recipe follows on the next page)

1. Preheat the oven to 450°F. and line an 11 x 17-inch baking pan with parchment paper.

2. To make the pâte à choux, sift the flour into a large bowl three times. Combine the milk, butter, sugar, salt, and nutmeg in a medium saucepan and bring to a boil over medium-high heat. Whisk briskly for about 10 seconds, remove from the heat, and stir in the flour using a wooden spoon. Return the pan to medium heat and cook the paste, stirring constantly, until it pulls away from the sides of the pan and has a satiny appearance, about 2 to 3 minutes.

3. Immediately transfer the dough to the bowl of electric mixer fitted with the paddle attachment and beat on low speed until the bowl is cool to the touch, about 7 to 10 minutes.

4. Mixing on medium speed, add 4 of the eggs, one at a time, making sure each egg is completely incorporated before adding the next. Turn off the mixer and run your finger through the paste. It should be wet, but your finger should leave a trail, which will slowly begin to fill again with paste. If the choux paste seems stiff and the trail remains, it is most likely too dry. If this is the case, add the remaining egg and egg yolk to obtain the proper consistency.

5. Fit a large pastry bag with a #16 straight tip and fill the bag one-quarter full with the choux paste. Pipe rounds, about 1 inch in diameter and ¼ inch high, onto the prepared baking sheet, place in the oven, and immediately reduce the temperature to 375°F. Bake until golden and puffed, about 15 minutes. When they are properly baked, the puffs will sound hollow when tapped on their bases. Set the choux puffs directly on a wire rack to cool completely.

6. To make the chocolate sauce, bring the milk to a boil in a medium saucepan over medium-high heat, stirring frequently. Reduce the heat to low, add the chocolate, and stir until it is completely melted. Remove the pan from the heat, stir in the butter and cream, and set aside to cool to room temperature.

7. To assemble the cream puffs, poke a small hole in the sides of each choux puff using a paring knife. Fit a pastry bag with a #10 straight tip, fill about one-third full with pastry cream, and pipe cream into each puff.

8. Dip the tops of each cream puff in the chocolate sauce and serve directly, or set aside in the refrigerator to allow the chocolate to become firm before serving.

Pastry Cream

Makes 3 cups

2 cups milk

½ cup sugar

¼ cup cornstarch

3 large eggs

½ teaspoon vanilla extract

2 tablespoons unsalted butter, softened

¼ cup water, chilled

2 tablespoons powdered gelatin

1. Combine the milk and ¼ cup of the sugar in a medium saucepan and bring to a boil over medium heat, stirring occasionally.

2. Meanwhile, whisk together the cornstarch, eggs, vanilla, and remaining ¼ cup of sugar in a large bowl.

3. Slowly pour the hot milk into the egg mixture, whisking constantly, until combined. Pour the mixture back into the saucepan and cook over medium heat, stirring constantly, until it thickens and just comes to a boil. Remove from the heat, pour into a medium bowl, and stir in the butter.

4. Pour the water into a small bowl, sprinkle the gelatin overtop, and set aside until the gelatin is soaked (bloomed), about 5 minutes. Melt the bloomed gelatin by setting the bowl in a larger bowl of warm water and stirring until the gelatin is melted and dissolved. Add the melted gelatin to the warm milk mixture, stirring to incorporate completely.

5. Cover the pastry cream with plastic wrap, setting the wrap directly on the surface of the cream, to prevent a skin from forming. Set aside until cooled to room temperature, about 30 minutes. Remove to the refrigerator and chill for at least 1 hour before serving. (The pastry cream will keep fresh sealed in an airtight container and stored in the refrigerator for up to 5 days.)

Black Forest Cake

SCHWARZWÄLDER KIRSCHTORTE

LITTLE NEED BE SAID ABOUT THIS CAKE, FOR IT IS KNOWN AROUND THE WORLD AND SERVED IN EVERY CAFÉ IN THE BLACK FOREST. IN FACT, VIRTUALLY EIGHTY PERCENT OF THE REGION'S CAFÉ SALES COME FROM BLACK FOREST CAKE ALONE! THE POPULARITY OF THIS CAKE IS HARDLY A MYSTERY. IT HAS COME TO PRACTICALLY SYMBOLIZE THE BLACK FOREST BECAUSE IT EPITOMIZES SOME OF THE MOST DELICIOUS AND ABUNDANT INGREDIENTS FOUND THERE.

LEST THE UBIQUITOUSNESS OF THIS DESSERT HAS DAMPENED YOUR INTEREST IN IT, I URGE YOU TO TRY THIS RECIPE. I'M CERTAIN YOU WILL COME TO UNDERSTAND WHY IT IS BELOVED BY SO MANY, AND YOU WILL JOIN THEM IN THEIR PASSION FOR THE CONFECTION.

GERMANS APPRECIATE GOOD-QUALITY DARK CHOCOLATE AND THIS IS ESPECIALLY SO IN THE BLACK FOREST, WHERE IT IS USED WIDELY IN CAKES AND CONFECTIONS ALIKE. THE REGION'S CREAM IS ALSO PARTICU-LARLY DELICIOUS, AS COWS FEED ON A VARIETY OF GRASSES AND WILD-FLOWERS AND PRODUCE RICH, FLAVORFUL MILK. AS FOR THE CHERRIES, SOUR CHERRIES (SAUERKIRSCHEN) GROW WILD THROUGHOUT THE BLACK FOREST AND ARE ALSO WIDELY FARMED. SO ABUNDANT ARE THEY, IN FACT, THAT IT IS QUITE COMMON FOR PEOPLE TO SELL THE WILD CHER-RIES THEY PICK DIRECTLY TO RESTAURANTS AND CAFÉS FOR A BIT OF EXTRA MONEY. SOUR CHERRIES ARE UNDOUBTEDLY BEST FOR THIS CAKE, BUT, AS THEY ARE DIFFICULT TO FIND IN THE UNITED STATES, I RECOM-MEND USING SWEET CHERRIES. LIKE THE CHERRIES, KIRSCHWASSER, OR CHERRY BRANDY, IS ESSENTIAL TO THE BLACK FOREST CAKE. THE PRO-DUCTION OF THIS AND OTHER POTENT EAUX DE VIE ORIGINALLY BEGAN AS A WAY OF MAKING USE OF THE REGION'S FERTILE ORCHARDS. IF YOU WISH TO PREPARE AN ALCOHOL-FREE VERSION OF THE CAKE, YOU CAN CER-TAINLY SUBSTITUTE SIMPLE SYRUP (SUGAR WATER) OR CHERRY JUICE, ALTHOUGH THE CAKE TRULY BENEFITS FROM THE EMPHATIC CHERRY PUNCH THAT THE KIRSCH LENDS TO IT.

CHEF'S NOTE: To make successful chocolate curls, bring a block of choco-late to room temperature and, using a vegetable peeler, slowly move the peeler across one of the flat sides of the chocolate. Keep the curls in the refrigerator so they remain firm until you are ready to use them.

Makes one 9-inch cake

CHERRY FILLING:

4 cups pitted sweet cherries

1½ cups Kirschwasser (cherry brandy/Schnaps)

1 cinnamon stick

1 vanilla bean

1 tablespoon cornstarch

1 tablespoon cold water

CHOCOLATE SPONGE CAKE:

¾ cup cake flour

4 tablespoons cornstarch

4 tablespoons cocoa powder

8 large eggs

1 cup sugar

1 tablespoon vanilla extract

Zest of 1 lemon

4 tablespoons unsalted butter, melted and cooled

CHERRY CREAM:

¼ cup Kirschwasser

1 quart heavy cream

1 (¼-ounce) packet granulated gelatin

½ cup confectioners' sugar

ASSEMBLY:

About ¾ cup Kirschwasser

1 cup heavy cream, whipped to soft peaks
 with 2 tablespoons confectioners' sugar

Semisweet chocolate curls, as needed (*see Chef's Note*)

BLACK FOREST CAKE

*Whip cream carefully. Slice cake into thirds.
Drizzle with Kirschwasser, and spread cherry
cream over surface. Spread thickened cherry filling over the cream, and arrange macerated cherries
on top. Assemble the cake, leave top layer plain.
Frost the cake with whipped cream. Press chocolate
curls into the sides of the cake. Pipe rosettes around
the edges of the cake.*

c

a

d

b

e

96

f

g

h

i

j

k

97

1. To make the cherry filling, begin at least one day before assembling and serving the cake. Stir together the cherries and Kirschwasser in a medium bowl. Add the cinnamon stick and vanilla bean, cover, and set aside at room temperature or in the refrigerator to macerate for 24 hours.

2. The next day, strain the macerating liquid into a small saucepan and reserve the cherries. Bring the liquid to a boil over medium heat, reduce the heat to medium low, and maintain at a simmer. Stir together the cornstarch and water in a small bowl and drizzle into the simmering liquid, stirring constantly until thickened. Remove the cherry filling from the heat and set aside to cool.

3. Preheat the oven to 375°F. and butter and flour two 8-inch cake pans.

4. To make the cake, sift together the flour, cornstarch, and cocoa powder three times into a large bowl and set aside momentarily.

5. Whisk together the eggs, sugar, vanilla, and lemon zest in a large bowl until just combined. Prepare a double boiler and maintain at a simmer. Pour the egg mixture into the top of the double boiler and heat to 200°F., or until warm to the touch, whisking constantly. Transfer the whipped eggs to the bowl of an electric mixer fitted with the whisk attachment and whip on medium-high speed until light yellow in color and tripled in volume.

6. Using a spatula, gently and gradually fold the sifted flour into the whipped eggs. When nearly all of the flour has been incorporated into the eggs, fold in the melted butter, adding it in a slow, steady stream. Do not over mix the batter or the cakes will be too firm and dense.

7. Divide the cake batter between the two prepared pans and bake for 30 to 35 minutes, until a toothpick inserted in the centers comes out clean.

8. To make the cherry cream, pour the Kirschwasser and 1/4 cup of the cream into a small bowl, sprinkle the gelatin overtop, and set aside until the gelatin is soaked (bloomed), about 3 minutes. Melt the bloomed gelatin by setting the bowl in a larger bowl of warm water and stirring until the gelatin is melted and dissolved. Add the melted gelatin to the warm milk mixture, stirring to incorporate completely.

9. Pour the remaining 3¾ cups of cream into the bowl of an electric mixer fitted with the whisk attachment and begin whipping on medium speed. Gradually incorporate the confectioners' sugar and continue whipping to form soft peaks. Add the gelatin, raise the mixing speed to high, and continue whipping to stiff peaks (image a, on page 96). (Watch the cream carefully, as over whipping will turn it to butter very quickly.)

10. To assemble the cake, slice each cake round horizontally into thirds (image b). Set one of the rounds on a cake plate, drizzle with Kirschwasser (image c), and spread a thin layer of cherry cream over the surface (image d). Spread a heaping tablespoon of thickened cherry filling over the cream, spreading it thinly (image e), and arrange some macerated cherries on top. Continue assembling the cake in this manner, leaving the top layer plain. Frost the cake with whipped cream, being especially generous on the top (image f). Carefully press chocolate curls into the sides of the cake (image g). Fit a pastry bag with a star tip if desired, fill with some of the whipped cream, and pipe rosettes around the edges of the cake (image h). Decorate with cherries and chocolate shavings (images j–k). Refrigerate for 1 to 2 hours before serving.

Bee Sting Cake

BIENENSTICH

1. To make the cake, combine the yeast, sugar, and milk in the bowl of an electric mixer, whisk with a wire hand whisk to incorporate the ingredients, and set aside to rest for 5 minutes.

2. Set the bowl on the mixer, fit it with a paddle attachment, and begin mixing on medium speed. Add the butter and salt, gradually incorporate the flour, and continue mixing for about 2 minutes. Remove the bowl from the mixer, cover with a towel, and set the dough aside to rest for about 30 minutes at room temperature.

3. Butter the sides of an 11 x 17-inch baking sheet and line with parchment paper. Press the rested dough onto the prepared baking sheet and set aside at room temperature to rise for another 30 minutes.

4. Preheat the oven to 400°F.

5. To make the almond-honey glaze, combine the butter, almonds, honey, and milk in a medium bowl.

6. Spread the glaze evenly over the risen dough and bake for about 30 minutes, or until a toothpick inserted in the center comes out clean. Set the cake on a wire rack to cool completely in the pan.

7. To assemble the bienenstich, slide the cake out of the pan, remove the parchment paper, and slice the cake in half horizontally so that the top and bottom half each measures 11 x 17 inches. Spread the pastry cream evenly over the bottom half of the cake and set the other half of cake on top.

8. Cut the cake into pieces of any size, to serve, although it is traditionally sliced into pieces measuring about 3 inches square.

LITERALLY TRANSLATED AS THE "STING OF A BEE," THIS UNIQUE CAKE IS A FAVORITE IN BLACK FOREST CAFÉS. ITS NAME DERIVES FROM THE GENEROUS AMOUNT OF HONEY IN THE GLAZE. APIARIES ARE PLENTIFUL IN THE BLACK FOREST, AND BEES, HAPPILY FEEDING ON THE WILDFLOWERS THAT CARPET THE REGION, PRODUCE MANY VARIETIES OF DELICIOUS HONEY.

SO POPULAR IS BIENENSTICH, IN FACT, THAT MANY FOLKS STUNG WITH CRAVINGS FOR THIS SOFT YEAST CAKE, WITH ITS BUTTERY ALMONDS AND RICH CREAM FILLING, GO TO GREAT LENGTHS TO QUELL THEM. THE DESSERT'S MOST PASSIONATE FANS ARE KNOWN TO SPEND ENTIRE AFTERNOONS HIKING TO CAFÉS RECOGNIZED FOR THEIR PARTICULARLY TASTY VERSIONS OF THIS CAKE.

Makes one 11 x 17-inch cake

CAKE:

1 ounce active dry yeast

5 tablespoons sugar

2 cups whole milk, warmed

4 tablespoons unsalted butter, softened

1/8 teaspoon salt

3 cups all-purpose flour

ALMOND-HONEY GLAZE:

1/4 pound (1 stick) unsalted butter, melted and cooled

3/4 cup sliced almonds

2/3 cup honey

1 tablespoon whole milk

ASSEMBLY:

6 cups Pastry Cream (page 94)

Meringues
with Ice Cream

SAHNE & EIS MERINGEN

Serves 8

MERINGUES:

4 large egg whites

1 tablespoon cream of tartar

¾ cup granulated sugar

1 cup confectioners' sugar, sifted

Zest of 1 orange, finely chopped

ASSEMBLY:

About 1½ cups vanilla ice cream

About 1½ cups chocolate ice cream

About 1½ cups strawberry ice cream

2 cups heavy cream

¼ cup sugar

1. At least 8 hours or the day before serving the meringues, preheat the oven to 150°F. and line a large baking sheet with parchment paper.

2. To make the meringues, combine the egg whites and cream of tartar in the bowl of an electric mixer fitted with the whisk attachment and whip on high speed to form soft peaks. Reduce the mixing speed to medium, slowly incorporate the granulated sugar, and continue whipping the meringue until it forms stiff peaks.

3. Remove the meringue from the mixer and, using a spatula, gently fold in the confectioners' sugar and orange zest.

4. Fit a large pastry bag with a #16 straight tip, fill halfway with meringue, and pipe about sixteen elongated ovals, about 3½ inches long and about 1¼ inches wide, onto the prepared baking sheet (images a–b on page 104). Bake the meringues for about 8 hours or overnight.

5. Remove the meringues from the oven and set them aside to cool to room temperature.

6. To assemble the meringues, begin by spooning about 3 tablespoons of each ice cream onto one meringue oval. The ice cream is not layered here; instead, each flavor is set next to the other, as the blocks of vanilla, chocolate, and strawberry ice creams appear in a half-gallon carton of Neapolitan ice cream, for example (image c). Place another meringue oval on top and set this "sandwich" on its side so that you see a band of ice cream flanked by the two meringues (image d). Repeat the process to create eight "sandwiches," set them on a baking sheet, and freeze until firm, about 30 minutes. (You might want to set each finished "sandwich" directly in the freezer while you complete the rest.)

7. Combine the cream and sugar in the bowl of an electric mixer fitted with the whisk attachment and whip on medium-high speed to firm peaks. Transfer the whipped cream to a pastry bag fitted with a straight tip. (Fill the bag about half full and refill as needed.)

8. Place each ice-cream-filled meringue on a serving plate so that the ice cream layer is visible. Pipe the whipped cream on top (images e–f) of the ice cream and serve immediately.

These lovely little meringue sandwiches are showcased in cafés, where they can be assembled, frozen, and then finished À LA MINUTE (at the last minute). They are not only delicious, but wonderful combinations of texture as well. The crunchy yet tender meringues, firm and creamy ice cream, and silky, airy whipped cream are wonderfully complementary and create a satisfying treat.

Plan to bake the meringues for at least eight hours or overnight. They need to have time to dry slowly and completely so that, ideally, they remain snow white. Keep an eye on them if possible. Meringues can brown rather easily, depending on the quirkiness of the oven. But not to worry—a little color is harmless and will actually give the meringues a pleasing, slightly caramel-like flavor.

In the Black Forest, we traditionally prepare this dessert with vanilla, chocolate, and strawberry ice creams, but feel free to use the number of varieties and flavor combinations you like best.

a

b

c

MERINGUES

Pipe meringue ovals onto the baking sheet and bake. Spoon ice cream onto oval, place another oval on top and set sandwich on side. Pipe whipped cream on top.

d

e

f

GASTHAUS
COMFORT FOOD

A S A LITTLE BOY, WHEN I WASN'T AT HOME OR AT SCHOOL, I WAS
WITH MY UNCLE WALTER AND AUNT RUTH AT THEIR GASTHAUS
ZUM BUCKENBERG. I EVEN SPENT MANY VACATIONS WITH THEM AT
the Gasthaus. I loved it there. I started in the kitchen peeling garlic when I was only four years
old and eventually worked my way up to tasks of greater responsibility. In addition to learning
a lot about cooking at my mother's side, her sister, my Aunt Ruth, also taught me a great deal.
As members of the Breuninger family, they shared a seemingly inherent skill for cooking, so it
was natural for my aunt to become cook at the Gasthaus when she married my Uncle Walter. I
learned a lot from him as well. He mainly worked in the butcher's shop at the Gasthaus, and I
acquired my basic butchering skills from him.

Uncle Walter, a master butcher and charcutier, was my role model growing up. We had
fun together, but I was also a great help to him. I started with small odds-and-ends jobs like
moving equipment and gathering ingredients. When I was a little older, he gave me more important jobs such as butchering rabbits and chickens. Eventually, Uncle Walter allowed me to
accompany him to the slaughterhouse. By age twelve I knew how to make sausages and had
even learned to bone a leg of veal, a massive cut of meat which rivaled me in size.

My early years at Gasthaus zum Buckenberg gave me a unique perspective on Gasthaus
culture and its significance in the Black Forest. Gasthaus, or Wirtschaft as it is also known, literally translates as "guest house." Depending on where they are located, these establishments
vary in size and often have rooms where travelers can stay the night. Regardless of whether or
not a Gasthaus has overnight accommodations or how large it is, it is almost always recognized
primarily for the comforting, hearty, and well-priced dishes the owners serve in their restaurant.
Gasthaus restaurants, like local taverns and family-owned restaurants in any community, are

Traditional German
Beer Steins

welcoming and offer consistent, well-prepared fare. Although only locals are afforded special seating at the *Stammtisch* (large round table)—a fixture in every Gasthaus—they and out-of-town visitors alike enjoy chatting over food and a glass of local beer, wine, or eau de vie.

As much as people enjoy home-style Gasthaus fare, they are as likely to visit for a refreshing local beer as they are for a good meal. **GASTHAUS RESTAURANTS AND BREWERIES ARE INTIMATELY CONNECTED IN THE BLACK FOREST. BREWERIES ACTUALLY FINANCE MANY GASTHAUS RESTAURANTS AND CONTRACT THEM TO SELL THEIR PRODUCTS.** Every town has at least one brewery. Some have as many as 10 to 12, and people throughout the region travel to neighboring communities to taste a variety of special brews.

Some Gasthaus restaurants, especially those in small towns and villages, offer fairly limited menus. During the day when restaurants are busiest, even small establishments serve a varied array of items. In the evenings, however, when business is quite a bit slower, they might only serve one or two hot dishes, such as a *Rostbraten* (steak) or *Fleishkäse* (pork and beef terrine), as well as several cold dishes like *Kartoffelsalat* (potato salad) and *Straßburger Wurstsalat* (bologna and cheese salad). Others, like my aunt and uncle's Gasthaus, have a large restaurant that could seat 200 for lunch and boasted a fairly extensive menu. No matter their size or location, however, almost every Gasthaus features at least one sausage special as well as an omelet of some kind, and all of the items are simply prepared and presented.

Gasthaus restaurants are particularly well known for the menu specials they offer throughout the week. Folks know when a particular Gasthaus is serving its *Gefüllte Kalbsbrust* (stuffed veal), *Gulasch*, or *Schlachtplatte*, for example, and make a trip just to partake of that dish. I remember many a weekend when I hiked four hours or more with my family just to enjoy a featured dish at a particular Gasthaus. We made a day of it, walking together and talking as we romped through forests and down quiet roads. We knew to arrive fairly early, as well. Most Gasthaus restaurants only prepare one batch of the daily specials, so when they're gone, patrons have to wait until the following week to satisfy their cravings.

During the week, most people enjoy large Gasthaus lunches but save dessert for the weekends when they have more time to sit and relax. Gasthaus restaurants actually

offer few desserts on weekdays. On Saturdays and especially on Sundays, however, cooks serve a variety of special sweets. Aunt Ruth featured a large spread of confections on Sunday afternoons for which she became quite renowned. She baked at least 12 cakes and tarts that included such delicious items as cheesecake, cherry cake, plum tart, apple-walnut cake, and Linzertorte. Of course, cafés are filled with weekend patrons as well, but especially in towns where there are few cafés, Gasthaus restaurants attract many customers. Some have even become well known for their particular specialties, and folks embark on long hikes or drives just to relax and indulge in freshly baked confections.

Like home kitchens, Gasthaus kitchens vary in size and, in my day especially, depended heavily on seasonal ingredients. Chefs de cuisine who worked in even large, elaborate kitchens traveled to markets almost every day to plan daily specials and purchase fresh produce. My aunt and uncle relied on their butcher's shop for meat and charcuterie and harvested fresh produce from their own gardens, but they supplemented their menus with seasonal items from the town's markets. To augment these fresh ingredients, my aunt relied on her pantry, which was always filled with large colorful jars of fruit syrups and preserved fruits and vegetables. Preserving and canning are year-round events in the Black Forest. The fall, however, is a particularly busy time for such activities. **LIKE EVERY FAMILY, WE ALL CONVENED AT THE GASTHAUS TO WORK IN THE ORCHARDS AND GARDENS DURING THE FALL HARVEST AND THEN MOVED TO THE KITCHEN TO DRY AND PRESERVE ALL WE HAD GATHERED.**

It is impossible to understand life in the Black Forest without having some knowledge of Gasthaus culture. These establishments are more than mere eateries or inns. They are centers of activity where locals gather to eat and drink together, as well as to celebrate significant events, such as weddings, confirmations, and seasonal festivals. The hospitality, hard work, and commitment to community that I experienced at the Gasthaus zum Buckenberg are inherent to the Black Forest way of life and have stayed with me all these years. At one time, I intended to return to the region and take over the Gasthaus when my aunt and uncle retired from the business. As it turned out, I was ultimately to take a different path. Soon after arriving in America, I met and married a beautiful woman from Nicaragua named Gloria. We had two children, Patrick and Elizabeth, and in 1974, I became a United States citizen. I am proud to have raised my family and pursued my culinary career in the United States. The truth is, though, I have never really left the Black Forest or the Gasthaus zum Buckenberg. I continue to carry with me memories of the place where I first realized that my passion for food and cooking was to become my life's work.

Bologna & Cheese Salad
with Mustard Vinaigrette

STRAßBURGER WURSTSALAT

THIS SALAD IS A GASTHAUS CLASSIC. IT COMES TOGETHER IN A SNAP AND RELIES ON BASIC, READILY AVAILABLE INGREDIENTS. IT IS ALWAYS MADE TO ORDER, SO THE TEXTURE OF EACH ITEM MAINTAINS ITS INTEGRITY AND FULL FLAVOR.

GASTHAUS MENUS OFFER SEVERAL VARIATIONS OF THIS DISH. THIS UPSCALE VERSION WITH SWISS CHEESE PAYS TRIBUTE TO THE CITY OF STRASBOURG AND THE REGION OF ALSACE IN NORTHEASTERN FRANCE. OMIT THE CHEESE, AND IT IS OFTEN SERVED SIMPLY AS **WURSTSALAT**. ANOTHER POPULAR VARIATION KNOWN AS **SCHWÄBISCHERWURST-SALAT** WAS INSPIRED BY SWABIA IN SOUTHWESTERN GERMANY AND INCLUDES THIN SLICES OF THE EVER-POPULAR SMOKED BLOOD SAUSAGE AND HEADCHEESE.

IN THE BLACK FOREST, THIS SALAD IS TRADITIONALLY SERVED IN THE LATE AFTERNOON AS A SNACK, APPETIZER, OR LIGHT MAIN COURSE, BUT IT WOULD ALSO BE DELIGHTFUL FOR LUNCH OR AS A LIGHT DINNER.

Schwäbischerwurstsalat

Serves 4

½ cup red wine vinegar

2 teaspoons Dijon mustard

¼ cup olive oil

1 red onion, peeled and finely sliced

2 dill pickles, sliced into thin strips
about 2 inches long and $\frac{1}{16}$ to ⅛ inch wide

2 tablespoons chopped fresh chives

Salt

Freshly ground black pepper

1 pound bologna, sliced into thin strips
about 2 inches long and ⅛ inch wide

8 ounces Swiss cheese, sliced into strips
about 2 inches long and ⅛ inch wide

1 head Bibb lettuce, cored and leaves separated,
for serving

1. Stir together the vinegar and mustard in a small bowl and drizzle in the olive oil, whisking to emulsify. Toss in the onion, pickles, and chives and season with salt and pepper.

2. Place the bologna and cheese in a medium bowl and pour the dressing overtop, tossing the salad to coat.

3. To serve, arrange two leaves of lettuce on each plate and spoon the salad on top.

WHENEVER I THINK ABOUT MAULTASCHEN, I AM HOME AGAIN. TO ME, THIS IS THE ULTIMATE COMFORT FOOD. THIS IS MY SOUL FOOD. MY MOTHER WOULD MAKE PILES OF THESE RAVIOLI IN A SINGLE DISCIPLINED SESSION, TAKING TIME AND CARE WITH THE DOUGH AND CUTTING IT IN VARIOUS SIZES TO STUFF WITH THE MEAT FILLING. MAULTASCHEN CAN BE LARGE OR SMALL, SAUTÉED AS I SUGGEST HERE, SIMMERED IN SOUP, OR CUT INTO STRIPS AND PREPARED LIKE HASH BROWNS. SOMETIMES MY MOTHER WOULD FLOAT THEM IN BEEF BOUILLON OR CHICKEN STOCK TO MAKE A DELICIOUS SOUP. PERSONALLY, I WILL EAT THEM ANYWHERE AT ANY TIME OF DAY. IN FACT, WHEN I USED TO TRAVEL HOME, MY MOTHER WOULD PREPARE MAULTASCHEN ESPECIALLY FOR ME AND SEND MY FATHER TO THE AIRPORT, PLATE IN HAND. AS SOON AS MY FEET HIT THE GROUND, I WOULD BEGIN TO INHALE THEM, AT THE SAME TIME THANKING HEAVEN THAT I WAS BACK IN THE BLACK FOREST.

Black Forest Ravioli

MAULTASCHEN

1. To make the noodle dough, pour the flour into a medium bowl and mix in the eggs, egg yolks, oil, and salt. Using your hands, knead the dough until it comes together and can be formed into a stiff ball. (Alternatively, mix and knead the dough in the bowl of an electric mixer fitted with the paddle attachment.) Wrap the dough in plastic wrap and set it aside to rest at room temperature for 1 hour.

2. To make the filling, melt the butter in a small sauté pan over medium heat, add the onion, and sauté until softened and translucent. Set aside for a few minutes to cool.

3. Combine the cooled onion, bread crumbs, meat, egg yolks, scallion, and parsley in a medium bowl, season with salt and pepper, and mix gently but thoroughly with your hands.

4. To assemble the Maultaschen, bring a large saucepan of salted water to a boil over high heat. Whisk together the egg and water in a small bowl to make an egg wash. Roll the noodle dough on a lightly floured surface to about $1/16$ inch (very thin) and cut it into twelve 6-inch squares. Divide the filling among the squares, brush the edges with the egg wash, and fold the four corners of each square into the center, pressing the seams firmly to seal.

5. Drop the Maultaschen, one at a time, into the boiling water and cook for approximately 5 minutes, or until they float to the surface. Remove them with a slotted spoon to an ice bath to cool. Drain the Maultaschen and set aside momentarily.

6. Melt the butter in a large sauté pan over medium-high heat. Place the Maultaschen in the pan and sauté on both sides until golden brown.

7. To serve, remove the Maultaschen to a serving platter and serve with potato salad.

Serves 6 to 8

NOODLE DOUGH:

4 cups all-purpose flour

4 eggs, lightly beaten

4 egg yolks, lightly beaten

1 tablespoon plus 1 teaspoon vegetable oil

1 tablespoon plus 1 teaspoon salt

FILLING:

1 tablespoon unsalted butter

$1/2$ yellow onion, peeled and finely chopped

$1/2$ cup soft bread crumbs

6 ounces ground pork

6 ounces ground beef

3 egg yolks

1 scallion, trimmed and finely chopped

1 tablespoon chopped fresh parsley

Salt

Freshly ground black pepper

ASSEMBLY:

1 egg

2 tablespoons water

4 tablespoons unsalted butter

Potato Salad, for serving (page 123) (optional)

Chicken Noodle Soup

HÜHNER NUDEL SUPPE

WE RAISED MANY CHICKENS AT HOME, MOSTLY FOR THEIR EGGS, WHICH WERE PRIZED FOR BAKING. OLDER CHICKENS THAT NO LONGER PRODUCED EGGS WERE THEN USED IN STEWS AND SOUPS LIKE THIS ONE. THESE CHICKENS NORMALLY WERE FATTIER THAN YOUNGER HENS, AND MY MOTHER USED THIS TO OUR ADVANTAGE; SHE RENDERED THE FAT TO MAKE SCHMALTZ TO BE USED AS A FLAVORFUL ALTERNATIVE TO BUTTER OR LARD IN OTHER DISHES.

I THINK THE BEST CHICKEN SOUPS ARE THE SIMPLEST, AND THIS ONE CERTAINLY IS BASIC. A BIT OF FRESH THYME ADDS A DELICATE FLAVOR THAT MARRIES BEAUTIFULLY WITH CHICKEN, AND THE EGG NOODLES LEND TEXTURE TO THE SOUP AND MAKE IT EVEN MORE SATISFYING.

Serves 6 to 8

1 tablespoon unsalted butter

1 medium onion, peeled and chopped

3 ribs celery, chopped

2 large carrots, peeled and chopped

3 quarts Chicken Stock (page 308)

1 sprig fresh thyme

1 pound boneless chicken (white or dark meat),
   cooked and chopped

8 ounces Egg Noodles (page 158), cooked and drained

Salt

Freshly ground black pepper

Chopped fresh parsley, for garnish

1. Melt the butter over medium heat in a medium saucepan, add the onion, and sauté for 3 to 5 minutes, until softened and translucent. Add the celery and carrots and sauté for 3 to 5 minutes more, until softened. Stir in the stock and thyme and bring to a boil over high heat. Reduce the heat to low and simmer for about 30 minutes, until the stock is reduced by one-third.

2. Lift out the thyme and add the chicken and egg noodles. Simmer until heated and season with salt and pepper.

3. Serve the soup in a tureen or in individual bowls garnished with parsley.

This soup has always been popular in France and Alsace, so it seems only natural that it has become a Gasthaus classic. Although it is prepared frequently in homes and cafés, this version is different as it relies on lentils to add body and richness to the broth. I first made this soup as an apprentice, and I think you will find it a satisfying medley of textures and flavors.

As usual when using lentils, plan ahead and begin preparing the soup the night before serving it. Any variety of lentils is fine here except the more delicate French lentils.

Oxtail Soup

OCHSENSCHWANZ SUPPE

Serves 6 to 8

½ cup lentils

3 pounds beef oxtails, cut into 1-inch pieces

2 tablespoons unsalted butter

1½ cups chopped onions

1 cup chopped carrots

1 cup chopped celery

1 tablespoon chopped garlic

¾ cup tomato paste

2 cups full-bodied red wine, such as Burgundy

2 quarts Beef Stock (page 310)

¼ cup chopped fresh parsley

1 teaspoon stemmed and chopped fresh rosemary

1 dried bay leaf

4 tablespoons unsalted butter

¼ cup all-purpose flour

Salt

Freshly ground black pepper

1. At least 8 hours before serving the soup, pour the lentils into a colander and rinse thoroughly, removing any stones or hard bits. Remove the lentils to a large bowl, add water until the lentils are covered by about 1 inch, and set aside at room temperature for 8 hours or overnight. The next day, or when ready to prepare the soup, drain and rinse the lentils and reserve.

2. Preheat the oven to 400°F.

3. Arrange the oxtail pieces in a medium roasting pan, place in the oven, and roast, stirring occasionally to prevent burning, for about 35 minutes, or until they are dark brown. Remove the pan from the oven, drain and discard any drippings, and set the pan and meat aside to cool slightly, about 15 minutes.

4. Melt the butter in a large saucepan or small stockpot over medium heat, add the onions, carrots, celery, and garlic, and sauté until the onions are translucent and all of the vegetables are slightly softened, about 5 minutes. Add the oxtails and stir in the tomato paste.

5. Pour in the wine to deglaze, stirring with a wooden spoon to loosen any browned bits on the bottom of the pan. Raise the heat to high, bring to a boil, and cook, stirring occasionally for about 10 minutes, or until the wine is reduced by half.

6. Add the stock, parsley, rosemary, and bay leaf and return to a boil over high heat. Reduce the heat to medium low and simmer for a total of about 2 hours, or until the meat falls off the bones.

7. Meanwhile, place the reserved lentils in a medium saucepan and add salted water just to cover. Bring to a boil and cook for about 10 to 15 minutes, or until the lentils are tender.

8. Drain the lentils and add them to the simmering soup during the last 30 minutes of cooking time. After 30 minutes, remove and discard the oxtail bones and bay leaf.

9. Melt the butter in a small saucepan over low heat, stir in the flour to make a roux, and cook for about 15 minutes, stirring frequently.

10. Bring the soup to a boil over high heat and add the roux a little at a time, stirring constantly to incorporate. Reduce the heat to medium and cook for 5 minutes more, until the soup has thickened slightly.

11. Season again with salt and pepper and serve in a tureen or in individual bowls.

Potato-Leek Soup

KARTOFFEL & LAUCH SUPPE

Serves 8

3 tablespoons unsalted butter

5 medium leeks (white part only),
    rinsed well and chopped (about 5½ cups)

1½ quarts Chicken Stock (page 308)

6 medium red-skinned potatoes (about 2 pounds),
    peeled and chopped

1 medium yellow onion, peeled and chopped

9 slices lean bacon, chopped (about ½ cup)

1 teaspoon dried marjoram

Salt

Freshly ground black pepper

2 cups Herb Croutons (page 31), for serving

This flavorful, satisfying soup is served throughout the year in the Black Forest. It is easy to prepare and relies on ingredients that are as readily available in the Gasthaus as they are in the home. Potatoes keep for months in root cellars, and leeks grown in the summer remain in the garden, where they freeze during the cold months.

I suggest serving this soup with herb croutons for additional flavor and texture, but if you wish not to do so, it is delicious and satisfying on its own.

1. Melt the butter in a large saucepan over medium-low heat, add the leeks, and sauté until softened, about 10 minutes.

2. Stir in the stock, add the potatoes, and simmer for about 30 minutes, until the potatoes are tender.

3. Meanwhile, heat a medium saucepan over medium heat, add the onion and bacon, and sauté until golden brown, about 5 minutes. Pour off the bacon drippings and stir the onion, bacon, and marjoram into the simmering soup.

4. Season the soup with salt and pepper and serve in a tureen or in individual bowls sprinkled with croutons.

Tripe Soup

KUTTELN SUPPE

1. At least 8 hours or the day before serving the soup, pour the beans into a colander and rinse thoroughly, removing any stones or hard bits. Remove the beans to a large bowl, add water until the beans are covered by about 1 inch, and set aside at room temperature for 8 hours or overnight. The next day, or when ready to prepare the soup, drain and rinse the beans and place them in an 8-quart saucepan. Pour in enough lightly salted water to cover and bring to a boil over high heat. Reduce the heat to medium low and simmer, covered, until the beans are tender, about 45 minutes. Drain the beans and reserve.

2. Place the tripe in the same saucepan, and pour in enough cold salted water to cover. Bring to a boil over high heat, reduce the heat to medium low, and simmer until tender, about 30 minutes. Drain the tripe thoroughly in a colander and set aside to cool for 15 minutes. Slice into $1/2$-inch strips and set aside.

3. Melt the butter in a large saucepan over medium heat, add the carrots, leek, celery, and garlic, and sauté until softened, stirring occasionally, about 5 minutes.

4. Add the tripe and beans and sauté for 5 minutes more.

5. Stir in the stock, wine, and bay leaf and bring to a boil over high heat. Reduce the heat to low, stir in the tomato paste, parsley, and thyme, and simmer until the beans begin to fall apart, about 30 to 45 minutes.

6. Serve the soup in a tureen or in individual soup bowls sprinkled with Parmesan cheese.

IN THE BLACK FOREST, TRIPE IS A DELICACY AND INCORPORATING IT IN A SOUP IS JUST ONE WAY TO PREPARE IT. THIS KIND OF HEARTY SOUP—FLAVORED WITH VEGETABLES, BEANS, HERBS, AND WINE—IS POPULAR IN NEARLY EVERY GASTHAUS, WHERE IT IS MOST COMMONLY SERVED AS A DAILY SPECIAL. ENJOY IT AS A FIRST COURSE, SATISFYING LUNCH OR, AS WE DO IN THE BLACK FOREST, AS AN EARLY EVENING MEAL WITH SOME BREAD OR ROLLS.

PLAN AHEAD WITH THIS SOUP, AS THE BEANS REQUIRE AT LEAST EIGHT HOURS OF SOAKING TIME.

Serves 6

$3/4$ cup dried cannellini beans (white Italian kidney beans)

1 pound beef honeycomb tripe

2 tablespoons unsalted butter

1 cup chopped carrots

1 large leek, trimmed, cleaned, and cut into strips about 2 inches long and $1/8$ inch wide (about 1 cup)

1 cup chopped celery

1 tablespoon chopped garlic

$1 1/2$ quarts Chicken Stock (page 308)

1 cup full-bodied red wine, such as Burgundy

1 dried bay leaf

$3/4$ cup tomato paste

1 tablespoon chopped fresh parsley

1 large sprig fresh thyme, stemmed and chopped

$1/4$ cup grated Parmesan cheese, for serving

Celery Root &
Carrot Salad

GEKOCHTER SELLERIE &
KAROTTEN SALAT

THIS SALAD IS AN EXAMPLE OF THE INGENUITY AND FRUGALITY TYP-
ICAL OF EVERY BLACK FOREST HOME AND RESTAURANT KITCHEN.
OUR GARDENS AND ROOT CELLARS WERE ALWAYS FILLED WITH
VEGETABLES, BUT WE WOULD NEVER HAVE BOILED THEM EXCLUSIVELY FOR
THIS DISH. INSTEAD, THESE VEGETABLES WERE ESSENTIALLY LEFTOVERS,
FIRST USED AS FLAVORFUL INGREDIENTS IN OTHER PREPARATIONS,
NAMELY BOILED MEAT DISHES OR SOUPS. BECAUSE THEY SIMMER IN RICH
MEAT BROTHS, THESE VEGETABLES DEVELOP A LOT OF FLAVOR AND TRANS-
FORM INTO DELICIOUS SALADS, TOSSED WITH A FEW FRESH VEGETABLES
AND A SIMPLE VINAIGRETTE. UPSCALE GASTHAUS RESTAURANTS SERVE
THESE SALADS FOR LARGE CELEBRATIONS, AND ALSO INCLUDE THEM IN
SALATPLATTEN—BEAUTIFULLY ARRANGED PLATES SHOWCASING A
VARIETY OF SALADS.

THE CELERY ROOTS AND CARROTS CALLED FOR HERE WERE COOKED
ALONGSIDE THE BEEF SHORT RIBS IN THE BEEF SALAD RECIPE (PAGE 129),
BUT FEEL FREE TO IMPROVISE AND USE VEGETABLES YOU HAVE SIMMERED
WITH A LARGER PIECE OF MEAT OR A CHICKEN IN THE SAME WAY.

Serves 8 to 10

Reserved celery roots and carrots
    from Beef Salad (page 129)

1 large red onion, peeled and thinly sliced

1 cup red wine vinegar

1 cup olive oil

1 tablespoon salt

1 teaspoon freshly ground white pepper

1 teaspoon hot pepper sauce

¼ teaspoon dried red pepper flakes

1 head Bibb lettuce, cored and leaves separated,
    for serving

Chopped fresh chives, for garnish

---

1. Peel the celery roots and carrots and slice into strips about 2 inches long and ⅛ inch wide. Place the strips in a large bowl and add the onion.

2. Whisk together the vinegar, oil, salt, pepper, hot pepper sauce, and red pepper flakes and pour over the vegetables, tossing gently to coat.

3. To serve, arrange 2 to 3 lettuce leaves on each plate, spoon some of the salad on top, and garnish with chives.

Beet Salad

ROTE RÜBEN SALAT

1. Place the beets in a large saucepan and pour in enough lightly salted water just to cover. Bring the water to a boil and cook for 25 to 30 minutes, or until the beets are just tender. Drain the beets in a colander and, when cool enough to handle, peel and cut them into 1-inch cubes.

2. Whisk together the olive oil, onions, vinegar, parsley, lemon juice, red pepper flakes, and mustard in a medium bowl. Add the beets, season with salt and pepper, and toss gently to coat. Set aside for a bit to marinate at room temperature or in the refrigerator while preparing the rest of the dish.

3. Fill a medium saucepan about ⅔ full with vegetable oil and heat to 375°F. Peel the carrot with a vegetable peeler to make thin strips, blot them dry with paper towels, and fry in the oil until golden, about 1 minute. Remove the carrots with a wire mesh strainer and drain on paper towels.

4. To serve, arrange leaves of romaine lettuce on a large serving platter and spoon the beet salad on top. Sprinkle with fried carrots and top with egg slices.

WE LOVE BEETS IN THE BLACK FOREST AND USE THEM IN A VARIETY OF SALADS AS WELL AS IN HOT AND COLD SOUPS. SINCE HOME AND PROFESSIONAL COOKS ALIKE KEPT LARGE AMOUNTS OF BEETS ON HAND IN ROOT CELLARS, THIS SALAD WAS AS POPULAR ON HOME TABLES AS IT WAS IN GASTHAUS DINING ROOMS.

MY MOTHER OFTEN PREPARED THIS SALAD, BUT I HAVE MADE IT A BIT FANCIER HERE, AS WE DID IN THE GASTHAUS, WITH THE ADDITION OF SLICED HARD-COOKED EGGS. THEY ARE A NICE TOUCH, BUT YOU CAN CERTAINLY OMIT THEM IF YOU WISH.

Serves 6

2 pounds fresh beets, stems trimmed to ½ inch

1 cup olive oil

½ cup finely chopped onions

¼ cup rice wine vinegar

1 tablespoon chopped fresh parsley

Juice of ½ lemon

½ teaspoon dried red pepper flakes

1 tablespoon Dijon mustard

Salt

Freshly ground black pepper

Vegetable oil, for frying

1 carrot, peeled

1 head romaine lettuce, cored and leaves separated

2 hard-cooked eggs, sliced (optional)

Potato Salad

KARTOFFELSALAT

Whant more can I possibly say about potato salad than that it is a Black Forest staple and that I absolutely adore it? Unlike most American potato salads, which are creamy and prepared with mayonnaise, you will notice that our version relies primarily on vinegar and onion for flavor and is moistened with oil and beef bouillon.

This salad is deliciously satisfying on its own or incorporated into a full meal by serving it with a fried egg. For a bit of variety, we also occasionally tossed in thin slices of crispy bacon and used some of the rendered fat in place of the vegetable oil.

1. Place the potatoes in a large saucepan and pour in enough salted water to cover. Bring to a boil over high heat and cook the potatoes for 20 to 25 minutes, until just tender. Drain the potatoes in a colander and, when cool enough to handle, peel and cut into ¼-inch-thick slices.

2. Combine the potatoes and onion in a medium bowl and add the vinegar and oil, tossing gently to coat.

3. Pour in the bouillon a little at a time, mixing gently until it is absorbed. (The salad should be moist but not drenched.) Season with salt and pepper and serve garnished with chives.

Serves 6

12 medium Yukon gold potatoes

1 large yellow onion, peeled and finely chopped

¼ cup red wine vinegar

¼ cup vegetable oil

1½ to 2 cups Beef Bouillon (*see Chef's Note*, and page 309)

Salt

Freshly ground white pepper

Chopped fresh chives, for garnish

CHEF'S NOTE: Gasthaus kitchens always have homemade beef bouillon on hand, but beef bouillon cubes dissolved in hot water are perfectly suitable for this dish.

THIS SPICY EASTERN EUROPEAN DISH WANDERED INTO THE BLACK FOREST DECADES AGO AND HAS REMAINED A FAVORITE EVER SINCE. THIS DISH MAKES FREQUENT APPEARANCES AT FESTIVALS SUCH AS OKTOBERFEST AND IS PRACTICALLY A FIXTURE ON MENUS IN COMFORTABLE, UNPRETENTIOUS GASTHAUS DINING ROOMS. IT IS TRADITIONALLY PREPARED WITH LAMB, BUT, AS LAMB IS EXPENSIVE IN THE BLACK FOREST, WE FREQUENTLY SUBSTITUTED CHICKEN, BEEF, OR PORK, ALL OF WHICH WORK JUST AS WELL. THE SKEWERS AND SAUCE COME TOGETHER QUITE QUICKLY AND EASILY.

Skewered Pork with Spicy Cream Sauce

SCHASHLIK IN WÜRZIGER PAPRIKA SOßE

1. To make the skewers, soak 4 bamboo skewers (8 to 12 inches long) in water for about 30 minutes. (You can skip this step by using metal skewers.) Place a piece of pork, bacon, onion, and pepper on each skewer, continuing the process until the ingredients are equally divided among the skewers. Season the skewers with salt and pepper, brush with vegetable oil, and set aside in a shallow casserole or pan to marinate in the refrigerator for 1 hour.

2. Melt the butter in a large sauté pan over high heat, place the skewers in the pan, and brown them on all sides, about 2 to 3 minutes per side. Remove the skewers, setting them aside momentarily, and return the pan to the stove.

3. To make the sauce, heat the butter remaining in the pan over high heat, toss in the garlic, and sauté until slightly softened, about 1 minute. Add the bacon, sautéing until crisp, then add the onion and pepper, sautéing until slightly softened, about 2 to 3 minutes.

4. Stir in the flour and paprika and add the wine to deglaze, stirring with a wooden spoon to loosen any browned bits on the bottom of the pan. Bring the wine to a boil and cook for about 5 minutes.

5. Stir in the cayenne pepper and red pepper flakes and season with salt and pepper. Return the skewers to the pan, reduce the heat to medium, and simmer for 5 to 10 minutes.

6. To serve, place the skewers on a platter or individual plates, stir the sour cream into the sauce, and spoon the sauce over the skewers, garnishing with chives.

Serves 4

PORK SKEWERS:

2 pounds pork tenderloin, cleaned, trimmed,
   and sliced into 2-ounce pieces

8 ounces bacon, cut into 2-inch pieces

2 medium onions, peeled and chopped into 2-inch pieces

2 large bell peppers, stemmed, seeded,
   and chopped into 2-inch pieces

Salt

Freshly ground black pepper

Vegetable oil

2 tablespoons unsalted butter

SAUCE:

1½ teaspoons finely chopped garlic

2 tablespoons finely chopped bacon

2 tablespoons chopped onion

2 tablespoons finely chopped green or red bell pepper

1 tablespoon all-purpose flour

1½ tablespoons Hungarian paprika

½ cup full-bodied red wine, such as Burgundy

¼ teaspoon ground cayenne pepper

¼ teaspoon dried red pepper flakes

Salt

Freshly ground black pepper

3 tablespoons sour cream

Chopped fresh chives, for garnish

Sausage & Smoked Meat Platter

SCHLACHTPLATTE

1. Pierce the onion with the bay leaf and cloves and place in a large stockpot. Add the pork knuckles, sprinkle in the salt, and pour water overtop to cover the knuckles by about 1 inch. Bring to a boil over high heat, reduce the heat to low, and simmer gently for about 2 hours, or until the pork is fully cooked. (When the pork is done, it will have shrunk back from the bone and a skewer will pierce it quite easily.) Remove the knuckles from the pot, reserving the cooking liquid, and set the knuckles aside in a small pot with some of the cooking liquid to keep warm.

2. Place the sausages and smoked pork chops in the reserved hot cooking liquid until heated, about 3 minutes. Do not boil.

3. Pour the half-and-half in a small bowl and melt the butter in a medium sauté pan over medium heat.

4. Remove the bratwurst links from the pot and pierce the skin in several places with a round toothpick or bamboo skewer. Dip the links in the half-and-half to coat, place them in the sauté pan, and sauté until well browned. Set aside to keep warm.

5. To serve, place the sauerkraut on a large platter, arrange the pork knuckles, sausages, and pork chops on top.

Serves 12 to 14

1 large yellow onion, peeled

1 dried bay leaf

3 whole cloves

12 pork knuckles (smoked if desired)

1 tablespoon salt

3 to 4 links knockwurst

3 to 4 links bratwurst

3 to 4 links blood sausage (optional)

3 to 4 links liver sausage (optional)

12 smoked pork chops (about 4 ounces each)

¼ cup half-and-half

2 tablespoons unsalted butter

4½ quarts Sauerkraut (page 164), for serving

Black Forest Digestif

It is difficult for me to convey the precise meaning of **SCHLACHTPLATTE**. More than a single recipe, it is a way of presenting specific foods, celebrating a particular event, and remembering a way of life. Basically, Schlachtplatte refers to the variety of sausages and cuts of meat prepared and served after a family has slaughtered a pig. Although virtually every family in my hometown was skilled at keeping livestock, even in my day, no one slaughtered their own pigs. It was just too big of a job. Instead, butchers like my Uncle Walter traveled to farms to complete the task. When this personal service ceased, folks would take their pigs to local butchers for the same purpose. In both cases, butchering a pig was a big event and called for a celebration we call **SCHLACHTFEST**. Literally translated as "festival of the butchering," the event is a time for family and friends to join in preparing and feasting upon pork in various forms—sausages, chops, etc.—always accompanied by large amounts of delicious sauerkraut.

I include Schlachtplatte here, because Gasthaus restaurants commonly offer it and, at various times during the year, hold Schlachtfest. When my aunt and uncle ran the Gasthaus zum Buckenberg, they had a butcher's shop and retail store on site, so it was natural for them to hold this event. Even Gasthaus restaurants without butcher's shops still celebrate this festival, taking pigs from their own farms to neighborhood butchers and serving a wide selection of pork items on their menus.

Today, Schlachtplatte is listed on restaurant menus throughout the year. Regardless of whether there is an accompanying festival, the presentation of delicious pork and tangy sauerkraut is a reminder of days gone by—of traditional foods and ways of life that were vital, and gave great joy, to generations of Black Forest communities.

Beef Salad

OCHSENFLEISCH SALAT

THIS TRADITIONAL BLACK FOREST DISH IS SERVED IN MODEST AND UPSCALE RESTAURANTS ALIKE. A FLAVORFUL COMBINATION OF MEAT, DIJON VINAIGRETTE, ONIONS, GARLIC, PICKLES, AND HORSERADISH, THE SALAD SPEAKS AS MUCH WITH AN ALSATIAN ACCENT AS IT DOES WITH A GERMAN ONE.

IN GASTHAUS RESTAURANTS, WE PREPARE BEEF SALAD TO ORDER AND SERVE IT AT ROOM TEMPERATURE SO IT MAINTAINS ITS FULL FLAVOR. IN ADDITION, IT IS A FAIRLY SUBSTANTIAL DISH, SO WE OFFER IT AS AN ENTRÉE SALAD, RATHER THAN AS AN APPETIZER, WITH SIDES OF HOME FRIES OR HEARTY BREAD OR ROLLS.

SINCE THIS RECIPE SERVES QUITE A FEW PEOPLE, I RECOMMEND MAKING IT FOR A SUNDAY BRUNCH OR SPECIAL OCCASION, AS THE LEFTOVERS WILL NOT FREEZE WELL.

Serves 8 to 10

SHORT RIBS:

5 to 7 pounds beef short ribs, bone in

½ yellow onion, peeled

1 dried bay leaf

3 whole cloves

6 scallions, trimmed

2 ribs celery

1 leek (white part only), trimmed

2 Roma tomatoes, cored

2 medium celery roots, thoroughly washed, but not peeled

3 large carrots, thoroughly washed, but not peeled

2 tablespoons salt

1 teaspoon fresh coarsely cracked black pepper

VINAIGRETTE:

½ cup Dijon mustard

1 cup extra virgin olive oil

1 cup red wine vinegar

ASSEMBLY:

3 red onions, peeled and thinly sliced

3 cloves garlic, peeled and coarsely chopped

3 kosher dill pickles, sliced into strips about 2 inches long and ⅛ inch wide

2 tablespoons salt

2 teaspoons freshly ground white pepper

1 head Bibb lettuce, cored and leaves separated, for serving

Chopped fresh chives, for garnish

Fried Horseradish (page 130), for garnish

1. Rinse the short ribs in cold water, place in a 9-quart stockpot, and fill the pot with water almost to the top. Pierce the onion with the bay leaf and cloves and place in the pot with the vegetables, salt, and pepper. Bring to a boil over high heat, skimming and discarding any foam that rises to the surface. Reduce the heat to medium low and simmer for about 20 minutes, or until the carrots are just tender. Carefully remove the carrots and set aside to cool. Simmer another 30 minutes, or until the celery roots are just tender. Carefully remove the celery roots and set aside to cool. Reserve the carrots and celery root for use in the Celery Root and Carrot Salad (page 120).

2. Continue to simmer the ribs until the beef is fully cooked. (When the beef is done, it will have shrunk about 2 to 2½ inches down the bone, and a skewer will pierce it quite easily.) Set the ribs aside to cool in the bouillon, about 45 minutes. Remove the ribs to a baking sheet or container, cover, and set in the refrigerator to chill. (At this point you can simply reserve the stock as it is for another use, such as the Potato Salad (page 123) or reduce it for later use. To make the reduction, strain the bouillon into a large saucepan and bring to a boil. Reduce the heat to medium high and simmer until reduced by half. Let cool and store in the refrigerator or freezer.)

3. To make the vinaigrette, whisk together the mustard and olive oil in a medium bowl and gradually whisk in the vinegar.

4. To assemble the salad, remove the chilled rib meat from the bones and slice into thin slices 1-inch square. Add the onions, garlic, pickles, salt, and pepper, tossing gently to combine. Pour the vinaigrette over the beef salad, tossing gently to coat and serve.

5. To serve, arrange 2 to 3 lettuce leaves on each plate, spoon some beef salad on top, and garnish with chives and fried horseradish.

Fried Horseradish

AUSGEBACKENER MEERRETTICH

1 cup vegetable oil, for frying
1 small horseradish, peeled and sliced as finely as possible into strips (about 2 inches long and ¹⁄₁₆ inch wide)

1. Heat the oil in a large sauté pan over high heat to 350°F. If you don't have a thermometer, drop one piece of horseradish in the pan. If it sizzles, then the oil is hot enough.

2. Add the horseradish, being careful to prevent splattering, and fry until golden brown, about 1 minute.

3. Remove the horseradish from the oil with a slotted spoon and set on paper towels to drain.

EVEN CHEFS DE CUISINE WHO WORKED IN LARGE, ELABORATE KITCHENS TRAVELED TO MARKETS ALMOST EVERYDAY TO PLAN DAILY SPECIALS AND PURCHASE FRESH PRODUCE. MY AUNT AND UNCLE RELIED ON THEIR BUTCHER'S SHOP FOR MEAT AND CHARCUTERIE AND HARVESTED FRESH PRODUCE FROM THEIR OWN GARDENS.

Tripe à la Mode

KUTTELN IN SENFSOBE

1. To make the tripe, bring a large saucepan of lightly salted water to a boil over high heat. Drop in the tripe and boil for 2 minutes. Remove the tripe, using a large slotted spoon, set on paper towels to drain and cool slightly, and slice into strips about 2 inches long and ⅛ inch wide.

2. Melt the butter in a large sauté pan over medium-low heat, toss in the garlic and shallots, and sauté until softened and translucent. (They should not brown at all.) Add the tripe and cook until any liquid it releases has evaporated. Remove from the heat and set aside.

3. To make the sauce, melt the butter in a sauté pan over medium heat, add the shallots, and sauté until softened and translucent, about 1 minute. (They should not brown at all.) Stir in the flour to make a smooth paste (roux) and remove from the heat. Whisk in the mustard, stock, demi-glace, cayenne pepper, season with salt and pepper, and bring to a boil over high heat. Reduce the heat to medium and simmer until reduced by one-fourth, about 8 to 10 minutes. Pour in the cream and simmer for 1 to 2 minutes more.

4. To finish the tripe, return the tripe to medium heat and add the vinegar to deglaze, stirring with a wooden spoon to loosen any browned bits on the bottom of the pan, and simmer just until heated.

5. To serve, arrange the tripe on a serving platter, pour the sauce overtop, and garnish with chives.

132

We love tripe in the Black Forest and consider any preparation a treat. This dish clearly pays tribute to the influence of French cuisine on the region. À LA MODE appears on menus throughout France and generally means "in the style of the chef." When I cooked in Gasthaus and Hotel kitchens throughout the Black Forest, the term always referred to a Dijon mustard sauce, as I have included in this recipe.

Sometimes we cooked tripe in marinara sauce or served it FRA DIAVOLO style, in a spicy tomato sauce. This mustard sauce was quite popular, too. It comes together rather quickly and is a flavorful, creamy combination of tart mustard, meaty demi-glace, spicy cayenne pepper, rich cream, and bright vinegar. We always served tripe à la mode as a special, usually on a Monday or Tuesday, never À LA CARTE. Like all "special" menu items, we cooked up just one large batch, and when we ran out customers anxiously waited until the following week when we prepared it again.

Serves 4

TRIPE:

2½ pounds honeycomb tripe

1 tablespoon unsalted butter

1 tablespoon finely chopped garlic

1 tablespoon finely chopped shallots

SAUCE:

3 tablespoons unsalted butter

1 cup chopped shallots

3 tablespoons all-purpose flour

3 tablespoons Dijon mustard

1 quart Beef Stock (page 310)

2 cups Demi-Glace (page 312) or prepared brown sauce

½ teaspoon ground cayenne pepper

1 tablespoon salt

½ teaspoon white pepper

½ cup heavy cream

TO FINISH THE TRIPE:

1 tablespoon white wine vinegar

Chopped fresh chives, for garnish

Marinated Beef Roast

SAUERBRATEN

1. Combine the vinegar, wine, garlic, onion, carrot, celery, bay leaves, juniper berries, cloves, and peppercorns in a large saucepan or casserole and bring to a boil over high heat. Remove from heat, gently drop in the roast, and set aside to cool slightly. Cover the saucepan and set aside in the refrigerator to marinate for about 3 days. (If the marinade does not cover the roast completely, be sure to turn the roast about every 12 hours to marinate evenly.)

2. After 3 days or when you are ready to proceed with the dish, remove the roast from the marinade and pat dry. Strain the marinade, reserving the vegetables and 3 cups of the marinade.

3. Preheat the oven to 350°F.

4. Combine the oil, salt, and pepper in a small bowl, rub over the roast, and set in a large casserole or medium roasting pan. Cover and roast for 1 hour.

5. Pour the reserved marinade into a small saucepan and bring to a boil over high heat. Reduce the heat to medium and simmer until reduced to about 2 cups.

6. Remove the roast from the oven and pour the reduced marinade into the pan to deglaze, stirring with a wooden spoon to loosen any browned bits on the bottom of the pan. Scatter the reserved vegetables around the roast and pour in the demiglace. Cover and roast for 30 to 45 minutes more, basting frequently.

7. To serve, place the roast on a serving platter. Strain the juices from the pan, stir in the sour cream to make a creamy sauce, and serve the sauce in a gravy boat on the side.

THIS DISH IS A FAVORITE NOT ONLY IN THE BLACK FOREST BUT THROUGHOUT SOUTHERN GERMANY AS WELL. THIS IS PROBABLY DUE TO THE TANGY, FULL-FLAVORED INGREDIENTS, SUCH AS VINEGAR, BAY LEAVES, JUNIPER BERRIES, AND CLOVES, FOR WHICH NEARLY EVERY GERMAN PALATE HAS A NATURAL AFFINITY. SAUERBRATEN COMBINES A VARIETY OF COOKING TECHNIQUES—SEVERAL DAYS OF MARINATING, SOME ROASTING, AND SOME BRAISING—WHICH RESULT IN A TENDER ROAST AND A FLAVORFUL SAUCE. THE MARINADE IS AN IMPORTANT COMPONENT THAT CAN BE USED IN EITHER OF TWO WAYS. MOST HOME COOKS PREFER A **BEIZE**, OR COLD MARINADE, AND SET THE BEEF TO MARINATE IN A COOL ROOT CELLAR FOR ABOUT 5 DAYS. GASTHAUS COOKS, ON THE OTHER HAND, PREFER TO START THE BEEF IN A HOT MARINADE, SUCH AS I SUGGEST HERE, AND THEN MOVE IT TO THE REFRIGERATOR TO MARINATE FOR ABOUT 3 DAYS. BOTH METHODS ARE FINE, BUT I THINK THE LATTER PENETRATES THE BEEF BETTER AND IN LESS TIME. SERVE SLICES OF SAUERBRATEN WITH ANY OF YOUR FAVORITE SIDES. I, OF COURSE, HAPPEN TO THINK THEY ARE BEST PAIRED WITH BLACK FOREST STAND-BYS: POTATO DUMPLINGS, SMASHED POTATOES, SPÄTZLE, OR BRAISED RED CABBAGE (PAGES 162, 156, 161, AND 159).

Serves 6

3 cups red wine vinegar

3 cups full-bodied red wine, such as Burgundy

3 cloves garlic, peeled and coarsely chopped

1 medium yellow onion, peeled and coarsely chopped

1 large carrot, peeled and coarsely chopped

2 ribs celery, coarsely chopped

3 dried bay leaves

¼ cup dried juniper berries

5 to 6 whole cloves

1 teaspoon freshly cracked black peppercorns

1 boneless beef chuck roast (about 6 pounds),
    rinsed in cold water and patted dry

¼ cup vegetable oil

2 teaspoons salt

1 teaspoon freshly ground black pepper

6 cups Demi-Glace (page 312) or prepared brown sauce

½ cup sour cream

Stuffed Cabbage

GEFÜLLTER WEIßKOHL

IN THE BLACK FOREST, STUFFED CABBAGE IS CELEBRATED AND ENJOYED IN MODEST AND UPSCALE SETTINGS ALIKE. TYPICAL OF MANY HOME COOKS, MY MOTHER PREPARED SUBSTANTIAL SIZE STUFFED CABBAGES, WHILE IN FORMAL RESTAURANTS WE OFTEN PRESENTED THREE PETITE STUFFED MORSELS ON A PLATE IN A MORE ELEGANT FASHION.

STUFFINGS FOR THIS DISH VARY WIDELY. SOME COOKS USE RICE TO LIGHTEN THE MIXTURE A BIT, WHILE OTHERS PREFER A HEARTIER STUFFING PREPARED SIMPLY WITH MEAT. I LIKE THE TEXTURE RICE GIVES TO THIS DISH, SO I HAVE INCLUDED IT HERE. IN ADDITION TO WRAPPING THE STUFFING IN CABBAGE, IT IS ALSO DELICIOUS STUFFED INTO PEPPERS.

THIS DISH IS ALMOST ALWAYS SERVED AS A GASTHAUS LUNCH ITEM AND OFFERED AS A WEEKLY SPECIAL. WARMING AND HEARTY, IT IS SATISFYING PRESENTED ON ITS OWN, OR, AS WE SOMETIMES DO IN THE BLACK FOREST, SERVED WITH RICE OR SMASHED POTATOES (PAGE 156).

Serves 6

STUFFING:

1 tablespoon unsalted butter

½ yellow onion, peeled and finely chopped

6 ounces ground pork

6 ounces ground beef

3 egg yolks

1 scallion, trimmed and finely chopped

1 tablespoon chopped fresh parsley

Salt

Freshly ground black pepper

1 cup cooked long grain white rice

ASSEMBLY:

1 large head green cabbage

6 slices bacon, cut in half widthwise

SAUCE:

2 tablespoons unsalted butter

1 tablespoon finely chopped garlic

¼ cup finely chopped bacon

¼ cup finely chopped onion

¼ cup finely chopped green bell pepper

3 tablespoons Hungarian paprika

2 tablespoons all-purpose flour

1 cup full-bodied red wine, such as Burgundy

½ teaspoon ground cayenne pepper

½ teaspoon dried red pepper flakes

Salt

Freshly ground black pepper

⅓ cup sour cream

1. To make the stuffing, melt the butter in a small sauté pan over medium heat, toss in the onion, and sauté until softened and translucent. Remove from heat and set aside to cool completely.

2. Combine the cooled onion and the remaining stuffing ingredients in a medium bowl, mixing well to combine, and set aside in the refrigerator.

3. Preheat the oven to 350°F.

4. To assemble the cabbage, bring a large saucepan of lightly salted water to a boil over high heat. Reduce the heat to medium high and maintain at a hearty simmer. Core the cabbage using a sharp knife (image a), gently drop into the water, and simmer until the outer leaves are slightly softened, about 2 to 3 minutes. Remove the softened outer leaves, setting them on a clean towel to drain. Continue this process, simmering the cabbage and removing the leaves until you have accumulated at least 24 leaves.

4. Place 2 leaves slightly overlapping on a work surface and set ¼ cup of the stuffing in the center (image b). Fold the leaves over the stuffing (images c–d) to seal tightly and set seal side down in a casserole or baking dish coated with nonstick cooking spray. Repeat the process with the remaining leaves and stuffing.

5. Place half a slice of bacon over each stuffed cabbage (image e) and bake until the bacon is crisp, about 20 minutes.

6. To make the sauce, melt the butter in a small sauté pan over medium heat, add the garlic, and sauté until golden about 1½ minutes. Add the bacon and sauté until crisp. Toss in the onions and bell peppers and sauté until softened and any liquid the vegetables release has evaporated, about 2 minutes.

7. Stir the paprika and flour into the bacon and vegetables until combined. Add the wine to deglaze, stirring with a wooden spoon to loosen any browned bits on the bottom of the pan, and simmer for 5 minutes. Stir in the cayenne pepper and red pepper flakes, season with salt and pepper, and simmer for an additional 5 to 10 minutes. Remove from the heat and stir in the sour cream.

8. To finish the cabbage, ladle the sauce over the stuffed cabbage, bake for 10 minutes more, and serve hot.

STUFFED CABBAGE

Place 2 leaves, slightly overlapping, on a work surface and set the stuffing in the center. Fold the leaves over the stuffing to seal tightly and set seal side down in a casserole dish.

c

a

b

d

e

Black Forest Beef Roulades

GESCHMORTE RINDER ROULADEN

1. Heat 2 tablespoons of the butter in a medium sauté pan over high heat. Add the onion and sauté until softened and translucent. Remove from the heat to cool completely.

2. Line up the beef slices on a work surface, laying them flat (image a, next page), and season with salt and pepper. Spread a generous teaspoon of mustard on each slice and sprinkle evenly with sautéed onion, parsley, and bacon (image b). Place a pickle spear on the edge of each strip (image c), roll tightly (image d), and tie with kitchen twine, or pierce with toothpicks to hold the rolls in place (images e–f).

3. Preheat the oven to 425°F.

4. Melt the remaining 2 tablespoons of butter in a medium ovenproof sauté pan over medium-high heat (the pan should be just large enough to snugly hold all the roulades). Season the roulades with salt and pepper, arrange them in the sauté pan, and brown well on all sides. Add the wine to deglaze, stirring with a wooden spoon to loosen any browned bits on the bottom of the pan, and simmer until the pan is nearly dry. Pour in the demi-glace, cover, and set in the oven to roast until the meat is fully cooked but still tender, about 30 minutes. (Check the roulades after about 15 minutes and be careful not to overcook them or they will fall apart.)

5. To serve, remove the twine or toothpicks from the roulades, arrange them on a platter or on individual plates, and garnish with parsley.

These tender roulades are another example of satisfying Black Forest comfort food. They are served at home almost as frequently as they are in restaurants, although the home cook usually purchases them already stuffed and rolled from the butcher. The meat must be sliced very thinly and evenly and this is most easily achieved using a professional meat slicer.

The stuffing for these roulades can be prepared with any number of ingredients. The stuffing I suggest here is particularly flavorful. Based on onion, bacon, pickles, and parsley, it is a terrific mix of richness and tartness that marries wonderfully with the beef.

Gasthaus restaurants often serve roulades as a special during the week, and some establishments have become particularly well known for the dish. So anticipated are the tender rolls of stuffed beef that some folks make special plans to visit these restaurants just to satisfy their cravings. They know to start out fairly early, though. As with most "special" menu items, restaurants prepare a single large batch of roulades, and once they're gone, guests have to wait until the following week to get their fix.

Serves 6

4 tablespoons unsalted butter

1 large white onion, peeled and sliced

6 slices lean beef top round, 8 to 10 inches long, 3 to 4 inches wide, and 1/4 inch thick

Salt

Freshly ground black pepper

2 to 3 tablespoons Dijon mustard

1 large bunch fresh curly-leaf parsley, stemmed and chopped

1 pound bacon, sliced into strips about 2 inches long and 1/8 inch wide

6 dill pickle spears

2 cups red wine

3 cups Demi-Glace (page 312) or prepared brown sauce

Fresh curly-leaf parsley sprigs, for garnish

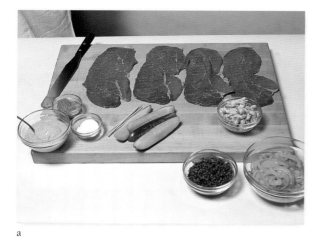

a

b

c

BLACK FOREST BEEF ROULADES

Season beef slices with salt and pepper. Spread mustard and sprinkle with onion, parsley, and bacon. Place pickle spear on edge of each strip, roll tightly, and pierce with toothpicks.

d

e

f

Cauliflower & Potato Casserole

BLUMENKOHL & KARTOFFEL GRATIN

THIS WARMING CASSEROLE IS PREPARED AT HOME AND IN GASTHAUS RESTAURANTS THROUGHOUT THE BLACK FOREST. IT IS A SIMPLE DISH THAT COMES TOGETHER QUICKLY AND GOES WELL WITH JUST ABOUT ANY ENTRÉE. I FIND IT PAIRS NICELY WITH ROASTS IN PARTICULAR.

1. Preheat the oven to 350°F.

2. Place the potatoes in a large saucepan and cover with cold water. Season lightly with salt and bring to a boil over high heat. Reduce the heat to medium and simmer until just tender, about 10 to 15 minutes.

3. Meanwhile, bring a large saucepan of lightly salted water to a boil over high heat, toss in the cauliflower, and boil until the florets are very soft, about 10 to 15 minutes.

4. Drain the potatoes and cauliflower and combine in a large bowl. Add the butter, sour cream, milk, and cheese, mash until smooth, and season with salt and pepper. Pour into a large buttered baking dish or casserole and sprinkle evenly with bread crumbs and paprika. Bake until golden brown and bubbly, about 30 minutes, and serve hot.

Serves 10 to 12

1½ pounds small Yukon gold potatoes, peeled

Salt

1 large head cauliflower, cut into florets

3 tablespoons unsalted butter, at room temperature

½ cup sour cream

½ cup milk

1 cup shredded Gruyère cheese

Freshly ground white pepper

¼ cup dry bread crumbs

1 teaspoon Hungarian paprika

New York Strip Steak with Caramelized Onions

SCHWÄBISCHER ROSTBRATEN

1. Melt the butter in a large sauté pan over medium heat, toss in the onions, and season with salt and pepper. Sauté until softened, reduce the heat to medium low, and continue to cook slowly, stirring frequently, until they are lightly browned and caramelized, about 5 minutes.

2. Meanwhile, pound the steaks to ¼ inch thick, make 3 equidistant slits in the fatty edge of each steak, and season with salt and pepper. (These slits prevent the steaks from shrinking.) Heat a large cast iron skillet or heavy-bottomed sauté pan over high heat and pour in a thin coating of oil, heating until very hot. (The oil will begin to shimmer slightly.) Place the steaks in the pan and sear on each side for about 2 minutes, or until cooked to medium-rare.

3. To serve, arrange the steaks on a serving platter, smother with caramelized onions, and sprinkle with scallions.

BLACK FOREST COOKING DOESN'T GET ANY SIMPLER THAN THIS SEARED STEAK SERVED WITH CARAMELIZED ONIONS. INTERESTINGLY ENOUGH, DESPITE HOW EASY IT IS TO PREPARE, WE RARELY MAKE IT AT HOME. THIS IS THE SORT OF SPECIAL DISH WE WOULD TRAVEL TO A GASTHAUS TO ENJOY, AND, IN FACT, MY AUNT AND UNCLE SERVED IT FREQUENTLY IN THEIR ESTABLISHMENT, GASTHAUS ZUM BUCKENBERG.

THIS STEAK IS PREPARED IN A VARIETY OF WAYS. ZIGEUNER ROSTBRATEN (GYPSY STYLE), IS SERVED WITH BACON AND ONIONS. GESCHMORTE ROSTBRATEN IS BRAISED AND COOKED UNTIL IT IS WELL DONE BUT TENDER. BY FAR THE MOST POPULAR VERSION IS THIS ONE, HOWEVER, SEARED AND SET SIMPLY ON A PLATE WITH ONIONS. OCCASIONALLY, ROLLS, POMMES FRITES (FRENCH FRIES), OR POTATO SALAD WILL BE SERVED ALONGSIDE, BUT PURISTS PREFER JUST TO FEAST ON THE STEAK.

WHETHER THE ROSTBRATEN IS SERVED ALONE OR WITH A SIDE DISH, IT IS ALWAYS COOKED TO MEDIUM-RARE. OF COURSE, YOU MIGHT LIKE YOUR STEAK RARE OR WELL-DONE. EVEN SO, IF YOU WANT TO SEAR IT PROPERLY, YOU MUST USE A CAST IRON SKILLET OR, AT THE VERY LEAST, A HEAVY-BOTTOMED SAUTÉ PAN. THIS ENSURES THAT THE STEAK OBTAINS THE BEAUTIFULLY DARK EXTERIOR FOR WHICH IT IS CELEBRATED.

Serves 6

¼ pound (1 stick) unsalted butter

6 large yellow onions, peeled and sliced

Salt

Freshly ground black pepper

6 New York strip steaks (about 14 ounces each), with at least 1 inch of the fat intact

Vegetable oil

6 scallions (green parts only), finely sliced on the diagonal, for garnish

AFTER WORLD WAR I, MANY HUNGARIANS MOVED TO FIND A BETTER LIFE IN SOUTHERN GERMANY AND SETTLED IN THE BLACK FOREST. THE MANY VARIETIES OF GOULASH I ENJOYED GROWING UP AND LEARNED TO PREPARE IN GASTHAUS KITCHENS ATTEST TO THE INFLUENCE OF HUNGARIAN CUISINE IN OUR REGION. HOME AND RESTAURANT COOKS LIKE TO SERVE THIS HEARTY DISH BECAUSE IT IS DELICIOUS AND INEXPENSIVE TO PREPARE. A LITTLE MEAT GOES A LONG WAY HERE AND ALMOST ANY KIND WILL DO. I SUGGEST USING BEEF HERE, BUT YOU CAN CERTAINLY PREPARE A **GEMISCHTES GULASCH** (MIXED GOULASH) BY INCORPORATING PORK AND/OR VEAL. COOKS ALSO OCCASIONALLY STRETCH THIS DISH BY ADDING POTATOES. MOST OFTEN INCLUDED IN TRADITIONAL HUNGARIAN GOULASHES, POTATOES ADD FLAVOR AND HELP TO THICKEN THE DISH. YOU WILL NOTICE THAT I DO NOT CALL FOR THEM IN THIS RECIPE, SIMPLY BECAUSE WE USUALLY OMITTED THEM. (IF YOU WISH TO ADD POTATOES, SEE THE CHEF'S NOTE.) INSTEAD, WE ADDED LOTS OF ONIONS, WHICH NOT ONLY IMPART RICH FLAVOR, BUT ALSO SERVE AS A MARVELOUS THICKENER. LASTLY ON THIS POINT, BECAUSE WE RELY ON THE ONIONS, FEW BLACK FOREST GOULASHES CALL FOR FLOUR OR CORNSTARCH TO HELP THICKEN THE DISH. I HAVE INCLUDED CORNSTARCH IN THIS RECIPE JUST IN CASE YOU FIND IT NECESSARY. SOME GOULASHES ARE SPICY WHILE OTHERS ARE QUITE MILD. FEEL FREE TO VARY THE AMOUNT OF PAPRIKA AND RED PEPPER FLAKES TO SUIT YOUR TASTE. IT IS IMPERATIVE THAT YOU USE HUNGARIAN PAPRIKA, HOWEVER, AS IT IMPARTS JUST THE RIGHT COMBINATION OF SWEET SPICINESS. IN ADDITION, I SUGGEST YOU TAKE THE TROUBLE TO USE FRESHLY GROUND CARAWAY SEEDS, AS THE PREPARED GROUND VARIETY IS VIRTUALLY TASTELESS. THIS GOULASH IS A HEARTY MIX OF SPICE AND TANG, WHICH IS BRIGHTENED AND REFRESHED WITH THE ADDITION OF FRESH LEMON ZEST AT THE END.

Hungarian Goulash

UNGARISCHES GULASCH

1. Heat the oil (or melt the butter) in a large shallow saucepan over medium-high heat.

2. Add the garlic and sauté until golden, about 4 to 5 minutes. Toss in the onions and sauté until softened and translucent, about 15 to 20 minutes.

3. Season the beef with salt and pepper, place the pieces in the sauté pan, and cook, stirring constantly, until the beef is browned evenly and the pan is nearly dry. Pour in 1 cup of the wine to deglaze, stirring with a wooden spoon to loosen any browned bits on the bottom of the pan, and raise the heat to high. Bring the wine to a boil and boil until it is reduced to the point where the pan is nearly dry again.

4. Stir in the tomato paste, add the remaining ½ cup of red wine, and boil until the pan is nearly dry once more.

5. Reduce the heat to medium low, add the paprika, and sprinkle in the flour. Pour in beef stock, whisking until smooth and to prevent lumps from forming, and add the red pepper flakes and caraway. Simmer for about 30 minutes, stirring often to prevent the paprika from burning.

6. Season the stew with additional salt and pepper if necessary and stir in the lemon zest just before serving.

Serves 6 to 8

½ cup vegetable oil,
    or ¼ pound (1 stick) unsalted butter

¾ cup coarsely chopped garlic

4 pounds white onions, peeled and coarsely chopped

4 pounds beef shoulder, cut into 2- to 2½ -inch cubes

Salt

Freshly ground black pepper

1½ cups full-bodied red wine, such as Burgundy

1½ cups tomato paste

¾ cup sweet Hungarian paprika

1½ cups all-purpose flour

3 quarts Beef Stock (page 310)

¾ tablespoon dried red pepper flakes, or to taste

1¼ tablespoons freshly ground caraway seeds

Cornstarch, as needed

Zest of 2 lemons, finely chopped

CHEF'S NOTE: Potatoes are sometimes included in goulash and are great for adding flavor and helping to thicken the stew. If you choose to try this variation, add 3 cups of peeled, chopped, or cubed potatoes in Step 5 along with the spices and stock.

Roasted Veal Shank

GEBACKENE KALBSHAXE

1. Preheat oven to 475°F.

2. To make the veal, season the veal shank with the salt, pepper, and paprika, drizzle with oil, and place in a small roasting pan or large casserole. Roast until golden brown, about 30 minutes. Cover with foil, reduce the oven temperature to 350°F., and roast for an additional 1½ hours. (The veal is properly cooked when the meat has shrunk, 5 to 6 inches of the bone are exposed, and the tendons have transformed into gelatin.) Remove the roast from the pan, cover it with foil, and set it aside to rest and keep warm. Reserve the pan.

3. To make the vegetables, bring a medium saucepan of salted water to a boil, drop in the carrots and boil (blanch) until bright in color and slightly softened, about 3 to 4 minutes. Lift out the carrots with a wire mesh strainer and set on paper towels to drain as the next batch is blanched. Repeat, one type at a time, with the remaining vegetables.

4. Melt the butter in the reserved roasting pan over medium heat. Toss in the vegetables, season with salt and pepper, and sauté until lightly browned and tender (but not too soft).

5. To serve, set the veal shank on a large platter, arrange the vegetables over and around it, and garnish with parsley.

I LOVE THIS DISH AND GET EXCITED JUST THINKING ABOUT IT. AS VISUALLY APPEALING AS IT IS DELICIOUS, IT WAS, AND STILL IS, A STANDARD ON SUNDAY MENUS IN UPSCALE GASTHAUS RESTAURANTS. THE SHANK MIGHT SEEM COLOSSAL AT FIRST, BUT THE BONE IS FAIRLY LARGE, AND THE MEAT SHRINKS AS IT ROASTS.

WE USED TO SERVE THIS DISH IN THE CLASSIC MANNER, REMOVED FROM THE BONE AND SLICED TABLESIDE ON A GUÉRIDON. AS I SUGGEST HERE, THE VEAL IS ALWAYS SERVED WITH LOTS OF TENDER, GORGEOUSLY ROASTED VEGETABLES.

Serves 4 to 6

VEAL SHANK:

1 veal shank (about 5 pounds), bone in,
    rinsed with cold water and patted dry

Salt

Freshly ground black pepper

⅛ teaspoon Hungarian paprika

2 tablespoons olive oil

VEGETABLES:

1½ cups chopped carrot

1½ cups chopped celery root

1 cup button mushrooms, quartered

4 ounces fresh green beans

½ head cauliflower, cut into florets

4 ounces snap peas

4 tablespoons unsalted butter

Salt

Freshly ground black pepper

Fresh parsley sprigs, for garnish

Veal Fricassée

EINGEMACHTES KALBSFLEISCH

1. Place the veal in a large saucepan or casserole, pour in the wine and water, and bring to a boil over high heat, skimming and discarding any foam that rises to the surface. Add the leeks, celery, onions, garlic, bouquet garni, salt, and pepper and return to a boil. Reduce the heat to medium low and simmer for 1 hour.

2. Remove the veal with a slotted spoon, strain the broth through a fine mesh strainer or cheesecloth into a large bowl, and discard the vegetables and bouquet garni. Return the broth to the saucepan and bring to a boil over high heat. Reduce the heat to medium and simmer until reduced by half, about 15 minutes.

3. Place the butter in a small bowl and knead in the flour, a bit at a time, to form a smooth paste (beurre manié). Whisk the beurre manié, a little at a time, into the simmering reduced broth and continue to simmer, stirring frequently, until the sauce is thickened and smooth, about 15 minutes. Strain the sauce again and return to the saucepan, maintaining at a low simmer over low heat.

4. Whisk together the heavy cream and egg yolks in a small bowl. Gradually stir into the sauce and fold in the reserved veal, simmering gently just until heated. Stir in the lemon juice and season with salt and pepper.

5. Serve the fricassée in a tureen or on a serving platter garnished with capers and parsley.

This fricassée is a classic example of the HAUSMANNSKOST (GOOD PLAIN FARE) SERVED IN MANY A GASTHAUS RESTAURANT. IT IS MOST OFTEN OFFERED AS A SPECIAL OF THE WEEK. IN ONE OF THE RESTAURANTS WHERE I WORKED, WE USED TO SHOWCASE IT ON WEDNESDAYS WITH SIMPLE NOODLES OR RICE.

FULL OF FLAVORFUL VEGETABLES AND HERBS, THIS CREAMY DISH IS PURE COMFORT FOOD. THE LEMON JUICE STIRRED IN JUST AT THE END AND THE GARNISH OF CAPERS ADD A BIT OF BRIGHTNESS AND TANG TO THE RICH SAUCE CLOAKING THE VEAL.

I HAVE SUGGESTED USING PIECES OF BONELESS VEAL SHOULDER HERE SO YOU DON'T HAVE TO CONTEND WITH PIECES OF BONE. IF YOU WISH, HOWEVER, ASK YOUR BUTCHER TO CUT THE VEAL PIECES WITH SOME OF THE BONES, AS THEY WILL ADD FLAVOR TO THE DISH AS IT COOKS.

Serves 8

5 pounds boneless veal shoulder, cut into 2-inch cubes

8 cups dry white wine, such as Chenin Blanc

8 cups water

4 leeks (white parts only), trimmed and chopped

2 ribs celery, chopped

2 large yellow onions, peeled and chopped

2 cloves garlic, peeled and chopped

1 Bouquet Garni (page 80)

3 tablespoons salt

1½ teaspoons freshly ground white pepper

6 tablespoons unsalted butter, at room temperature

1 cup all-purpose flour

½ cup heavy cream

4 egg yolks, lightly beaten

Juice of 2 large lemons (about ¼ cup), strained

Salt

Freshly ground black pepper

¼ cup small (nonpareil) capers in brine, strained, for garnish

Chopped fresh parsley, for garnish

149

Stuffed Veal Breast Grandmother Style

GEFÜLLTE KALBSBRUST GROßMUTTER ART

I F FOOD ELICITS FLASHES OF MEMORY, THIS DISH FLOODS MY BRAIN WITH FULL-COLOR SCENES FROM THE PAST. MY MOTHER PREPARED IT SOMETIMES FOR OUR BIG SUNDAY DINNER AFTER CHURCH, AND IT WAS A FAVORITE FOR WEDDINGS AND BANQUETS AT MY AUNT RUTH AND UNCLE WALTER'S ESTABLISHMENT, GASTHAUS ZUM BUCKENBERG.

I WILL NOT LEAD YOU ASTRAY AND SUGGEST THAT THIS IS AN EASY DISH. BECAUSE VEAL BREASTS ARE RATHER LARGE AND THE DISH IS TIME CONSUMING AND REQUIRES A NUMBER OF STEPS, STUFFED VEAL BREAST IS TYPICALLY PREPARED FOR A CROWD OR CELEBRATORY EVENT. IF, HOW-EVER, YOU ARE PREPARED TO SPEND SOME TIME IN THE KITCHEN AND PRESENT A DISH THAT WILL EARN YOU GREAT ACCLAIM, I SUGGEST YOU TRY THIS ONE.

THE STUFFING IS A CLASSIC AND VERY DELICIOUS, BUT YOU CAN CER-TAINLY VARY THE FLAVORS WITH MEAT OR MUSHROOMS AS WE SOMETIMES DID. AS FOR THE VEAL, YOUR BUTCHER WILL BONE AND CLEAN IT FOR YOU. THIS IS SUCH A HEFTY JOB THAT ONLY BUTCHERS ARE SUITED FOR THE TASK. IN MY DAY, THEY SOLD VEAL BREASTS WHOLE AS WELL AS STUFFED AND OVEN-READY.

CALL IN SOME FAMILY MEMBERS AND MAKE THIS DISH TOGETHER. I GUARANTEE THE EXPERIENCE OF PREPARING AND FEASTING UPON IT WILL BE QUITE MEMORABLE FOR YOU AS WELL.

CHEF'S NOTE: If you are fortunate enough to have a butcher who will give them to you, ask him to give you the pieces of rib bones that he removed from the breast. They are not absolutely necessary, but they are a terrific addition to the *mirepoix* (bed of vegetables) that cushions the veal in the roasting pan. In the old days, when the roasting pan sat directly on the floor of the oven, they prevented the vegetables from burning. They also added great flavor to the sauce, which is why I highly recommend using them.

Serves 8 to 10

HERBED BREAD STUFFING:

1 cup milk

2 medium 1- to 2-day-old baguettes, cut into ¼-inch cubes

1½ pounds bacon, chopped

2 tablespoons unsalted butter

2 medium onions, peeled and finely chopped

2 bunches fresh parsley, finely chopped

4 whole eggs

4 egg yolks

½ cup mixed chopped fresh herbs, such as tarragon, basil, thyme, and chives

¼ teaspoon freshly grated nutmeg

Salt

Freshly ground black pepper

ASSEMBLY:

1 boneless veal breast (about 5 to 7 pounds), cleaned and trimmed

2 large onions, peeled and chopped (about 1½ cups)

2 cloves garlic, peeled and smashed

3 large carrots, peeled and chopped (about 2 cups)

1 medium celery root, peeled and chopped (about 2 cups)

Salt

Freshly ground black pepper

½ teaspoon Hungarian paprika

SAUCE:

4 cups Demi-Glace (page 312) or prepared brown sauce

½ cup sour cream

½ cup heavy cream

Salt

Freshly ground black pepper

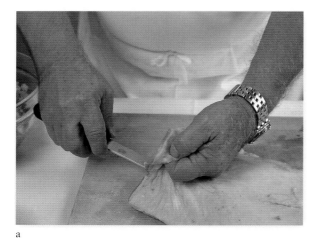

a

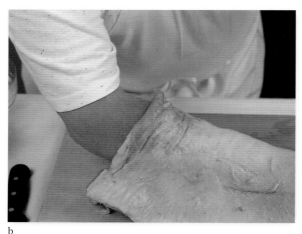

b

c

Cut a slit in side of veal, insert fingers and create a pocket for stuffing. Season, then fill pocket with stuffing and sew closed.

d

e

f

1. To make the stuffing, bring the milk to a boil in a small saucepan over high heat. Place the bread cubes in a large bowl and pour enough of the milk over the bread, tossing to coat the cubes, until the bread is just moistened (you might not need all of the milk). Set aside while preparing the other ingredients.

2. Heat a medium sauté pan over medium-high heat, add the bacon, and sauté until crisp and golden. Remove the bacon to paper towels to drain.

3. Melt the butter in a medium sauté pan over medium-high heat, add the onions, and sauté until translucent and slightly softened. Stir in the parsley and sauté for 1 minute more. Remove from the heat and set aside to cool.

4. Toss the bacon, onion and parsley mixture, eggs, egg yolks, chopped herbs, and nutmeg together with the moistened bread, season with salt and pepper, and set aside for about 30 minutes.

5. Preheat the oven to 350°F.

6. To assemble the veal breast, cut a slit about 2 inches long in one side of the veal (just below where the rib bones rested) using a paring knife (image a). Insert your fingers and then your hand into the slit, gently moving it around to create a pocket for the stuffing (image b). Season well (image c), then fill the pocket with stuffing (image d) and sew it closed using a kitchen needle and twine (image e). Massage the breast with oil (image f).

7. Arrange the onions, garlic, carrots, and celery root in the bottom of a large roasting pan, season the veal with salt, pepper, and paprika, and set it on top of the vegetables. Cover the pan with foil and roast for about 2½ hours until it is about three-quarters of the way done. Remove the foil, raise the oven temperature to 400°F., and roast for 1 hour more, until the veal is well browned and crisp.

8. Remove the veal from the pan, cover loosely with foil, and set aside to rest for about 15 minutes.

9. To make the sauce, set the roasting pan over high heat and bring the juices and vegetables to a boil. Reduce the heat to medium, stir in the demi-glace, and simmer until reduced by about half. Strain the reduction into a medium saucepan, stir in the sour cream and heavy cream (off of the heat to prevent the sauce from breaking), and season with salt and pepper if necessary.

10. To serve, slice the veal and arrange the slices on a serving platter. Spoon some of the sauce overtop and serve the remaining sauce in a gravy boat on the side.

Braised Rabbit Legs

HASENPFEFFER

If truth be told, we never prepared this dish with just rabbit legs in the Black Forest. Always frugal and mindful of waste, we used the whole rabbit for a traditional Hasenpfeffer (rabbit stew). Everybody kept rabbits in my day and they were plentiful on every farm. I admit that sometimes I would get a bit too attached to the adorable creatures, and when Fluffy went missing I became worried. My carnivorous side soon took over, though, and I confess I looked forward to the delicious dish to come.

Home and Gasthaus cooks alike prepare rabbit in all sorts of ways, showcasing it in ragoûts, as well as in well-known dishes such as HASENGULASCH (goulash with rabbit). Again, this Hasenpfeffer is based on the traditional stews we often prepared in the Black Forest, but I have varied it slightly. We typically used rabbit blood as a thickening agent, but I have eliminated it for contemporary palates. We also often flavored the stew with bacon, which I have left out of this version in order to lighten the dish a bit. The stew has plenty of flavor without it. Finally, rather than cooking the vegetables for a long time as called for in the traditional recipe, I have added them near the end of the cooking time so they maintain their texture and fresh flavor.

Begin preparing this dish at least four hours or the night before you plan to serve it so the rabbit has time to marinate. Hasenpfeffer pairs nicely with potatoes, or, if you wish to be a bit more traditional, serve spätzle or egg noodles, as we usually did. They are perfect for soaking up the flavorful sauce.

Serves 8

5 pounds rabbit legs, skinned (*see* Sources, page 320)

3 cups full-bodied red wine, such as Burgundy

½ cup vegetable oil

4 tablespoons unsalted butter

4 ribs celery, chopped

2 carrots, peeled and chopped

1 large onion, peeled and chopped

3 cloves garlic, peeled and chopped

1 dried bay leaf

6 cups Demi-Glace (page 312) or prepared brown sauce

3 tablespoons chopped fresh parsley

1 sprig fresh thyme, stemmed and chopped

2 medium zucchini, trimmed and chopped

2 medium yellow squash, trimmed and chopped

½ small red cabbage, chopped (about 1 cup)

1 cup sliced white button mushrooms

2 large plum tomatoes, seeded and chopped

Salt

Freshly ground black pepper

1. At least 4 hours or the day before serving the dish, cut each rabbit leg in half at the joint (or ask your butcher to do so). Place the pieces in a medium bowl and pour in 2 cups of the wine. Cover with plastic wrap and set aside in the refrigerator to marinate for at least 4 hours or overnight.

2. The next day or when you are ready to proceed with the dish, remove the rabbit pieces from the wine (discarding the wine) and pat dry on paper towels. Heat the oil and 2 tablespoons of the butter in a large heavy-bottomed sauté pan or skillet over high heat, add the rabbit, and sauté on each side for about 1½ minutes, until golden brown. Reduce the heat to medium.

3. Add the celery, carrots, onion, and garlic to the rabbit and sauté until the vegetables are softened, about 5 to 8 minutes. Stir in the remaining 1 cup of wine, bay leaf, demi-glace, parsley, and thyme. Bring to a boil over high heat, reduce the heat to medium low, and simmer until the rabbit is still tender but no longer pink, about 20 minutes. Remove from the heat and set aside momentarily.

4. Melt the remaining 2 tablespoons of butter in a large sauté pan over medium heat, add the zucchini, yellow squash, and red cabbage, and sauté until just softened, about 5 minutes. Toss in the mushrooms and tomatoes and cook until the mushrooms are just softened, about 5 minutes more.

5. Return the rabbit to medium heat, stir in the sautéed vegetables, and simmer for about 5 to 7 minutes.

6. Season with salt and pepper and serve on a large platter.

Smashed Potatoes

ZERDRÜCKTE PELLKARTOFFEL

THESE POTATOES ARE A DELICIOUS ACCOMPANIMENT TO A VARIETY OF DISHES. I PARTICULARLY LIKE YUKON GOLD, AS THEIR CREAMY CONSISTENCY AND NATURALLY BUTTERY FLAVOR REMINDS ME OF THE POTATOES WE GREW IN ABUNDANCE IN THE BLACK FOREST.

SMASHED, OR ROUGHLY MASHED, POTATOES HAVE BEEN POPULAR FOR YEARS, BUT THIS RECIPE IS UNIQUE WITH THE ADDITION OF FRESH SHALLOTS AND PARSLEY.

Serves 8

2 pounds Yukon gold potatoes, halved (quartered if large)
1 tablespoon olive oil
½ cup sour cream
¼ cup finely chopped shallots
1 bunch fresh chives, chopped (about ¼ cup)
Salt
Freshly ground white pepper

1. Bring a large saucepan of salted water to a boil over high heat. Add the potatoes and cook for 10 to 15 minutes until fork-tender.

2. Drain the potatoes and pour into a large serving bowl. Add the oil, sour cream, shallots and chives and smash roughly with a potato masher or the back of a large spoon. (You want the potatoes to maintain some texture.)

3. Season with salt and pepper to taste.

Creamed Green Beans

GRÜNE BOHNEN IN RAHMSOßE

W E ENJOYED FRESH, SIMPLY PREPARED GREEN BEANS DURING THE SUMMER WHEN THE VINES IN OUR GARDENS STOOD HEAVILY DRAPED WITH THE SLENDER BRIGHT GREEN VEGETABLES. AFTER THE WARM MONTHS, HOWEVER, WE LEFT ANY SURPLUS OF THAT YEAR'S CROP TO DRY ON SHEETS IN THE SUN AND STORED THE DEHYDRATED BEANS IN THE LARDER FOR USE IN FALL AND WINTER DISHES. SHRIVELED AND DRY, THESE GREEN BEANS WERE HARDLY AS ATTRACTIVE AS THEIR FRESH COUNTERPARTS. SOAKED IN WATER AND THEN TOSSED WITH DELICIOUS CREAM SAUCE, THOUGH, THESE BEANS MADE UP IN FLAVOR WHATEVER THEY LACKED IN APPEARANCE.

TODAY, OF COURSE, WE CAN PURCHASE FRESH GREEN BEANS AND PREPARE THEM IN THIS MANNER THROUGHOUT THE YEAR. THE ONIONS, GARLIC, AND BIT OF CAYENNE PEPPER GIVE THESE BEANS A DELIGHTFUL LITTLE KICK, WHICH NICELY COMPLEMENTS THE RICH BÉCHAMEL SAUCE.

Serves 4 to 6

1½ pounds fresh green string beans, trimmed

1 tablespoon unsalted butter

1 medium onion, peeled and finely chopped (about ½ cup)

1 clove garlic, peeled and chopped

½ cup Béchamel Sauce (page 313)

¼ cup heavy cream

Small pinch of cayenne pepper

Salt

Freshly ground white pepper

Chopped fresh parsley, for garnish

1. Bring a large saucepan of lightly salted water to a boil over high heat, add the beans, and cook until just tender, about 5 to 8 minutes. Drain the beans and set aside momentarily.

2. Melt the butter in a medium saucepan over medium heat, add the onions and garlic, and sauté until translucent and slightly softened, about 3 minutes.

3. Slowly stir in the béchamel sauce, cream, and cayenne pepper. Add the beans, tossing gently to coat with the sauce, and season with salt and pepper.

4. Serve in a large serving bowl garnished with parsley.

Egg Noodles

EIER NUDELN

LIKE SPÄTZLE, EGG NOODLES ARE SERVED THROUGHOUT THE BLACK FOREST. MY MOTHER PREPARED THEM REGULARLY, AND I DID AS WELL IN GASTHAUS AND HOTEL KITCHENS. THEY ARE SIMPLE YET FLAVORFUL AND PAIR WELL WITH JUST ABOUT ANY STEW, CASSEROLE, OR RAGOÛT. TO ENJOY THESE NOODLES IN THEIR PUREST FORM, TOSS THEM WITH SOME BUTTER AND SALT AS I SUGGEST HERE.

1. Combine the flour, eggs, egg yolks, and oil in the bowl of an electric mixer fitted with the paddle attachment. Mix on medium speed until the dough comes together and forms a stiff ball. Remove the dough, wrap in plastic wrap, and set aside to rest at room temperature for 1 hour.

2. On a lightly floured surface, flatten the dough to about $1/4$ inch thick and roll with a rolling pin until very thin, about $1/16$ inch thick. Cut the dough into strips of noodles about $1/2$ inch wide and 2 inches long.

3. Bring 2 quarts of salted water to a boil in a large saucepan, add the noodles, and cook until al dente, about 2 minutes.

4. To serve, strain and pour the noodles into a large serving bowl. Add the butter, tossing to coat, and season with salt.

Serves 8

2 cups all-purpose flour

2 eggs, lightly beaten

2 egg yolks, lightly beaten

2 teaspoons vegetable oil

2 tablespoons unsalted butter

Salt

CHEF'S NOTE: If you plan to dry this pasta and store it for later use, replace about $1/4$ cup of the all-purpose flour with semolina flour. This will make the dough a bit more durable. Arrange the freshly cut strips of dough on a parchment-lined baking sheet and set aside to dry completely, about 2 hours. Seal the dried pasta in an airtight container and it will keep for several weeks.

Flatten the dough with a rolling pin and cut into strips of noodles.

Braised Red Cabbage

SÜß-SAUREM ROTKOHL

Serves 8

2 tablespoons unsalted butter

1 medium shallot, peeled and chopped

1 clove garlic, peeled and chopped

2½ to 3 pounds red cabbage, cored and shredded (about 10 cups)

½ cup full-bodied red wine, such as Burgundy

1¼ cups balsamic vinegar

½ cup sugar

Salt

Freshly ground black pepper

IN THE BLACK FOREST, BRAISED CABBAGE IS MOST OFTEN PREPARED SIMPLY AND IS TART AND SAVORY LIKE SAUERKRAUT. SOMETIMES HOME COOKS ADD A BIT OF SLICED AND SAUTÉED APPLE, BUT ONLY UPSCALE GASTHAUS RESTAURANTS SERVE A DELICIOUSLY SWEET AND SOUR BRAISED CABBAGE LIKE THIS ONE. I ACTUALLY LEARNED TO PREPARE THIS DISH WHILE WORKING AT BEAU RIVAGE IN NEUCHÂTEL, SWITZERLAND, AND UPON MY RETURN TO THE BLACK FOREST, I SERVED A VERSION OF IT AT THE GASTHAUS ZUM BUCKENBERG. THIS SATISFYING, FLAVORFUL CABBAGE IS PARTICULARLY DELICIOUS WITH STEWS, RAGOÛTS, AND ROASTS OF GAME, BEEF, OR PORK.

1. Melt the butter in a large sauté pan over medium heat, add the shallot and garlic, and sauté until golden, about 1 minute.

2. Add the cabbage, tossing several times, and pour in the wine to deglaze, stirring with a wooden spoon to loosen any browned bits on the bottom of the pan.

3. Stir in the vinegar and sugar and season with salt and pepper. Bring to a boil over high heat, stirring constantly to prevent the sugar from burning, reduce the heat to medium low, and simmer until the liquid is reduced by three-fourths, about 10 minutes. (The reduction will be concentrated and have a light syrup consistency.)

SPÄTZLE

Scrape the dough into a potato ricer or a colander with large holes and press the dough into the boiling water. Lift the cooked spätzle out of the water with a large slotted spoon.

a

b

c

d

e

Spätzle

1. Combine the flour, eggs, salt, and nutmeg in the bowl of an electric mixer fitted with the paddle attachment. Mix on medium speed until combined and slowly pour in the water, mixing until the batter is smooth. Mix for about 5 minutes more, until the batter is elastic.

2. Bring 2 quarts of lightly salted water to a boil in a large saucepan over high heat. Scrape the dough into a potato ricer or a colander with large holes and press the dough into the boiling water (image a) (with a large spoon or spatula if using a colander). Alternately, place dough on a small cutting board and scrape dough into boiling water (images b–d). Cook until the spätzle are tender but still firm, stirring occasionally, about 3 to 4 minutes. They will rise to the surface when done.

3. Lift the cooked spätzle out of the water with a large slotted spoon (image e), shake off the excess water and place directly onto a serving platter. (You can also drain the spätzle in a colander.)

CHEF'S NOTE: If you make the spätzle ahead of time, cool them off in an ice bath after cooking. Once cool, transfer the spätzle to an airtight container and toss with a bit of vegetable oil before sealing so they don't dry out. To reheat, either shock them in boiling water or sauté them in butter until golden brown.

My mother prepared spätzle all the time at home, and I continued to do so in the Gasthaus and hotel kitchens where I worked. Literally translated as "little sparrows," these tender dumplings are even more popular than potatoes in the Black Forest.

We prepared many varieties of spätzle, flavoring them with paprika, pepper, herbs, cheese, or even bits of sausage. The dough is quite forgiving and lends itself well to just about any flavorful ingredient. Spätzle also marries well with virtually any sauce, which is yet another reason for its wide popularity. Most often it is just tossed with butter as I have suggested here.

If this is your first time making spätzle, this recipe is a good place to start. In traditional Black Forest style, I have called for just a bit of nutmeg to be mixed in to this soft, elastic dough. You can shape the dumplings in a number of ways. I learned to cut them by hand on a board as my mother did (images b–d). This can be a bit tricky, however, so I suggest using a potato ricer or large-holed colander. If you think you'll be making the dumplings often, you might purchase a spätzle machine (see Sources, page 320). These contraptions are widely available today in most kitchen supply stores and make an easy job of shaping the dough.

Serves 4

2 cups all-purpose flour

4 large eggs

1 teaspoon salt

¼ teaspoon freshly grated nutmeg

1 cup cold water

Potato Dumplings

KARTOFFEL KNÖDEL

1. Place the bread in a large bowl, pour the milk overtop, tossing to coat, and set aside until soggy, about 2 to 3 minutes. Using your hands, squeeze the milk out of the bread, discarding the milk, and set the bread in another large bowl.

2. Stir the grated potatoes, onions, parsley, salt, pepper, nutmeg, and marjoram into the bread, add the eggs, mixing to combine, and shape the dough into 24 round dumplings about 1½ inches in diameter (image a).

3. Bring 2 quarts of lightly salted water to a boil in a large saucepan over high heat. Dredge the dumplings in flour, coating generously, and slip them gently into the water (image b). Return the water to a boil, reduce the heat to medium, and cover the pan, simmering until the dumplings expand and float to the surface, about 15 minutes (image c).

4. Remove the dumplings with a slotted spoon or a spider (images d–e). Serve on a large platter, garnished with chopped parsley (image f).

IT IS SAID THAT THE BEST AND MOST VARIED KNÖDEL (DUMPLINGS) ARE FOUND IN OUR NEIGHBORING REGION, BAVARIA. THIS MIGHT BE SO, BUT IT IS ALSO UNDENIABLE THAT POTATO DUMPLINGS ARE ANOTHER TYPICAL EXAMPLE OF THE QUICKLY PREPARED, SATISFYING DISHES WE OFTEN ENJOYED IN THE BLACK FOREST. THEY ARE SOMEWHAT DECEIVING, HOWEVER. AS BASIC AS THEY ARE, EVEN MY MOTHER, AN EXPERIENCED COOK, OFTEN SAID THEY WERE A LOT OF WORK. THE RECIPE IS HARDLY COMPLICATED, BUT THE MOST SUCCESSFUL DOUGH RELIES ON THE DETAILED EYE OF A WATCHFUL COOK WHO WILL ENSURE THAT IT IS NEITHER TOO WET NOR TOO DRY. IN ADDITION, ONCE THE DOUGH COMES TOGETHER, SHAPING THE DUMPLINGS REQUIRES A FAIRLY LIGHT TOUCH.

LEST YOU SHOULD BE DETERRED, FEAR NOT. THESE DUMPLINGS ARE WORTH THE EFFORT AND ARE WONDERFUL ACCOMPANIMENTS TO RICH STEWS AND RAGOÛTS, DISHES THAT DRENCH THE TENDER MORSELS WITH FLAVORFUL SAUCE. AT HOME AND IN GASTHAUS RESTAURANTS, WE SERVED THEM BESIDE THESE DISHES AS WELL AS ALONGSIDE HEARTY BRAISED MEATS. BECAUSE THEY REQUIRE A BIT OF CARE AND ATTENTION, IT WAS, AND STILL IS, COMMON FOR GASTHAUS RESTAURANTS TO SERVE THEM AS MUCH ANTICIPATED SPECIALS DURING THE WEEK.

Serves 8

15 slices day-old white sandwich bread, crusts removed

1 cup whole milk

7 large red-skinned potatoes, peeled and grated (about 2 cups)

2 medium yellow onions, peeled and grated (about 1 cup)

About ⅓ cup chopped fresh parsley

1 tablespoon salt

¼ teaspoon freshly ground white pepper

⅛ teaspoon freshly grated nutmeg

⅛ teaspoon dried marjoram

3 large eggs, beaten well

All-purpose flour, for dredging

POTATO DUMPLINGS

Shape the dumplings by hand and slip them gently into boiling water. They're ready when they float to the surface.

a

b

c

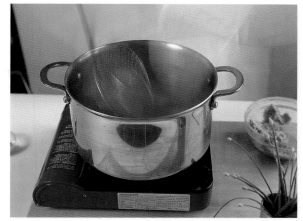

d

e

f

163

Sauerkraut

Serves 6

In the Black Forest, sauerkraut is prepared with a particular variety of white cabbage called **FILTERKRAUT** known for its unique cone shape and delicate texture. Along with our other cabbages, Filterkraut grew abundantly in our gardens and we took advantage of the plentiful harvests to make sauerkraut ourselves. To assist us with the task, a man used to travel through town with a cart and a hand-cranked machine that sliced the cabbage into the very thin strips that are essential for preparing sauerkraut. I can still see the huge vats of salted cabbage that sat in our root cellar fermenting slowly into the tangy vegetable we enjoyed time and again.

We prepared many varieties of sauerkraut at home and in the Gasthaus kitchens where I worked. This recipe features the wonderful combination of salty bacon, pungent garlic, sweet onions, apples, and wine, the nutty and slightly anise flavor of caraway seed, and the satisfying texture of potato. Sauerkraut is almost exclusively a cold weather dish, and it is a wonderful accompaniment to many fall and winter favorites, including roasted and braised pork. My mother often served it at home with sausages for a simple but hearty meal.

3 tablespoons unsalted butter

9 slices lean bacon, diced

2 medium onions, peeled and chopped

1 clove garlic, peeled and chopped

4 cups prepared sauerkraut, rinsed and drained (bagged and refrigerated is best)

1½ cups Chicken Stock (page 308)

1 cup white wine, such as Riesling or Gewürztraminer

½ teaspoon caraway seeds

2 large apples, peeled, cored, and thinly sliced

1 large red-skinned potato, peeled and grated (about ⅓ cup)

Salt

Freshly ground white pepper

---

1. Melt the butter in a large saucepan over medium heat, add the bacon, and sauté until crisp, about 3 minutes.

2. Stir in the onions and garlic and sauté until golden brown, about 5 minutes.

3. Stir in the sauerkraut, stock, wine, and caraway seeds and bring to a boil over high heat. Reduce the heat to medium low and simmer until the stock is reduced by three-quarters, about 30 minutes.

4. Incorporate the apples and potato, simmer until they are very soft, about 30 minutes more, and season with salt and pepper.

Apple-Walnut Cakes

APFEL & WALNUß KUCHEN

1. At least 8 hours or the day before serving the cakes, toss together the apples and B & B in a medium bowl, adding more liqueur if necessary to liberally coat the apples and prevent them from discoloring. Cover and set aside in the refrigerator to macerate for at least 8 hours or overnight.

2. The next day or when you are ready to make the cakes, preheat the oven to 350°F. and butter and flour eight 4-ounce 3 x 1½-inch ramekins.

3. Sift together the flour, cinnamon, baking soda, and nutmeg into a medium bowl.

4. Combine the brown sugar, oil, and eggs in the bowl of an electric mixer fitted with the paddle attachment and mix on medium speed until smooth. Reduce the mixing speed to low and gradually add the sifted dry ingredients, mixing just until combined. Remove the bowl from the mixer and fold in the walnuts and macerated apples.

5. Divide the batter among the prepared ramekins and arrange them on a baking sheet. Bake the cakes until slightly puffed and golden brown and a skewer inserted in the centers comes out clean, about 20 to 25 minutes. Serve the cakes warm or place the ramekins on a wire rack to cool.

CHEF'S NOTE: Toasted nuts have more flavor than raw nuts and are easy to prepare. The method is similar for all nuts, but you might have to alter the baking time depending on the size and oil content of each variety. For walnuts, spread the nuts in a single layer on a baking sheet and toast in a 350°F. oven until golden brown, about 20 minutes. Remove the toasted nuts to a plate or second baking sheet to cool completely.

APPLES AND WALNUTS GROW ABUNDANTLY IN THE BLACK FOREST AND ARE DELICIOUS IN THESE PRETTY LITTLE CAKES. LIKE MY MOTHER AND ALL THE WOMEN IN HER FAMILY, MY AUNT RUTH WAS A WONDERFUL BAKER AND SERVED SIMPLE BUT DELICIOUS TREATS TO GUESTS OF THE GASTHAUS ZUM BUCKENBERG, WHICH SHE RAN WITH MY UNCLE WALTER. MOST FOLKS ENJOYED SUBSTANTIAL LUNCHES AT THE GASTHAUS DURING THE WEEK BUT REFRAINED FROM DESSERTS UNTIL THE WEEKENDS. IT WAS THEN, ESPECIALLY ON SUNDAYS, THAT MY AUNT WOULD PREPARE MANY CAKES AND TARTS FOR VISITORS WHO WANTED A BIT OF SOMETHING SWEET IN THE AFTERNOON. SHE OFTEN PREPARED APPLE-WALNUT CAKE AND IT WAS ALWAYS A BIG SELLER.

I HAVE MADE THIS CAKE A BIT FANCIER BY BAKING IT IN INDIVIDUAL RAMEKINS, BUT, IF YOU PREFER, YOU CAN MAKE A SINGLE CAKE AS MY AUNT ALWAYS DID. THIS RECIPE WILL MAKE ONE 8-INCH CAKE. BE PREPARED TO PLAN AHEAD WITH THIS RECIPE AS WELL. THE APPLES SHOULD MACERATE WITH THE LIQUEUR FOR AT LEAST EIGHT HOURS TO SOAK UP AS MUCH FLAVOR AS POSSIBLE.

Serves 8

2 medium McIntosh of Granny Smith apples, peeled, cored, and chopped (about 2 cups)

½ cup B & B (spicy herbal liqueur), or as needed

1 cup sifted all-purpose flour

1 tablespoon ground cinnamon

1 teaspoon baking soda

1 teaspoon freshly grated nutmeg

1 cup packed light brown sugar

¾ cup vegetable oil

2 large eggs

¾ cup walnuts, toasted, and chopped (*see Chef's Note*)

Chocolate-Almond Cake

SCHOKOLADE & MANDEL KUCHEN

1. Preheat oven to 350°F. and butter and flour one 8½ x 4½ x 4½-inch loaf pan.

2. Prepare a double boiler and maintain at a simmer over low heat. Place the chocolate in the double boiler and heat gently, stirring occasionally, until melted and smooth. Remove from the heat and set aside.

3. Place the almond paste in the bowl of an electric mixer fitted with the paddle attachment and beat on medium speed until smooth. Gradually add the butter and mix until smooth. Incorporate the eggs one at a time and add the vanilla, stopping at least once to scrape down the sides of the bowl. Mix until smooth. Reduce the mixing speed to low and incorporate the flour.

4. Remove the bowl from the mixer and fold about one-third of the batter into the melted chocolate. Pour the plain batter into the prepared pan, spoon the chocolate batter overtop, and carefully swirl the two together with a skewer to create a marble design. Bake until the cake is firm on top, has pulled away from the sides of the pan, and a skewer inserted in the center comes out clean, about 30 to 40 minutes. Cool the cake in the pan on a wire rack for 30 minutes before removing from the pan.

THIS LOAF CAKE WAS ALWAYS POPULAR AT THE GASTHAUS ZUM BUCKENBERG. ITS MARBLED APPEARANCE MAKES PRETTY SLICES, AND IT IS A DELICIOUS COMBINATION OF ALMONDS AND CHOCOLATE. THIS CAKE ALSO KEEPS FRESH FOR SEVERAL DAYS, ALTHOUGH IT IS SO TEMPTING THAT I HARDLY THINK IT WILL LAST THAT LONG.

Makes one 8-inch loaf cake

3 ounces semisweet chocolate, roughly chopped

10½ ounces almond paste

½ pound (2 sticks) unsalted butter, at room temperature

6 large eggs

1½ teaspoons vanilla extract

½ cup sifted all-purpose flour

Rhubarb-Strawberry Pie

RHABARBER & ERDBEER KUCHEN

WE LOVE RHUBARB AND STRAWBERRIES IN THE BLACK FOREST. RHUBARB HAS A FAIRLY LONG GROWING SEASON THAT ACTUALLY EXTENDS INTO THE FALL. STRAWBERRIES, HOWEVER, GROW ABUNDANTLY BUT HAVE A VERY SHORT SEASON THAT ONLY STRETCHES BETWEEN MAY AND JUNE. WHEN THE VIBRANTLY RED BERRIES BEGIN DOTTING THE LANDSCAPE, THEREFORE, WE TAKE FULL ADVANTAGE OF THE OPPORTUNITY TO PRESERVE THEM, BAKE WITH THEM, AND EAT THEM FRESH.

OUR WILD STRAWBERRIES ARE PARTICULARLY WONDERFUL. MANY FOLKS SPEND AFTERNOONS AND WEEKENDS PICKING THEM IN THE FORESTS AND THEN SELL THEM TO HOTEL AND GASTHAUS KITCHENS. MY AUNT RUTH BARTERED WITH THESE FOLKS QUITE A FEW TIMES, TRADING VARIOUS CUTS OF BEEF AND PORK FROM HER KITCHEN FOR BUSHELS OF RIPE WILD STRAWBERRIES.

THIS PIE COMES TOGETHER EASILY AND IS DELIGHTFUL ON ITS OWN OR SERVED WITH A DOLLOP OF **SCHLAGSAHNE** (WHIPPED CREAM).

Makes one 9-inch pie

2 pounds fresh rhubarb, leaves removed and chopped into 1-inch pieces (about 4 cups)

2 pints (4 cups) fresh strawberries, hulled and quartered

1/2 cup packed light brown sugar

1/4 cup granulated sugar

1/4 cup cold water

2 tablespoons cornstarch

Juice of 1/2 lemon

1 pound Pâte Brisée (page 315)

CHEF'S NOTE: When buying rhubarb, choose smaller (about 1 inch thick), bright red stalks that are firm and crisp without blemishes. Larger stalks will work fine, but will have to be peeled before using.

1. Preheat the oven to 350°F. and butter a 9 x 1 1/2-inch pie plate.

2. Combine the rhubarb, strawberries, sugars, water, cornstarch, and lemon juice in a large bowl, tossing to mix well.

3. Lightly dust a work surface with flour and roll the pâte brisée into a circle about 10 inches in diameter. Fit the pastry into the prepared pie pan, being careful not to stretch it, and trim the edges to extend 1/2 inch beyond the pan. Neatly fold this 1/2-inch edge and crimp decoratively.

4. Fill the pastry with rhubarb and strawberry filling and bake until the top is golden and bubbly. Cool completely on a wire rack before serving.

Crème Caramel

Serves 6

CARAMEL:

1 cup sugar

CUSTARD:

½ cups sugar

5 large eggs

2 cups light cream

½ cup heavy cream

½ teaspoon vanilla extract

1. Preheat the oven to 325°F.

2. To make the caramel, melt the sugar in a medium saucepan and over medium-low heat, watching closely and shaking the pan occasionally to prevent the sugar from burning. Simmer until clear and syrupy, about 2 to 3 minutes. Reduce the heat to low and simmer, stirring occasionally, until light amber in color, about 5 minutes more. Immediately remove the caramel from the heat and divide equally among six 4-ounce, 3 x 1½-inch ramekins. Do this carefully as the sugar is very hot at this point. Quickly tilt each ramekin to coat the bottom evenly and set aside for the caramel to become firm.

3. Arrange the ramekins in a medium roasting pan and set aside.

4. To make the custard, whisk together the sugar and eggs in a large bowl.

5. Combine the light and heavy creams and vanilla in a medium saucepan and bring to a boil over medium-high heat. Remove from the heat and gradually pour the hot cream into the sugar and eggs, whisking constantly. Strain the custard through a fine mesh strainer and divide among the prepared ramekins.

6. Carefully pour boiling water into the roasting pan until it reaches halfway up the sides of the ramekins. Carefully transfer the roasting pan to the oven and bake the custards until just set, about 30 to 40 minutes. Remove the custards from the water bath and cool completely on a wire rack. Cover with plastic wrap and chill in the refrigerator for at least 1 hour before serving.

7. Before serving the crème caramel, remove the custards from the refrigerator and bring to room temperature (about 20 minutes). Carefully run a paring knife around the edge of each crème caramel to loosen from the ramekin. Invert onto individual dessert plates, slowly lift off the ramekins, allowing the caramel to pool around the custard, and serve immediately.

IF TRUTH BE TOLD, MY AUNT RUTH NEVER MADE OR SERVED CRÈME CARAMEL AT THE GASTHAUS ZUM BUCKENBERG. IN FACT, I WAGER IT WAS ABSENT FROM MOST GASTHAUS KITCHEN REPERTOIRES. THIS DESSERT OBVIOUSLY HAS A FASHIONABLE FRENCH FLAIR THAT WAS SIMPLY UNCHARACTERISTIC OF BASIC GASTHAUS DINING. EVERY ONCE IN A WHILE, HOWEVER, FANCY DESSERTS LIKE THIS ONE WOULD TURN UP AT LOCAL RESTAURANTS. USUALLY, IT WAS BECAUSE THE COOK (MOST OFTEN THE SON OR A RELATIVE OF THE OWNERS) HAD COMPLETED AN APPRENTICESHIP PROGRAM IN UPSCALE HOTEL KITCHENS. I HAD THIS EXPERIENCE MYSELF. AFTER APPRENTICING IN SWITZERLAND, I RETURNED HOME TO WORK AT THE GASTHAUS ZUM BUCKENBERG, WHERE I OCCASIONALLY SERVED ELEGANT DESSERTS LIKE CRÈME CARAMEL. EVEN THOUGH IT STOOD OUT AMONG THE SIMPLER DESSERTS ON THE MENU, EVERYONE ENJOYED THIS CREAMY CUSTARD DRAPED IN AMBER-COLORED CARAMEL.

Apple-Raisin Turnovers

APFEL & ROSINEN TASCHE

1. Preheat the oven to 350°F. and line a baking sheet with parchment paper.

2. Toss together the apples, lemon juice, and raisins in a medium bowl.

3. Stir together the flour, sugar, cinnamon, and nutmeg in a small bowl.

4. Melt the butter in a small saucepan over medium heat. Remove from the heat and whisk in the honey and vanilla. Pour over the apples and raisins, tossing to combine, and stir in the spiced flour and sugar.

5. Lightly dust a work surface with flour and roll the puff pastry to a ¼-inch thick 12 x 18-inch rectangle, trimming the edges as necessary. Cut the pastry first in half lengthwise and then cut each half into thirds.

6. Place about 1 heaping tablespoon of apple butter in the center of each square and top with apple filling. Whisk together the eggs, water, and salt in a small bowl to make an egg wash. Lightly brush the edges of the pastry squares with egg wash, fold into triangles, and press the edges with the tines of a fork to seal.

7. Arrange the turnovers on the prepared baking pan and make three ½-inch slits on the top of each turnover. Brush the turnovers with the egg wash and chill in the refrigerator for 30 minutes.

8. Combine the brown sugar and cardamom in a small bowl, brush the chilled turnovers again with egg wash, and sprinkle with the spiced sugar. Bake the turnovers until golden brown, about 20 minutes, and serve hot.

THESE FLAKY TURNOVERS ARE LIKE EXTRA SPECIAL INDIVIDUAL APPLE PIES. MY AUNT RUTH SERVED SIMILAR TURNOVERS ON SUNDAYS AT THE GASTHAUS ZUM BUCKENBERG, BUT TO TELL THE TRUTH, SHE PURCHASED THEM FROM THE CAFÉ ACROSS THE STREET. THEY WERE DELICIOUS AT ROOM TEMPERATURE OR WARMED IN THE OVEN.

I HAVE SUGGESTED USING PUFF PASTRY HERE, BUT YOU CAN CERTAINLY USE PÂTE BRISÉE OR OTHER PIE DOUGH, AS MOST COOKS DO IN THE BLACK FOREST.

Serves 6

4 Gala or Granny Smith apples, peeled, cored, and chopped into 1-inch cubes

Juice of ½ lemon

1 cup golden raisins

¼ cup all-purpose flour

1 cup plus 2 tablespoons granulated sugar

1 tablespoon ground cinnamon

⅛ teaspoon freshly grated nutmeg

4 tablespoons unsalted butter

2 tablespoons honey

2 teaspoons vanilla extract

3 pounds prepared puff pastry or Pâte Brisée (page 315)

½ cup apple butter

3 large eggs

1 tablespoon water

⅛ teaspoon salt

½ cup packed light brown sugar

⅛ teaspoon ground cardamom

Clafouti Tart

MIRABELLEN TÖRTCHEN

1. Butter and flour one 10 x 2-inch cake pan and set aside in the refrigerator to chill.

2. To shape the pastry, dust a work surface generously with flour and roll the pâte sucrée into a circle ¼ inch thick and about 12 inches in diameter. Transfer the dough to the prepared cake pan, carefully and neatly pressing the pastry against the sides of the pan. Dock (prick) the surface all over with a fork and chill in the refrigerator for 30 minutes.

3. Preheat the oven to 350°F.

4. Place a piece of foil over the chilled pastry, pour dried beans or pie weights overtop, and bake the pastry until the sides begin to brown, about 10 minutes. Remove the pastry from the oven, carefully lift out the foil and weights, and place on a rack to cool.

5. To make the filling, whisk together the eggs, egg yolks, and sugar in a medium bowl until thick and light yellow in color. Whisk in the flour and set aside momentarily. In another medium bowl, whisk together the milk and sour cream. Pouring in a steady stream, whisk the milk mixture into the lightened sugar and eggs.

6. To assemble the tart, pour the filling into the cooled pastry. Arrange the plums on top and sprinkle with sugar. Bake until the filling puffs and is lightly browned, about 25 to 30 minutes. Set aside to cool for 1 hour.

7. To remove the tart from the pan, carefully run a paring knife around the crust to loosen it from the edges of the pan. Place a plate upside down on top of the pan and quickly invert the tart and plate. Tap lightly on the bottom of the pan and carefully lift it off the tart. Set a cake plate on top of the inverted tart and invert once again.

THIS TART GIVES A NOD TO THE CLASSIC FRENCH CLAFOUTI, PREPARED WITH FRUIT AND A CREAMY, SOMETIMES CAKE-LIKE, CUSTARD THAT PUFFS UP AROUND IT AS IT BAKES. I HAVE SIMPLY ADDED A BOTTOM PASTRY TO THIS COMFORTING, COUNTRY-STYLE DESSERT, MAKING IT A BIT MORE ELEGANT AND TYPICAL OF THE CONFECTIONS I SERVED IN GASTHAUS RESTAURANTS.

USE ANY FRUIT YOU LIKE HERE. I HAVE SUGGESTED MIRABELLE PLUMS, AS THEY ARE TYPICAL OF THE BLACK FOREST, BUT GRAPES, PEACHES, BERRIES, AND CHERRIES ARE ALSO DELICIOUS IN CLAFOUTI. REMEMBER THAT THE FRUIT NEED NOT BE PICTURE PERFECT. IT IS CUT INTO PIECES AND COVERED WITH FILLING, SO A FEW BRUISES OR IMPERFECTIONS ARE OF NO CONSEQUENCE.

Makes one 10-inch tart

1 pound Pâte Sucrée (page 315),
     chilled for at least 3 hours

4 large eggs

3 large egg yolks

1 cup sugar

¼ cup cake flour

3 cups milk

1 cup sour cream or crème fraîche

About 1¼ pounds mirabelle plums,
     pitted and halved (about 3 cups)

3 tablespoons sugar

Apricot Tea Cookies

APRIKOSEN GEBÄCK

APRICOTS GROW ABUNDANTLY IN THE BLACK FOREST, WHERE WE ENJOY THEM FRESH, DRIED, IN BAKED GOODS, AND PRESERVED. THIS RECIPE CALLS FOR COMBINING TWO FLAVORFUL PREPARATIONS: BUTTERY COCONUT-ALMOND COOKIES AND SWEET APRICOT PRESERVES. THESE COOKIES PRESENT A HARMONY OF FLAVORS THAT ARE DELICIOUS WITH COFFEE OR TEA OR, ARRANGED IN PRETTY TINS, MAKE FOR SWEET HOLIDAY GIFTS.

Makes 3 dozen

5 cups all-purpose flour, sifted

2 teaspoons baking powder

$\frac{1}{2}$ teaspoon salt

1 pound (4 sticks) unsalted butter, softened

$\frac{3}{4}$ cup granulated sugar

2 large eggs

1 cup sliced almonds, toasted

1 cup apricot preserves

$\frac{1}{4}$ cup flaked coconut, toasted

(see Chef's Note, page 72)

1. Line baking sheets with parchment paper.

2. Sift together the flour, baking powder, and salt into a medium bowl.

3. Place the butter in the bowl of an electric mixer fitted with the paddle attachment and begin mixing on medium speed. While mixing, add the sugar in a steady stream and continue mixing until light and fluffy, stopping at least once to scrape down the sides of the bowl. Add the eggs one at a time and continue to mix until incorporated, again stopping at least once to scrape down the sides of the bowl.

4. Reduce the mixing speed to low and gradually incorporate the sifted dry ingredients, mixing until just combined. Add the almonds, $\frac{1}{2}$ cup of the preserves, and coconut, mixing until incorporated. Wrap the dough in plastic wrap and chill in the refrigerator for at least 1 hour.

5. Preheat the oven to 350°F.

6. Shape the dough into 1-inch balls and place 1 inch apart on the prepared baking sheets. Make an indentation (using your thumb is best) in the center of each ball and fill with about $\frac{1}{2}$ teaspoon of the remaining preserves. Bake until the edges of the cookies are lightly browned, about 12 to 15 minutes. Set the cookies on wire racks to cool completely and store in an airtight container.

Almond Cookies

MANDEL GEBÄCK

1. Butter and flour one 24-cup mini muffin pan (or use two pans with 12 muffin cups each) and set aside to chill in the refrigerator.

2. Melt the butter in a small saucepan over medium heat, simmering until it is light brown and has a nutty aroma. Remove from the heat and set immediately in an ice bath to prevent it from burning. Gradually and carefully stir in the amaretto (it might splatter a bit) and set aside to cool at room temperature.

3. Place the toasted almonds in the bowl of a food processor fitted with the blade attachment and pulse until finely ground. (Watch the nuts carefully to prevent them from turning into a paste.) Add the sugar, flour, and honey and process to the consistency of coarse meal. Transfer the mixture to an electric mixer fitted with the paddle attachment.

4. Place the egg whites in a medium bowl and whisk briefly just to loosen. Begin mixing the almond mixture on medium speed and gradually add the egg whites, mixing until incorporated. Gradually pour in the cooled browned butter, mixing until just incorporated, and chill the batter in the refrigerator for about 1 hour.

5. Preheat the oven to 400°F.

6. Fill each cup of the prepared muffin pan about half full with chilled batter. Bake with the oven door slightly ajar until the cookies are light golden, about 10 minutes. Place the muffin pan on a wire rack, remove the cookies when completely cool, and store in an airtight container.

THESE DELICIOUS, CRUNCHY ALMOND COOKIES ARE NOT EXCLUSIVE TO THE BLACK FOREST, BUT WE DO MAKE AND ENJOY THEM FREQUENTLY. LIKE THE ITALIANS, WHOSE DELICATE AMARETTI COOKIES ARE CELEBRATED THROUGHOUT THE WORLD, WE ARE FOND OF USING ALMONDS IN THIS RECIPE. FOR A TOTALLY DIFFERENT, BUT EQUALLY WONDERFUL FLAVOR, TRY SUBSTITUTING HAZELNUTS, AS WE OFTEN DO, AND SEE WHICH YOU PREFER.

Makes 2 dozen cookies

6½ tablespoons unsalted butter

2 tablespoons amaretto (almond flavored liqueur)

½ cup toasted almonds

1 cup sugar

½ cup pastry flour

1 tablespoon honey

6 large egg whites

BLACK FOREST COOKIE TRAY INCLUDES
APRICOT TEA COOKIES, ALMOND COOKIES, AND PINE NUT COOKIES

Pine Nut Cookies

PIGNOLI GEBÄCK

In the Black Forest, Gasthaus restaurants most frequently offer plates of cookies at weddings, confirmations, and other large celebrations, along with coffee or tea. These buttery almond cookies are made extra special with the addition of pine nuts. Italy is perhaps most well known for these (PIGNOLI) nuts, but we use them often in the Black Forest as well, given the region's large number of pine trees.

1. Preheat the oven to 325°F. and line baking sheets with parchment paper.

2. Combine the almond paste and honey in the bowl of an electric mixer fitted with the paddle attachment and mix on medium speed until soft and smooth, stopping occasionally to scrape down the sides of the bowl. Reduce the mixing speed to low and add the butter, one cube at a time, until half the butter is incorporated. Scrape down the sides of the bowl, begin mixing again, and incorporate the remaining butter. Scrape down the sides of the bowl once more, add the sugar, and mix on medium speed until smooth and fluffy. Add the eggs and egg yolks one at a time and mix until smooth.

3. Reduce the mixing speed to low and gradually add the flour and almonds, mixing until just combined. Add the pine nuts mixing again until just incorporated.

4. Drop tablespoons of the batter about 1 inch apart onto the prepared baking sheets and bake until the edges of the cookies are light golden, about 7 minutes. Cool the cookies on the baking sheets and store in air-tight containers for up to one week.

Makes 2 dozen cookies

6½ ounces prepared almond paste

6 tablespoons honey

½ pound (2 sticks) unsalted butter, cut into cubes, at room temperature

½ cup sugar

4 large eggs

4 large egg yolks

1¼ cups plus 2 tablespoons sifted all-purpose flour

1 cup finely ground toasted almonds

2 cups pine nuts, toasted and cooled (*see Chef's Note*)

CHEF'S NOTE: Like all nuts, pine nuts toast easily and very quickly. For best results, spread the nuts on a large baking sheet and toast in a 350°F. oven for about 7 minutes, or until they are lightly browned, watching carefully and shaking the pan at least once or twice. Remove the toasted nuts right away to a plate to cool, as they will continue to brown if left on the hot baking sheet.

FASHIONABLE
HOTEL DINING

WHEN I WAS GROWING UP IN THE BLACK FOREST, DELICIOUS, THOUGHTFULLY PREPARED FOOD WAS ALWAYS AT HAND. MY MOTHER'S COOKING, THOUGH MOST OFTEN FAIRLY SIMPLE, WAS fresh, flavorful, and satisfying. Cafés offered specialty pastries and artfully presented savory bites well worth a day's hike. Gasthaus restaurants prided themselves on basic hearty fare and daily specials we often waited all week to savor. And then there were the hotels. They were in a different league altogether. Hotels were, and still very much are, paragons of elegant dining, where serious culinary connoisseurs and the social elite celebrate classic menus and refined hospitality.

My experience cooking in hotels started early. In my day, many families still adhered to old-world traditions and encouraged their children to choose an occupation early in life. I had always loved cooking, so after I finished eighth grade I began my journey towards becoming a chef. I was just fourteen years old. Excited and anxious to learn from classically trained chefs, my parents sent me to apprentice and attend the culinary academy at the Hotel Post in Nagold. Like other elite hotels of its kind, the Hotel Post was famous for its pedigreed chefs, French inspired menus, and celebrated clientele, which included a host of prime ministers and Napoleon Bonaparte himself.

Naturally, many aspiring chefs desired to apprentice at the Hotel Post, but limited openings prevented many from doing so. I, in fact, was fortunate to be admitted. The year I arrived, there was no room left for me on the upper levels of the hotel where all the staff lodged. I made the best of it, though, and found a room across the street above a gas station. Actually, living outside the hotel worked to my advantage. Local folks soon learned of my butchering abilities and I began moonlighting on the side, often butchering deer at a moment's notice and sometimes late at night. Occasionally, I made even more money selling some of the meat and prized skin I was able to keep. I welcomed any extra money in my pocket, considering we only earned $20

The Hotel Post
The Sommerberg Hotel
sits atop a tree-lined hill
in Bad Wildbad.

a month as apprentices. In truth, though, we needed very little spending money. We had few days off and spent the majority of our time in the kitchen.

Life at the Hotel Post was all consuming for the three years I apprenticed there. A large, experienced staff ran it with precision and according to the highest standards. In the dining room, the maitre d', professional waiters, and bar men (who had committed all conceivable drinks to memory) maintained order and elegance. The tables were always draped with crisp white linens and bedecked with shining silver flatware, sparkling crystal, and fine china. The kitchen was equally disciplined and orderly. The executive chef was in charge of a huge brigade of chefs and apprentices who were not only responsible for cooking, but also for the many kinds of food preparation that the classic menu required.

Like many upscale establishments of its kind, the Hotel Post was completely self-sufficient and demanded many hours from the kitchen staff. There was so much work to be done that, typical of classically run kitchens, we all worked double shifts six days a week. Similar to centuries-old taverns in Europe and America, we butchered our own meat, made our own sausages, and tended to our own smoke house. We spent countless hours preparing pastry and delicate desserts in a separate pastry kitchen. We cared for our own orchards that produced an abundance of fruit, including apples, plums, and berries. Occasionally, we were even required to give up a cherished day off from work to harvest the produce. We also kept large root cellars filled with staples like potatoes, horseradish, and celery roots that grew in our extensive gardens. I recall we did have several women who cared for the gardens, but we pickled and preserved fruits and vegetables ourselves and even made our own eau de vie.

When my apprenticeship ended at the Hotel Post, I graduated from the culinary academy and received my *Gehilfenbrief* (chef's certificate). I was finally a professional chef and could work anywhere in Europe. Before settling in one location, though, I decided to travel and gain more experience working as a *commis* (an assistant chef of sorts) in a variety of hotels and restaurants. I first went on to assist with the reopening of the Sommerberg Hotel in

Bad Wildbad—another gorgeous hotel that literally sat on the top of a mountain and catered to an upscale clientele. From there, I went on to work in Switzerland, France, and Italy, eventually completing seven years of intensive training.

In my day, especially, hotels reflected the most admired fashion of cooking and dining—that of France. It is undeniable that French cuisine greatly influenced the dishes we prepared in Nagold and Bad Wildbad. To be a great chef anywhere in Europe, one had to intimately know and be able to prepare classic French recipes. We studied the techniques and dishes of the famous nineteenth-century French chef and "master of modern cookery," Auguste Escoffier, and we gained command of the extensive terminology set forth in culinary reference books like *Le Répertoire de La Cuisine*, first published in 1914.

It is thus hardly surprising that many of the recipes I present in this chapter speak with a pronounced French accent. Dishes like steak tartare, coquilles St. Jacques, venison ragoût à la forestière, boeuf bourguignonne, and crème brûlée appeared regularly on our hotel menus and have become some of my favorites. As much as we admired French cooking, however, we were still loyal to the traditions and ingredients native to our own Black Forest and incorporated them whenever we could. As a result, we prepared items like herring bonne femme, utilizing our beloved pickled herring; paupiettes of brook trout, featuring our most famous fish; pork medallions with lager and chanterelles, prepared with our much loved golden lager; and *Zwetschgenkuchen* (plum tart), in which the region's favorite plums are showcased in classic French pastry.

My years as a young chef in hotels were filled with much hard work but many rewards, as well. Like many new chefs, when I returned home from my travels, I worked at the family restaurant as *chef de cuisine*. There, at the Gasthaus zum Buckenberg in Pforzheim, I utilized many of my new skills and served fancy dishes every so often like chocolate soufflé or frog's legs Provençal. It was always obvious when a young chef returned to the family Gasthaus after years of classic training, because elegant items would periodically appear on the otherwise modest menus.

For the most part, though, refined classic dishes remained within the heralded domains of hotel chefs' exclusive repertoires. These menu items were complicated and often required costly ingredients as well as the labor of numerous cooks and apprentices. Patrons expected exquisite food and service and happily paid for the experience.

Elegant hotel dishes are about as far removed from comforting home food as they can be. Each accurately represents the culinary traditions of the Black Forest, however, and shows the depth and breadth of our respect and passion for the table.

Smoked Trout &
Asparagus Salad

GERÄUCHERTE FORELLE & SPARGEL SALAT

WHEN I WORKED AT THE HOTEL POST IN NAGOLD, THIS WAS THE MOST POPULAR SALAD ON THE MENU. IT WAS HARDLY SURPRISING. TROUT IS ADORED THROUGHOUT THE BLACK FOREST, AS IS ASPARAGUS—ESPECIALLY IN THE SPRING AND EARLY SUMMER WHEN THE REGION IS FLOODED WITH IT.

THIS LIGHT AND FRESH SALAD, DRESSED WITH A EUROPEAN-STYLE SAUCE AND ELEGANTLY BRIGHTENED WITH FRIED LEMON ZEST, IS DELICIOUS FOR LUNCH OR AS AN APPETIZER AT DINNER. AS WE DID AT THE HOTEL POST, I SUGGEST SERVING THE SALAD IN RADICCHIO CUPS, BUT IT IS ALSO LOVELY PRESENTED IN MARTINI GLASSES OR TOGETHER WITH BLACK FOREST CRACKER BREAD (RECIPE FOLLOWS). TO MAKE THE SALAD REALLY SNAZZY, SPOON SOME CAVIAR OR SALMON ROE ON TOP.

---

1. To make the dressing, stir together the mayonnaise, ketchup, vinegar, curry, Cognac and horseradish in a small bowl and season with salt and white pepper.

2. To make the fried lemon zest, heat the oil in a small saucepan to 375°F. Add the lemon zest and fry until golden brown, about 2 to 3 minutes. Remove with a slotted spoon and set aside to drain on paper towels.

3. To make the salad, combine the white and green asparagus, onion, cucumber, tomatoes, and mushrooms in a large bowl, tossing to incorporate, and gently fold in the dressing and trout.

4. To serve, set some radicchio leaves on each plate to form a small cup and spoon in some salad. Sprinkle some of the fried lemon zest on top and garnish with chives and capers.

Serves 6

DRESSING:

¾ cup Mayonnaise (page 314)

1 tablespoon ketchup

2 tablespoons red wine vinegar

⅛ teaspoon curry powder

1 tablespoon Cognac

1 level teaspoon grated horseradish

Salt

Freshly ground white pepper

FRIED LEMON ZEST:

1 cup vegetable oil

Zest of 1 lemon, sliced into thin strips

SALAD:

8 ounces white asparagus, blanched and cut into slices about 3 inches long and ⅛ inch thick

1 pound green asparagus, blanched and cut into slices about 3 inches long and ⅛ inch thick

1 red onion, peeled and thinly sliced

½ large English cucumber, seeded and sliced (about 1 cup)

3 Roma tomatoes, seeded and sliced

3 white button mushrooms, sliced

3 smoked trout fillets, skinned, boned, and cut into 1-inch pieces

2 heads radicchio, cored and leaves separated

Chopped fresh chives, for garnish

Small capers, for garnish

Black Forest Cracker Bread

KNÄCKEBROT

1. Preheat the oven to 375°F. Grease the backs of two 11 x 17-inch baking sheets with vegetable shortening.

2. Combine the water, yeast, and honey in the bowl of an electric mixer fitted with the dough hook attachment and mix on low speed until well combined. Add the olive oil, flour, and salt and continue mixing until incorporated. Increase the speed to medium and mix the dough until it forms a stiff ball. (If the dough is too wet, add a bit more flour.)

3. Remove the dough from the bowl, divide in half, and stretch each half over the back of one of the prepared baking sheets (image a).

4. Beat the two eggs together with the tablespoon of water to make an egg wash. Brush the dough with the egg wash and sprinkle with equal amounts of the caraway seeds, poppy seeds, and salt (image b). Bake until golden brown, about 25 minutes. Cool the bread directly on the baking sheets and break into pieces to serve (image c).

I DECIDED TO OMIT A CHAPTER ON BREAD IN THIS BOOK, AS GERMAN BREADS GENERALLY REQUIRE FAIRLY LENGTHY DISCUSSIONS. I JUST HAD TO INCLUDE THIS RECIPE FOR CRACKER BREAD, HOWEVER. WE PREPARED IT OFTEN DURING MY APPRENTICESHIPS IN HOTEL KITCHENS AND SERVED IT ALONG WITH OTHER BREADS IN BREADBASKETS. CRISP AND FLAVORFUL, THIS BREAD IS BAKED IN LARGE SHEETS AND RESEMBLES MIDDLE EASTERN LAVASH.

THIS RECIPE CALLS FOR FLAVORING THE BREAD WITH SALT, POPPY SEEDS, AND CARAWAY SEEDS, BUT THE OPTIONS ARE VIRTUALLY ENDLESS. YOU MIGHT TRY CURRY POWDER OR PAPRIKA, WHICH ARE ALSO DELICIOUS.

CRACKER BREAD PAIRS NICELY WITH STEWS, SOUPS, AND SALADS. FOR A DRAMATIC AND ATTRACTIVE PRESENTATION, BREAK THE BAKED BREAD HAPHAZARDLY INTO LARGE PIECES AND ARRANGE THEM IN BASKETS.

Makes two 11 x 17-inch baking sheets

1¼ cups water

1½ tablespoons dry active yeast

2 tablespoons honey

6 tablespoons olive oil

3 cups bread flour, sifted

1½ teaspoons salt

2 eggs

1 tablespoon water

1 tablespoon caraway seeds

1 tablespoon poppy seeds

1 tablespoon kosher salt

BLACK FOREST CRACKER BREAD

Divide dough in half, and stretch each half over the back of the baking sheet. Sprinkle with equal amounts of the caraway seeds, poppy seeds, and salt.

a

b

c

Waldorf Salad

SALAT WALDORF

THIS SALAD IS A CLASSIC THE WORLD OVER AND IS SERVED IN NEARLY ALL BLACK FOREST HOTELS. IT IS DELICIOUS PAIRED WITH FOIE GRAS OR WITH A SLICE OF RICH PÂTÉ OR TERRINE.

Serves 4

4 large Granny Smith apples, peeled, cored,
    and thinly sliced (about 2 inches long and $1/16$ inch wide)

1 medium celery root, peeled and thinly sliced
    (about 2 inches long and $1/16$ inch wide)

Juice of 1 large lemon (about $1/4$ cup)

$1/2$ cup chopped walnuts

$1/4$ cup Mayonnaise (page 314)

2 tablespoons heavy cream

$1/4$ teaspoon Worcestershire sauce

$1/8$ tablespoon curry powder

Salt

Freshly ground white pepper

Chopped fresh parsley, for garnish

1. Toss the apples and celery root with lemon juice in a medium bowl.

2. Stir together the walnuts, mayonnaise, cream, Worcestershire sauce, and curry powder in a small bowl.

3. Pour the mayonnaise over the apples, toss gently to combine, and season with salt and white pepper. Cover and refrigerate until well chilled, about 1 hour, before serving.

French Lentil Salad

FRANZÖSICHER LINSEN SALAT

1. To make the salad, at least 4 hours before serving, put the lentils in a large bowl, pour water overtop to cover by about 1 inch, and set aside to soak.

2. Drain the lentils, place them in a large saucepan, and add the carrots, onion, garlic, bay leaf, thyme, salt, and pepper. Pour in enough water to cover by about 1 inch and bring to a boil over high heat. Reduce the heat to low and simmer until the lentils are just tender, checking frequently to prevent overcooking, about 10 minutes.

3. Drain the lentils in a colander, discarding the cooking liquid, bay leaf, and thyme. Pour the lentils and vegetables into a bowl and set to chill in the refrigerator for about 1 hour.

4. Heat a small saucepan over medium heat, add the bacon, and sauté until crisp, about 3 minutes. Drain the bacon on paper towels.

5. To make the dressing, whisk together the chives, onion, oil, vinegar, mustard, garlic, salt, and pepper in a large bowl.

6. To assemble the salad, gently toss together the cooled lentils and dressing and set aside at room temperature for about 30 minutes to allow the flavors to mingle.

7. To serve, season with additional salt and pepper if necessary and pour into a large serving bowl. Garnish with parsley.

THIS DISH IS CONSIDERED MORE OF AN APPETIZER THAN A MERE SALAD IN HOTEL RESTAURANTS AND IT IS ALWAYS PAIRED WITH OTHER ITEMS. WHEN I WAS AN APPRENTICE, FOR EXAMPLE, WE SERVED IT ALONGSIDE VEAL SAUSAGES OR SLICED BREAST OF DUCK. FLAVORED WITH GARLIC, HERBS, MUSTARD, AND BACON, LENTIL SALAD AT ONCE DISPLAYS ITS FRENCH AND SOUTHERN GERMAN CHARACTER. ALTHOUGH WE COMMONLY SERVED THIS DISH IN SOME OF THE BLACK FOREST'S MOST ELEGANT RESTAURANTS, IT IS PERFECTLY SUITED TO THE HOME KITCHEN, AS THE SALAD COMES TOGETHER EASILY AND IS QUITE ECONOMICAL.

Serves 8

SALAD:

4 cups French lentils

2 carrots, peeled and cut into strips
about 2 inches long and 1/8 inch wide

1 medium yellow onion, peeled and chopped

2 large cloves garlic, peeled and chopped

1 dried bay leaf

3 sprigs fresh thyme

1 teaspoon salt

1/2 teaspoon freshly ground black pepper

9 slices lean bacon, chopped

DRESSING

1 bunch fresh chives, chopped

1 red onion, peeled and finely chopped

1/2 cup olive oil

1/4 cup red wine vinegar

2 tablespoons Dijon mustard

3 cloves garlic, peeled and chopped

1 teaspoon salt

1/2 teaspoon freshly ground black pepper

1/2 bunch fresh parsley sprigs, for garnish

Steak Tartare

TATAR BEEFSTEAK

Parisian brasseries and elegant Black Forest hotels and restaurants share an affinity for this classic dish. Patrons of both types of restaurants expect to see it on their menus. As in Paris, hotels throughout the Black Forest serve steak tartare with a variety of side dishes and ingredients, including POMMES FRITES (French fries), caviar, and even egg yolks from quail, rather than from the more common chicken. Egg yolks are traditional to Parisian and Black Forest steak tartare, but you can certainly omit them if you wish.

For the best result, I recommend purchasing only the freshest, leanest, finest quality beef tenderloin, freshly ground by a reputable butcher.

1. Combine the mustard, oil, Worcestershire sauce, hot pepper sauce, and 1½ tablespoons each of the capers, onion, and parsley in the bowl of a food processor fitted with the blade attachment and purée until smooth.

2. Place the beef in a medium bowl and add the purée, paprika and Cognac, tossing gently to combine. (Aggressive mixing will make the tartare tough.) Divide the tartare into four portions and roll each into a ball. Press into patties and score decoratively with crosshatches using the back of a knife.

3. To serve, set each tartare in the center of a plate, arrange anchovies as well as the remaining capers, onion, and parsley around it, and, if desired, top the tartare with an egg yolk.

Serves 4

1½ tablespoons whole-grain mustard

1½ tablespoons olive oil

1½ tablespoons Worcestershire sauce

Hot pepper sauce, to taste

3½ tablespoons capers

3½ tablespoons chopped yellow onion

3½ tablespoons chopped fresh parsley

⅛ teaspoon Hungarian paprika

¼ cup high quality Cognac

1 pound ground beef tenderloin

Anchovy fillets, for serving

4 egg yolks, for serving (optional)

CHEF'S NOTE: Consuming raw or undercooked meats, poultry, seafood, shellfish, or eggs may increase the risk of food borne illness to young children, seniors and those with compromised immune systems.

Vols-au-Vent with Sweet-breads, Salsify, & Saffron-Cream Sauce

PASTETCHEN MIT KALBSBRIESLE, SCHWARZWURZEL & SAFRAN RAHMSOße

Serves 6

3 pounds veal sweetbreads

1 onion, peeled and studded with three whole cloves

1 dried bay leaf

2 pounds salsify

Juice of 2 lemons

6 tablespoons unsalted butter

3 shallots, peeled and finely chopped

3 tablespoons all-purpose flour

3 cups white wine

2 cups heavy cream

½ teaspoon saffron threads

Salt

Freshly ground white pepper

6 Vols-au-Vent (page 80), for serving

1. Place the sweetbreads in a large saucepan, cover with cold salted water, and add the studded onion and bay leaf. Bring to a boil over medium-high heat and lower the heat to medium low. Simmer for 30 to 45 minutes, skimming any foam that rises to the surface, until the sweetbreads are fully cooked and easily pierced with a knife. Drain the sweetbreads, reserving the cooking liquid, and set in cold water to cool. Peel off the outer membrane, pull apart the pieces where they naturally separate, and set aside in the refrigerator.

2. Strain the cooking liquid, return it to the saucepan, and bring to a boil over high heat. Lower the heat to medium and simmer until reduced by three-quarters. Strain and set aside. (The cooked sweetbreads and cooking liquid can be refrigerated overnight at this point if you wish.)

3. Trim and peel the salsify and rinse thoroughly. Cut on the diagonal into 1-inch pieces, place in a large bowl, and toss with lemon juice to prevent them from discoloring.

4. Melt 3 tablespoons of the butter in a large sauté pan over medium heat, add the shallots, and sauté until slightly softened, but not colored. Toss in the salsify and sauté until just tender, about 3 to 5 minutes. (If the salsify is very fresh, it will cook quite quickly.) Remove from the heat and set aside momentarily.

5. Place the remaining 3 tablespoons of butter in a small bowl and knead in the flour, a bit at a time, to form a beurre manié.

6. Stir together the white wine, cream, saffron, and reduced sweetbread liquid in a medium saucepan and bring to a boil over medium-low heat. Stir in the beurre manié a little at a time until incorporated and the sauce thickens. Season with salt and pepper. Add the salsify and sweetbreads, mixing gently, and simmer until heated.

7. To serve, set a vol-au-vent on each plate and fill with the sweetbreads and sauce.

THIS ELEGANT APPETIZER IS A FAVORITE IN THE BLACK FOREST. SWEETBREADS ARE STILL CONSIDERED VERY MUCH A DELICACY IN THE REGION, AND SALSIFY GROWS IN NEARLY EVERY GARDEN. WHEN I WORKED AT THE HOTEL POST, WE OFTEN SERVED THESE PRETTY VOLS-AU-VENT AS STARTERS AT LARGE EVENTS AND CELEBRATIONS. THE PREPARATION IS SLIGHTLY LABOR INTENSIVE, BUT THE END RESULT IS QUITE WORTH THE EFFORT.

Herring *à la Bonne Femme*

HERING NACH HAUSFRAUEN ART

The French term **À LA BONNE FEMME** translates as "in the style of the good wife," referring to food that is flavorful, homey, and uncomplicated. This classic appetizer is simple to prepare and filled with flavor, just as its name implies. The dish features a variety of flavors and textures. From the crunchy apples, to the tender herring, to the creamy sour cream, it is satisfying and quintessentially representative of the Black Forest.

1. Toss together the apples and juice of 1 lemon in a medium bowl. Drain the apples, discarding the excess liquid, and combine with the herring and onion.

2. Whisk together the sour cream, Worcestershire sauce, and remaining lemon juice in a medium bowl. Season with salt and white pepper and gently fold into the herring, apples, and onions.

3. To serve, arrange 3 or 4 lettuce leaves on a plate to form a cup. Fill with some of the herring salad and garnish with red and yellow peppers.

Serves 6 to 8

4 small Granny Smith apples, peeled, cored, and finely chopped

Juice of 2 lemons

1 (18-ounce) jar herring marinated in white wine, drained and cut into 2-inch pieces

2 large white onions, peeled and chopped

1½ cups sour cream

1 teaspoon Worcestershire sauce

⅛ teaspoon salt

½ teaspoon white pepper

2 heads Bibb lettuce, cored and leaves separated, for serving

½ red bell pepper, cored, seeded, and finely chopped, for garnish

½ yellow bell pepper, cored, seeded, and finely chopped, for garnish

Smoked Salmon Frittata

GERÄUCHERTER LACHS FRITTATA

1. Heat 2 tablespoons of the olive oil in a large sauté pan over medium heat, toss in the garlic, onion, mushrooms, and peppers, and sauté until softened, about 5 minutes. Remove from the heat and set aside in the refrigerator to chill.

2. Stir together the eggs, pasta, cheese, herbs, and chilled sautéed vegetables in a large bowl and season with salt and pepper. Heat the butter and remaining olive oil in a small sauté or omelet pan over medium-high heat and add about one-quarter of the egg mixture, shaping it into a cake about 1 inch thick and 3 inches in diameter. Brown on each side for about 5 minutes (image below), then remove the frittata to a covered plate to keep warm. Repeat three more times with the remaining mixture.

3. To serve, set each frittata in the center of a plate and place a slice of salmon decoratively on top. Garnish with chives and serve with sour cream or crème fraîche.

Serves 4

1 cup olive oil

1 tablespoon finely chopped garlic

2 tablespoons finely chopped onion

1 cup finely chopped portobello mushrooms

2 tablespoons finely chopped green bell pepper

2 tablespoons finely chopped red bell pepper

8 large eggs, lightly beaten

4 cups cooked angel hair pasta,
    chilled for at least 30 minutes

½ cup grated Parmesan cheese

1 teaspoon stemmed and finely chopped fresh thyme

1 teaspoon finely chopped fresh basil

¼ teaspoon dried oregano

Salt

Freshly ground black pepper

2 tablespoons unsalted butter

4 slices smoked salmon (about 3 ounces each)

Chives, cut into 3-inch-long pieces, for garnish

Sour cream or crème fraîche, for serving (optional)

This frittata represents the coming together of basic Italian fare and elegant Black Forest hotel cuisine. Italian frittatas are generally modest dishes prepared with eggs and an assortment of vegetables and cheese. In elegant Black Forest hotels, these large frittatas are prepared as appetizers, the size of silver dollars, and are served with delicacies like smoked salmon as well as tangy crème fraîche and fresh herbs.

In my day, smoked salmon was a very special and expensive restaurant item. In fact, it was so costly that it was locked away to curb the fishy appetites of slippery restaurant staff. Fortunately, smoked salmon is widely available today and is easily paired with this fresh, flavorful frittata.

Creamy Tomato-Basil Soup

TOMATEN BASILIKUM RAHMSUPPE

HOME COOKS AND RESTAURANT CHEFS ALIKE MAKE A VARIETY OF TOMATO SOUPS IN THE BLACK FOREST. THIS RECIPE IS DELICIOUS ANYTIME OF YEAR, AS IT RELIES ON THE CONCENTRATED FLAVOR OF TOMATO PASTE. OF COURSE, BASIL PAIRS PERFECTLY WITH TOMATOES, AND THE FRESH HERB LENDS BRIGHTNESS TO THIS RICH AND TANGY CREAM SOUP.

1. Melt 1 tablespoon of butter in a medium saucepan over medium heat, add the onion, and sauté until light golden and softened, about 4 minutes. Add the garlic and sauté until golden, about 1½ minutes more.

2. Stir in the stock, wine, and tomato paste and bring to a boil over high heat. Add the cream, return the soup to a boil, and incorporate the basil.

3. Melt the remaining 4 tablespoons of butter in a small saucepan over low heat, stir in the flour to form a roux, and cook, stirring frequently, until golden brown, about 15 minutes.

4. Gradually stir the roux into the soup and reduce the heat to medium low. Add the tomatoes and simmer for about 5 minutes until slightly thickened.

5. Season with salt and pepper and serve in individual bowls garnished with a dollop of crème fraîche and a basil leaf.

Serves 6 to 8

5 tablespoons unsalted butter

1 small onion, peeled and finely chopped

1 clove garlic, peeled and chopped

1½ quarts Vegetable Stock (page 311) or Chicken Stock (page 308)

1 cup dry white wine, such as Sauvignon Blanc

¾ cup tomato paste

1 cup heavy cream

2 tablespoons chopped fresh basil

¼ cup all-purpose flour

3 Roma tomatoes, seeded and finely chopped

Salt

Freshly ground black pepper

Crème fraîche, for garnish

Fresh basil leaves, for garnish

CHEF'S NOTE/VARIATION: Tomato-basil soup is delicious on its own for a modest or upscale first course. To dress it up a bit, try presenting the soup as we often did at the Sommerberg Hotel in Bad Wildbad. Pour the soup into bowls, cover it with puff pastry dough, and bake until golden. When you are ready to serve, cut into the pastry and spoon a dollop of crème fraîche on top.

Cream of Cucumber Soup

GURKEN RAHMSUPPE

This simple but lovely soup is based on a traditional French recipe and is one of my favorites. We prepared many elegant soups in the hotel kitchens where I apprenticed and, as we did for every recipe, we learned the proper French terminology for each one. In Europe, cold creamy cucumber soup is traditionally called CRÈME DORIA, in dedication to a member of the famous Genoese Doria family who frequented the Café Anglais in Paris in the nineteenth century.

My version includes many of the same ingredients, but the salmon roe is a unique touch. If you wish to exclude it you can, but it is awfully pretty paired with the light green purée.

1. At least 4 hours before serving, melt the butter in a 6-quart saucepan over medium heat, add the onion, and sauté until translucent and slightly softened, about 2 minutes. Add the cucumbers and sauté, stirring constantly, until translucent and any liquid they release has evaporated. Stir in the potatoes and sauté for 2 minutes more.

2. Add the stock, raise the heat slightly to medium high, and cook until the potato pieces have completely broken down and are no longer visible, about 25 minutes. Remove from heat and pour about one-third at a time into a blender, puréeing until smooth. Pour into a bowl or container, cover, and set aside in the refrigerator to chill completely, 4 hours or overnight.

3. When ready to serve, add the cream, stirring until well combined. If the soup is too thick, incorporate milk to reach your desired consistency. Stir in the dill and season with salt and pepper.

4. To serve, place 1 tablespoon of cucumber strips in the center of each soup bowl and ladle the soup around it. Set 1 teaspoon of salmon roe on top of the cucumber and sprinkle with chives.

Serves 8

1 tablespoon unsalted butter

1 medium onion, peeled and finely chopped

8 cups peeled, seeded, and chopped English cucumbers

2 cups peeled and chopped Yukon gold potatoes

2 quarts Chicken Stock (page 308)
  or Vegetable Stock (page 311)

1 cup heavy cream

Milk, as needed

2 tablespoons chopped fresh dill

Salt

Freshly ground white pepper

1 medium English cucumber, peeled, seeded, and cut into strips about 2 inches long and $\frac{1}{8}$ inch wide (about 1½ cups), for serving

Salmon roe, for garnish (optional)

Finely chopped fresh chives, for garnish

Mushroom Bisque

WILDE PILZ SUPPE

1. Melt the butter in large Dutch oven or casserole over medium heat, add the mushrooms, and sauté for about 5 minutes. Remove from the heat, set aside to cool for 15 minutes, and transfer to the bowl of a food processor fitted with the blade attachment. Process until puréed and set aside.

2. Combine the stock, bay leaf, and garlic in a large saucepan, bring to a boil over high heat, and continue to boil until reduced by half, about 45 minutes.

3. Stir in the sherry and cream, remove the bay leaf, and boil until again reduced by half, about 30 minutes.

4. Stir in the mushroom purée, reduce the heat to medium low, and simmer for about 10 minutes.

5. Season with salt and pepper, serve in a soup tureen or soup bowls, and garnish with parsley.

GIVEN THE ENORMOUS NUMBER OF WILD MUSH-ROOMS AVAILABLE IN THE BLACK FOREST, JUST ABOUT EVERY HOTEL RESTAURANT SERVED MUSH-ROOM BISQUE. LOCAL MUSHROOM GATHERERS, IN FACT, OFTEN CAME TO THE KITCHEN DOOR TO SELL US BASKETS FILLED WITH FUNGI, FRESH FROM THAT DAY'S PICKING.

I ENCOURAGE YOU TO TRY THIS RECIPE AND USE IT AS A BASIC TEMPLATE, VARYING THE FLAVORS AS YOU WISH. I PARTICULARLY LIKE USING PORCINI MUSHROOMS (ALSO CALLED CÈPES) IN THIS SOUP, FOR EXAMPLE, BUT I SUGGEST YOU USE WHATEVER VARIETY IS FRESHEST AND MOST APPEALING TO YOU IN YOUR MARKET.

REFRIGERATE LEFTOVERS IN AIRTIGHT CONTAINERS FOR UP TO ONE WEEK. THIS SOUP CAN ALSO BE FROZEN, BUT THE MUSHROOMS HAVE A TENDENCY TO BECOME MUSHY WHEN REHEATED.

Serves 10 to 12

2 tablespoons unsalted butter

2 pounds assorted fresh mushrooms, such as portobello, porcini, and chanterelles, chopped

4 quarts Vegetable Stock (page 311)

1 dried bay leaf

2 large cloves garlic, peeled and minced

1 cup dry sherry

2 quarts heavy cream

Salt

Freshly ground white pepper

Chopped fresh parsley, for garnish

Carrot Soup with Tapioca

KAROTTEN SUPPE MIT TAPIOCA

Serves 8

2 tablespoons unsalted butter

1 large onion, peeled and finely chopped

2 pounds carrots, peeled and finely chopped

2 pounds Yukon gold potatoes,
   peeled and finely chopped

1½ quarts Chicken Stock (page 308)

Salt

Freshly ground white pepper

¼ cup pearl tapioca,
   cooked according to package directions

Chopped fresh parsley, for garnish

Champagne or sparkling wine, for garnish

THIS ELEGANTLY SIMPLE SOUP HAS QUITE A REFINED PEDIGREE. INSPIRED BY THE TOWN OF VICHY, IN CENTRAL FRANCE, IT PAYS TRIBUTE TO THE DELIGHTFUL **CAROTTES À LA VICHY**, A VEGETABLE DISH OF THINLY SLICED CARROTS COOKED AND GLAZED WITH A BIT OF BUTTER, SUGAR, AND WATER AND FINISHED WITH CHOPPED PARSLEY. THE WATER IS THE MOST SPECIAL INGREDIENT HERE; THE TRADITIONAL RECIPE CALLS FOR USING VICHY'S SPARKLING MINERAL WATER THAT NATURALLY BUBBLES IN THE SPRINGS AROUND THE FAMOUS SPA CITY.

THE ADDITION OF TAPIOCA MAKES THE SOUP EXTRA SPECIAL. ALTHOUGH AMERICANS MOST OFTEN ASSOCIATE TAPIOCA WITH SWEET PUDDING, EUROPEANS USE THE SMOOTH, TENDER PEARLS IN SAVORY DISHES, TOO. COMBINING THE CREAMY SOUP WITH THE JEWEL-LIKE, TRANSLUCENT TAPIOCA RESULTS IN A DELICIOUS AND ELEGANT DISH.

1. Melt the butter in a large saucepan over medium-high heat, add the onion, and sauté until translucent and softened, about 5 minutes. Add the carrots and sauté for another 5 minutes, stirring occasionally. Toss in the potatoes and sauté for 2 more minutes.

2. Pour in the stock and bring to a boil over high heat, continuing to boil until the potatoes and carrots are tender, about 20 minutes. Remove from the heat and, working with about one-third of the soup at a time, pour into a blender. Purée until smooth, return to the saucepan, and season with salt and pepper.

3. To serve, place about 1 tablespoon of tapioca in the bottom of each bowl and ladle the soup overtop. Garnish with parsley and, at the last moment, tableside, a drizzle of Champagne or sparkling wine.

French Onion Soup

FRANZÖSICHE ZWIEBEL SUPPE

Onion soup is one of those dishes that just about everyone adores. Warming and satisfying, it is as welcoming on home dinner tables as it is in fancy hotel restaurants.

This version is one of my favorites. I like to refer to it as "Nagolder Onion Soup," as it is based on the recipe we prepared at the Hotel Post in Nagold. We served a similar onion soup at the Sommerberg Hotel in Bad Wildbad. I especially remember it from my days as Chef de Garde when I periodically worked alone (with a few dish washers and servers) in the kitchen late at night. Late-night crowds always ordered simpler dishes like sandwiches, goulash, and, of course, onion soup.

One particular late-night experience led me to invent a new and tasty variation of the soup for which I became rather well known. I was, as usual, working by myself when I received an order for onion soup. After much searching, I found that we were out of French bread and could not prepare croutons. You can imagine my dismay, as every onion soup aficionado knows the crispy bits of bread are essential to traditional onion soup. So, I regained my composure and decided to use a single large **MAULTASCHE** (ravioli, page 113) instead. The soup was a hit! So much so, in fact, that guests began to regularly request the Maultaschen version.

In this recipe, I suggest traditionally enhancing the basic soup with creamy Gruyère cheese. I encourage you, though, to vary the soup as you please and add croutons (or Maultaschen!) if you wish. Refrigerate leftovers in airtight containers for up to one week. This soup can also be frozen, but the vegetables have a tendency to become mushy when reheated.

Serves 8 to 10

½ pound (2 sticks) unsalted butter

4 pounds yellow onions (about 16), peeled and thinly sliced

3 tablespoons all-purpose flour

4 cups very dry white wine, such as Chenin Blanc

2 quarts Beef Bouillon (page 309)

Salt

Freshly ground black pepper

4 cups grated Gruyère cheese

1. Melt the butter in a large saucepan over medium heat, add the onions, and sauté until golden brown, about 15 minutes. Sprinkle the onions with flour and stir to form a paste (roux).

2. Add the wine to deglaze, stirring with a wooden spoon to loosen any browned bits on the bottom of the pan, and stir until all of the flour has been incorporated and the liquid is smooth. Add the bouillon and bring to a boil, reduce the heat to medium, and simmer for about 30 minutes.

3. Preheat the broiler.

4. Ladle the soup into individual ovenproof bowls and divide the cheese among them. Set the bowls under the broiler until the cheese has melted, watching carefully to keep it from burning, and serve bubbly hot.

Creamy
Cucumber Salad

GURKENSALAT MIT RAHM

1. Place the cucumber slices in a medium bowl and sprinkle with a light coating of salt. Cover with plastic wrap and refrigerate until chilled and the cucumbers have released their water, about 1 hour. Drain the cucumbers in a colander, rinse with cold water, and gently squeeze the slices with your hands to remove any excess liquid.

2. Stir together the sour cream, onion, vinegar, paprika, and chili powder in a medium serving bowl, add the drained cucumber slices, and toss gently to combine.

3. To serve, season with pepper and additional salt if necessary and garnish with chives.

VARIOUS CUCUMBER SALADS ARE OFTEN SERVED IN THE BLACK FOREST AS PART OF WHAT THE FRENCH CALL SALADES COMPOSÉES (COMPOSED SALADS). IN FRANCE, THESE SALADS ARE TOSSED WITH DRESSING AND BEAUTIFULLY ARRANGED ON A SINGLE PLATE. IN THE BLACK FOREST, THE TERM IS USED SLIGHTLY DIFFERENTLY, REFERRING TO SMALL SERVINGS OF NUMEROUS SALADS SERVED IN INDIVIDUAL PLATES AND THEN ASSEMBLED ON A LARGER SERVING PLATE. THE VARIETY HERE IS ENDLESS AND OFTEN INCLUDES SUCH ITEMS AS POTATO SALAD, TOMATO SALAD, BEET SALAD, AND PICKLED CAULIFLOWER. THE FINAL DISH CAN BE FAIRLY LARGE AND QUITE A COMPOSITION OF COLOR, TEXTURE, AND FLAVOR.

THIS RECIPE IS BASED ON A TRADITIONAL CREAMY CUCUMBER SALAD, BUT I HAVE ADDED MY OWN TWIST WITH THE ADDITION OF SPICY PAPRIKA AND CHILI POWDER. I LIKE THE HEAT AND FLAVOR THEY IMPART, BUT IF YOU PREFER THE MORE TYPICALLY BLACK FOREST VERSION YOU CAN CERTAINLY OMIT THEM.

Serves 4

1 large English cucumber, or 4 small cucumbers, peeled and thinly sliced (about 4 cups)

Salt

$\frac{1}{2}$ cup sour cream

1 medium red onion, peeled and finely chopped

1 tablespoon cider vinegar

$\frac{1}{8}$ teaspoon Hungarian paprika

$\frac{1}{8}$ teaspoon chili powder

Freshly ground black pepper

Chopped fresh chives, for garnish

Dandelion Salad with Bacon Vinaigrette

LÖWENZAHN SALAT MIT SPECK

WHEN I APPRENTICED IN HOTEL KITCHENS, WE FREQUENTLY PREPARED DANDELION SALADS. THE SPIKY GREENS GREW FREELY AROUND THE PROPERTIES AND, AS AN APPRENTICE, IT WAS MY JOB TO PICK THEM FRESH FOR EACH DAY'S MENU. DANDELION GREENS ARE SLIGHTLY BITTER AND TANGY AND THUS ARE PERFECTLY PAIRED WITH RICH, FLAVORFUL BACON VINAIGRETTE.

Serves 8

6 slices lean bacon, cut into thin strips

¼ cup balsamic vinegar

2 cloves garlic, peeled and chopped

½ red onion, peeled and finely chopped

2½ pounds fresh dandelion greens, torn into bite-size pieces

2 cups Herb Croutons (page 31)

Salt

Freshly ground black pepper

1. Heat a medium saucepan over medium heat, add the bacon, and cook until crisp, about 3 minutes. Remove the bacon, setting aside momentarily, and whisk in the vinegar, garlic, and onion to combine and make a vinaigrette.

2. To serve, place the dandelion greens and croutons in a large salad bowl, toss with the bacon vinaigrette and bacon strips, and season with salt and pepper.

CHEF'S NOTE: Freshly picked dandelion greens are best for this salad, but if you pick your own, be sure to choose only the light green leaves. Most high-quality food markets carry dandelion greens, so you need not take the trouble to traipse about the yard.

Bibb Lettuce with Raspberry Vinaigrette

KOPFSALAT MIT HIMBEER VINAIGRETTE

THIS SALAD CELEBRATES TENDER GREEN **KOPFSALAT** (BIBB LETTUCE) AND RASPBERRY VINEGAR, A TRADITIONAL CONDIMENT PREPARED WITH BLACK FOREST RASPBERRIES. WE OFTEN SERVED RASPBERRY VINAIGRETTE ON SALADS AT THE SOMMERBERG HOTEL IN BAD WILDBAD, BUT MUSTARD VINAIGRETTES PREPARED WITH DIJON MUSTARD WERE POPULAR IN MANY HOTELS, AS WELL. EITHER WOULD BE DELICIOUS HERE, OR YOU COULD VARY THE DISH FURTHER AND USE ANOTHER FRUIT-BASED VINAIGRETTE, SUCH AS BLUEBERRY. YOU CAN, OF COURSE, MAKE THIS SALAD WITH OTHER LETTUCE VARIETIES, TOO, ALTHOUGH I MUST ADMIT THAT I AM PARTIAL TO THE TENDERNESS AND DELICATE FLAVOR OF BIBB LETTUCE.

Serves 6

½ cup raspberry vinegar

2 teaspoons balsamic vinegar

1 teaspoon sugar

1 teaspoon Dijon mustard

1½ cups olive oil

Salt

Freshly ground white pepper

3 heads Bibb lettuce, cored and leaves separated

1. Whisk together the raspberry vinegar, balsamic vinegar, sugar, and mustard in a medium bowl. Slowly drizzle in the oil, whisking constantly, and season with salt and pepper. Cover and chill in the refrigerator for at least 10 minutes.

2. To serve, roughly tear the lettuce leaves and place them in a large serving bowl. Whisk the chilled dressing again and pour over the lettuce, tossing gently to coat.

Gratin of Scallops

COQUILLES ST. JACQUES/JAKOBS MUSCHELN

1. Arrange the scallop shells in a large baking dish or on a large baking sheet and preheat the broiler.

2. Melt 3 tablespoons of the butter in a large sauté pan over medium-high heat, add the shallots, and sauté until softened and translucent, about 1 minute. Add the scallops to the pan, pour in the wine, and season with salt and pepper. Reduce the heat to low and simmer gently until the scallops are opaque but still slightly translucent and very tender, about 2 to 3 minutes. (Overcooking will cause the scallops to be rubbery and tasteless.) Remove the pan from the heat momentarily and take the scallops out of the pan, setting each one in a shell. Reserve the cooking liquid.

3. Place the remaining 1½ teaspoons of butter in a small bowl and knead in the flour to form a beurre manié. Return the scallop cooking liquid to medium heat, add the cream, and simmer until reduced by one-quarter. Stir in the beurre manié a little at a time until incorporated. Add the curry powder and anisette and simmer until the sauce is slightly thickened.

4. Drizzle a spoonful of sauce over each scallop, top with a generous dollop of hollandaise sauce, and sprinkle with Parmesan cheese. Set the scallops under the broiler, watching carefully, and broil until golden brown.

5. Serve each shell on a plate and garnish with mesclun and a lemon wedge.

THIS CLASSIC DISH IS A FAVORITE IN ELEGANT BLACK FOREST HOTEL RESTAURANTS. IT WAS PARTICULARLY SPECIAL IN MY DAY WHEN RESTAURANTS PURCHASED COSTLY SCALLOPS FROM FRANCE. THIS RECIPE IS BASED ON THE TRADITIONAL FRENCH PREPARATION, TO WHICH I HAVE ADDED A BIT OF CURRY POWDER, HOLLANDAISE SAUCE, AND ANISETTE, A MUCH-LOVED LIQUEUR IN THE BLACK FOREST.

Serves 4

24 large scallops in the shell, cleaned,
    removed from the shells, and shells reserved
3 tablespoons plus 1½ teaspoons unsalted butter
2 large shallots, peeled and finely chopped
1½ cups dry white wine, such as Sauvignon Blanc
Salt
Freshly ground white pepper
1½ teaspoons all-purpose flour
1 cup heavy cream
¼ teaspoon curry powder
1 teaspoon anisette (sweet licorice-flavored liqueur)
1½ cups Hollandaise Sauce (page 311)
2 cups grated Parmesan cheese
Mesclun (mixed young salad greens), for garnish
1 lemon, cut into 4 wedges, for garnish

Poached Salmon
with Tomatoes &
Dill Cream Sauce

POCHIERTER LACHS MIT TOMATEN & DILL SOßE

1. Place the salmon in a shallow dish, pour the lemon juice and Worcestershire overtop, and season with salt and white pepper, turning the fish to coat.

2. Melt 2 tablespoons of the butter in a large sauté pan over medium heat, add the shallots, and sauté until softened and translucent, about 1 minute. Toss in the mushrooms and sauté until slightly softened, about 2 minutes. Add the wine and arrange the salmon in the pan. Cover and simmer until the fillets are opaque and cooked to medium-rare (still slightly pink in the center), about 7 minutes. Remove from the heat, lift the salmon out of the pan onto a serving platter, and cover to keep warm while finishing the dish.

3. Add the dill and cream to the poaching liquid and simmer over medium-high heat until reduced by one-quarter.

4. Place 1½ tablespoons of the remaining butter in a small bowl and knead in the flour, a bit at a time, to form a beurre manié. Stir the beurre manié a little at a time into the reduced sauce until incorporated and the sauce thickens.

5. Melt the last tablespoon of butter in a medium pan over medium-high heat. Toss in the tomatoes, season with salt and white pepper, and sauté for about 2 minutes.

6. Arrange the tomatoes on top of the salmon and spoon the sauce overtop. Place a dollop of hollandaise sauce on each fillet and garnish with dill.

206

Serves 4

4 salmon fillets (8 to 10 ounces each),
   skinned and pin bones removed

Juice of 1 lemon

⅛ teaspoon Worcestershire sauce

Salt

Freshly ground white pepper

4½ tablespoons unsalted butter

3 large shallots, peeled and chopped (about ½ cup)

About 5 white button mushrooms, sliced (about ½ cup)

2 cups white wine

2 tablespoons chopped fresh dill, or 1 teaspoon dried

1 cup heavy cream

1½ tablespoons all-purpose flour

8 Roma tomatoes, blanched, skinned, seeded,
   and quartered (*see Chef's Note*)

¼ cup Hollandaise Sauce (page 311), for serving

Fresh dill sprigs, for garnish

CHEF'S NOTE: To prepare the tomatoes, bring a large saucepan of water to a boil and prepare a large bowl of ice water. Core each tomato at the stem end using a sharp-tipped paring knife and slice a shallow cross on each one at the smooth end. Set the tomatoes in the boiling water for about 1 minute, lift them out using a slotted spoon or wire mesh strainer, and place them immediately in the ice water. Peel the tomatoes (the skin will come off easily) and slice them in half lengthwise. Remove the seeds and slice each half again lengthwise into quarters.

THIS DISH IS SO SIMPLE TO PREPARE YET IT MAKES FOR AN ELEGANT FISH COURSE. IN MY DAY, SALMON WAS EXPENSIVE, AS RESTAURANTS SHIPPED IT IN FROM NORWAY. IT WAS ALWAYS POPULAR AMONG RESTAURANT GUESTS, HOWEVER, ESPECIALLY WHEN WE PREPARED IT WITH FRESH HERBS, VEGETABLES, AND CREAM SAUCE AS IT IS HERE.

ALTHOUGH THIS DISH IS A BIT LABOR INTENSIVE, IT IS ACTUALLY SIMPLE TO PREPARE. THE SHRIMP ARE WRAPPED WITH THIN STRIPS OF CHICKEN AND COOKED WITH MUSHROOMS, WINE, HERBS, CREAM, SAFFRON, AND ANISETTE TO CREATE A CREAMY, FLAVORFUL, AND ELEGANT ENTRÉE THAT IS PERFECT FOR ANY SPECIAL OCCASION.

Chicken-Wrapped Shrimp with Creamy Saffron-Herb Sauce

GARNELEN ROULADEN MIT
SAFRAN-KRÄUTER RAHMSOßE

Serves 4

2 whole chicken breasts, skinned, boned,
   and cut into 4 halves

Salt

Freshly ground white pepper

1 tablespoon chopped fresh oregano, or 1 teaspoon dried

1 tablespoon chopped fresh basil, or 1 teaspoon dried

1 tablespoon stemmed and chopped fresh thyme,
   or 1 teaspoon dried

20 jumbo shrimp, peeled, de-veined, and tails removed

4½ tablespoons unsalted butter

2 tablespoons anisette (anise-flavored liquor)

4 large shallots, peeled and finely chopped (about 1 cup)

About 6 white button mushrooms, quartered (about 1 cup)

2 cups dry white wine, such as Sauvignon Blanc

1½ tablespoons all-purpose flour

1 cup heavy cream

¼ teaspoon saffron threads

2 tablespoons mixed chopped fresh herbs,
   such as parsley, chives, basil, and thyme

1. Slice each chicken breast half lengthwise into 5 strips (for a total of 20 strips) (image a). Place each strip between pieces of parchment or wax paper and pound with a mallet or the bottom of a heavy pan until the pieces are flat and thin, at least ⅛ inch thick (image b). Season with salt, white pepper, oregano, basil, and thyme (image c).

2. Wrap each piece of chicken around a shrimp, skewer with a toothpick to form secure bundles, and season with additional salt and white pepper (images d–e).

3. Melt 3 tablespoons of the butter in a large sauté pan over medium-high heat, add the chicken and shrimp bundles, and sauté until golden brown. Remove the bundles from the pan, add the anisette to deglaze, stirring with a wooden spoon to loosen any browned bits on the bottom of the pan, and simmer for about 1 minute.

4. Add the shallots and sauté until softened and translucent, about 1 minute. Add the mushrooms, sauté until slightly softened, about another 2 minutes, and pour in the wine to deglaze the pan once more.

5. Return the bundles to the pan, reduce the heat to medium, and simmer until the chicken is fully cooked but still tender, about 5 to 7 minutes. Lift the bundles out of the sauce and arrange on a serving platter. Remove the toothpicks and cover with foil to keep warm while finishing the dish.

6. Place the remaining 1½ tablespoons of butter in a small bowl and knead in the flour to form a beurre manié. Stir the beurre manié into the sauce a little at a time until incorporated and add the cream and saffron, simmering until slightly thickened.

7. To serve, toss the herbs into the sauce and pour over the chicken and shrimp.

209

CHICKEN-WRAPPED SHRIMP WITH CREAMY SAFFRON-HERB SAUCE

Slice chicken breast and pound thin. Season, then wrap around shrimp and secure with a toothpick.

a

b

c

d

e

Sautéed Trout Meunière

FORELLE MÜLLERIN ART

1. Preheat the oven to 450°F.

2. Season each trout inside and out with salt and pepper and arrange in a shallow dish. Drizzle with Worcestershire sauce and lemon juice set aside in the refrigerator to marinate for about 5 to 10 minutes.

3. Melt the butter in a large sauté pan over medium heat. Pat the trout dry and open flat to expose both fillets. Dredge in flour and set in the pan, skin side down, sautéing on each side for about 2 to 3 minutes until golden brown.

4. Place the pan in the oven and bake the trout until fully cooked, about 5 to 8 minutes. Remove the trout to a serving platter while finishing the dish.

5. Place the sauté pan over medium heat and cook the butter until dark brown, about 1 minute.

6. To serve, arrange lemon slices over the trout, drizzle with browned butter, and garnish with parsley.

THIS QUINTESSENTIALLY FRENCH DISH HAS ALSO BECOME A STANDARD ON MANY HOTEL MENUS IN THE BLACK FOREST. MEUNIÈRE, FRENCH FOR "MILLER'S WIFE," IS YET ANOTHER OF THOSE SNAZZY FRENCH CULINARY TERMS THAT REFERS TO A PARTICULAR PREPARATION. IN THIS CASE, IT DENOTES FOOD (USUALLY FISH) THAT IS SEASONED, DUSTED WITH FLOUR, AND SERVED WITH A SIMPLE BROWNED BUTTER SAUCE, LEMON, AND PARSLEY.

TROUT IS SO POPULAR THAT IT IS SERVED IN A VARIETY OF WAYS IN GASTHAUS AND HOTEL RESTAURANTS ALIKE. TRUITE AU BLEU (BLUE TROUT) IS BY FAR THE MOST FAMOUS TROUT DISH IN THE BLACK FOREST. WHEN COOKED, THE TROUT TAKES ON A BRILLIANT BLUE HUE FOR WHICH IT IS NAMED. TRUITE AU BLEU IS PREPARED IN A CLASSIC FRENCH MANNER, WHICH INSISTS ON A FRESHLY CAUGHT, CAREFULLY HANDLED FISH— TOUCHING IT WITH BARE SKIN WILL PREVENT IT FROM TURNING BRIGHT BLUE. THE TROUT IS THEN SIMPLY POACHED WITH SALT AND VINEGAR AND SERVED IN AN ELEGANT SILVER VESSEL WITH BOILED POTATOES, PARSLEY, AND USUALLY HOLLANDAISE SAUCE AND MELTED BUTTER.

UNLIKE BLUE TROUT, THIS RECIPE REQUIRES LITTLE FUSS. TROUT ARE WIDELY AVAILABLE IN FISH MARKETS, AND IF SOME OF YOUR GUESTS ARE A SQUEAMISH ABOUT FISH HEADS, YOU CAN EVEN PURCHASE THEM WITH THE HEADS REMOVED.

THIS TROUT IS DELIGHTFULLY SIMPLE, BUT YOU CAN PERK IT UP SLIGHTLY TO CREATE YET ANOTHER CLASSIC DISH KNOWN AS GRENOBLOISE. SIMPLY TOSS SOME CAPERS AND FINELY CHOPPED LEMON BITS INTO THE BROWNED BUTTER AT THE END.

Serves 4

4 whole trout (about 1 pound each), boned and cleaned

Salt

Freshly ground white pepper

1 teaspoon Worcestershire sauce

Juice of 1 lemon

4 tablespoons unsalted butter

1 cup all-purpose flour, for dredging

1 lemon, peeled, sliced into rounds, and seeded, for garnish

Chopped fresh parsley, for garnish

Paupiettes
of Brook Trout

FORELLEN ROULADEN

THIS DISH PAYS TRIBUTE TO THE MANY CLASSIC FRENCH RECIPES AND NUMEROUS TROUT DISHES PREPARED IN THE BLACK FOREST. PAUPIETTE IS A FRENCH TERM THAT REFERS MOST OFTEN TO A THIN SLICE OF MEAT ROLLED AROUND A FILLING AND THEN FRIED, BAKED, OR BRAISED IN WINE OR STOCK. IT IS ALSO OCCASIONALLY WRAPPED ON THE OUTSIDE WITH BACON FOR ADDITIONAL FLAVOR.

IN MY BLACK FOREST VERSION, TROUT REPLACES MEAT AND AN ELE-GANT GREEN LEEK IS TIED AROUND THE PAUPIETTE IN PLACE OF THE ROBUST BACON. TROUT IS MUCH LOVED THROUGHOUT THE REGION, AND CHEFS AND DINERS ALIKE CONSIDER IT A SERIOUS BUSINESS. MANY RESTAURANTS MAINTAIN THEIR OWN TROUT PONDS AND TANKS AND SOME EVEN PERMIT DINERS TO PICK OUT THEIR OWN FISH. AT THE HOTEL POST IN NAGOLD, OUR TROUT SHARED A TANK IN THE COURTYARD WITH CARP.

THESE PAUPIETTES ARE SPECIAL AND SERVED ALMOST EXCLUSIVELY AT LARGE ELEGANT DINNERS. WE OFTEN FEATURED THEM AS THE FISH COURSE ON SYLVESTER NIGHT (NEW YEAR'S EVE) MENUS, FOR EXAMPLE. THEY TAKE A BIT OF TIME TO PREPARE, BUT YOUR GUESTS ARE SURE TO BE PLEASED WITH THIS BEAUTIFUL, FLAVORFUL DISH.

Serves 4

STUFFING:

1 teaspoon unsalted butter

2 tablespoons finely chopped onion

1 tablespoon finely chopped green bell pepper

1 tablespoon finely chopped red bell pepper

8 ounces jumbo lump crabmeat,
    bits of shell and cartilage removed

2 eggs

1/2 cup fine dry bread crumbs (see Chef's Note)

Juice of 1/2 small lemon

1/8 teaspoon dried thyme

1/8 teaspoon dried oregano

1/8 teaspoon dried basil

1 teaspoon salt

1/8 teaspoon freshly ground white pepper

PAUPIETTE ASSEMBLY:

1 large leek, trimmed and cut in half,
    separating the green and white parts

4 fresh brook trout fillets (6 to 8 ounces each),
    skinned and pin bones removed

Salt

Freshly ground white pepper

4 tablespoons unsalted butter

4 large shallots, peeled and finely chopped (about 1 cup)

1 cup thinly sliced white button mushrooms

2 cups dry white wine, such as Sauvignon Blanc

3 tablespoons all-purpose flour

1 1/2 cups heavy cream

1 tablespoon chopped fresh parsley

4 teaspoons salmon or sturgeon roe, for garnish

CHEF'S NOTE: Dry bread crumbs are certainly available in every supermarket, but it is easy to make them at home and they are much more flavorful than the canned variety. Simply grate day-old French bread and store the crumbs in airtight containers. Although Asian panko crumbs are all the rage at the moment, they are not suited to this sort of classic recipe. For best results, stick to the traditional bread crumbs whether they are store bought or homemade.

a

b

c

PAUPIETTES OF BROOK TROUT

Score side of fillet and season. Place stuffing in center of fillet and roll ends securely. Peel back layers of leek, wrap around fillet, and secure with strip of green leek. Tie in a knot.

d

e

f

1. For the stuffing, melt the butter in a small sauté pan over medium heat, add the onions, and sauté until translucent. Stir in the bell peppers and sauté until softened and any liquid they release has evaporated, about 2 minutes. Remove from the heat and set in the refrigerator to cool completely.

2. Combine the cooled vegetables, crabmeat, eggs, bread crumbs, lemon juice, herbs, salt, and pepper, mixing gently until incorporated. Cover and refrigerate for at least 30 minutes.

3. To assemble paupiettes, bring a medium saucepan of lightly salted water to a simmer over medium heat. Add the white and green parts of the leek and poach until tender and the white part is softened. Remove the leek from the poaching liquid, slice the green part lengthwise into thin strips, and set aside until cool enough to handle.

4. Score the skin side of each trout fillet (the side formerly covered with skin) several times using a paring knife and season with salt and white pepper (images a–b). Place the stuffing in the center of each fillet and roll the ends securely around it (image c). Peel back the layers of the cooled leek (the white part), wrap one or two layers around each fillet, and secure with a strip of green leek, tying it in a knot (images d–e). Set the assembled paupiettes aside momentarily (image f).

5. Melt 1 tablespoon of the butter in a large sauté pan over medium heat, add the shallots, and sauté until softened and translucent, about 1 minute. Add the mushrooms and sauté until softened and any liquid they release has evaporated, about 2 minutes.

6. Add the wine to deglaze, stirring with a wooden spoon to loosen any browned bits on the bottom of the pan. Place the paupiettes in the pan, cover, and cook over high heat for about 2 to 3 minutes. Reduce the heat to medium and simmer until the trout is fully cooked but still tender, about 7 to 10 minutes. Do not overcook. (The trout is fully cooked when it appears opaque.)

7. Remove the paupiettes from the pan, cover loosely with foil, and set aside to keep warm while finishing the dish.

8. Place the flour and remaining 3 tablespoons of butter in a small bowl and knead together to form a beurre manié. Add the cream to the pan, stir in the beurre manié a little at a time until incorporated and the sauce thickens, and add the parsley.

9. Set each paupiette on a plate, spoon some of the sauce overtop, and garnish with salmon roe.

Steamed Mussels with Creamy Mustard Broth

GEDÄMPFTE MUSCHELN MIT SENF RAHMSOßE

STEAMED MUSSELS ARE SERVED WITH A VARIETY OF SAUCES THROUGHOUT ALSACE AND FRANCE. THEY ARE ALSO POPULAR IN THE BLACK FOREST, WHERE THE MUSSELS ARE OFTEN FLAVORED WITH GARLIC, SHALLOTS, MUSTARD, AND CREAM AS THEY ARE IN THIS RECIPE. LAGER, OF COURSE, IS ALSO A VITAL COMPONENT OF THIS DISH AND CONTRIBUTES A UNIQUE CHARACTER TO THE SAUCE. ALTHOUGH WE TRADITIONALLY USE LAGER IN THE BLACK FOREST, IF YOU HAVE TROUBLE FINDING IT, ANY LIGHT-STYLE GOLDEN BEER WILL DO.

Serves 4

2 tablespoons unsalted butter

4 large shallots, peeled and finely chopped (about 1 cup)

About 6 cloves garlic, peeled and finely chopped (about ½ cup)

1 (12-ounce) bottle Pilsner

4 tablespoons Dijon mustard

¼ cup stemmed and chopped fresh thyme

1 cup heavy cream

4 pounds mussels, scrubbed and de-bearded

Salt

Freshly ground black pepper

Chopped fresh parsley, for garnish

Toasted French bread, for serving

---

1. Melt the butter in a large casserole dish or heavy-bottomed saucepan over medium-high heat, add the shallots and garlic, and sauté until softened and translucent, about 1 minute.

2. Pour in the beer, whisk in the mustard and thyme, and bring to a boil. Stir in the cream and drop in the mussels. Cover, raise the heat to high, and cook, stirring occasionally, just until the mussels have opened, about 5 to 10 minutes. Remove and discard any mussels that remain closed and season the broth with salt and pepper if necessary. (The mussels will naturally make the dish slightly salty.)

3. To serve, arrange the mussels on a large serving platter or in individual bowls and pour the creamy broth overtop. Garnish with parsley and serve with toasted bread.

CHEF'S NOTE: Before cooking, discard any open mussels. Mussels that refuse to open even after they are cooked are not suitable for eating. Simply discard them.

Brook Trout Amandine

FORELLE IN MANDELN GEBRATEN

ERE IS YET ANOTHER TROUT RECIPE IN THE CLASSIC FRENCH STYLE. IT IS ELEGANT IN ITS SIMPLICITY, FEATURING THE FRESH AND RICH FLAVORS OF TROUT, BUTTER, ALMONDS, AND LEMON. JUST BE CAREFUL WHEN SAUTÉING THE FISH, AS THE ALMONDS CAN BURN QUITE QUICKLY.

1. Score the skin side of each trout fillet (the side formerly covered with skin) several times using a paring knife, season both sides with salt and pepper, and arrange in a shallow dish. Drizzle with Worcestershire sauce and lemon juice and set aside to marinate for about 3 minutes.

2. Place the flour, eggs, and almonds in separate shallow dishes. Pat the trout fillets dry and begin coating them first with flour, then with egg, and finally with almonds.

3. Melt the butter in a large sauté pan over medium heat, place the fillets in the pan, and sauté on each side for about 3 minutes or until golden, watching carefully to prevent the almonds from burning.

4. To serve, arrange the fillets on a serving platter or individual plates and place the lemon segments on top. Drizzle with the butter from the pan and garnish with parsley.

Serves 4

8 trout fillets (6 to 8 ounces each),
   skinned and pin bones removed

Salt

Freshly ground white pepper

1 teaspoon Worcestershire sauce

Juice of 1 lemon

1 cup all-purpose flour, for dredging

2 eggs, beaten

2 cups sliced almonds

4 tablespoons unsalted butter

1 lemon, peeled, sectioned, and seeded for garnish

Chopped fresh parsley, for garnish

Frog's Legs Provençal

FROSCHSCHENKEL PROVENÇAL

1. To make the sauce, heat the oil over medium heat in a large sauté pan, add the garlic, and sauté until golden, about 1 minute. Add the onion and sauté until softened and translucent, about one minute more. Toss in the tomatoes and continue to cook until softened and any liquid they release has evaporated. Pour in the wine and stir in the basil and thyme sprig, simmering until the pan is almost dry. Remove the thyme, season with salt and pepper, and set aside to keep warm while finishing the dish.

2. To make the frog's legs, rinse the legs in cold water and pat dry. Season with salt and pepper, arrange in a shallow dish, and drizzle with Worcestershire sauce and lemon juice. Set aside to marinate for about 3 minutes.

3. Melt the butter in a large sauté pan over medium heat. Pat the frog's legs dry and dredge the frog's legs in flour, shaking to remove any excess. Set in the pan and sauté on each side for about 2 minutes until fully cooked and golden brown.

4. To serve, spoon the Provençal sauce into the center of a serving platter, arrange the frog's legs on top, and garnish with parsley.

FROG'S LEGS ARE AS POPULAR IN THE BLACK FOREST AS THEY ARE IN FRANCE AND IT IS COMMON TO SEE THEM ON HOTEL RESTAURANT MENUS. THE SAUCE IN THIS DISH OBVIOUSLY GIVES A NOD TO PROVENCE WITH FRAGRANT AND FRESH INGREDIENTS INCLUDING OLIVE OIL, GARLIC, TOMATOES, AND FRESH HERBS. IT PAIRS NICELY WITH THE DELICATE FROG'S LEGS—SO WELL, IN FACT, THAT WE LIKE TO SERVE IT WITH FRIED FROG'S LEGS, TOO.

IN MY TIME, WE ACTUALLY HAD FROG FARMS IN THE BLACK FOREST, WHERE WE OBTAINED THE LEGS FRESH, BUT THEY ARE ALSO AVAILABLE FROZEN. SIMPLY THAW THEM IN THE REFRIGERATOR BEFORE PROCEEDING WITH THE RECIPE.

Serves 4

PROVENÇAL SAUCE:

¼ cup extra virgin olive oil

1 tablespoon finely chopped garlic

1 large yellow onion, peeled and finely chopped

5 large Roma tomatoes, peeled, seeded, and chopped

1 cup dry white wine, such as Sauvignon Blanc

3 large basil leaves, sliced into thin strips,
    or ¼ teaspoon dried

1 sprig fresh thyme

Salt

Freshly ground white pepper

FROG'S LEGS:

32 pair frog's legs

Salt

Freshly ground white pepper

1 teaspoon Worcestershire sauce

Juice of 1 lemon

2 tablespoons unsalted butter

1 cup all-purpose flour, for dredging

Fresh parsley sprigs, for garnish

Pork Medallions with Lager & Chanterelles

SCHWEINEMEDALLIONS MIT BIER & PFIFFERLINGEN

1. At least 4 hours or the day before serving the dish, place the pork in a large shallow dish, cover with 3 cups of the lager, and add the salt and pepper. Add the thyme, cover with plastic wrap, and set in the refrigerator to marinate for at least 4 hours or overnight.

2. The next day or when you are ready to proceed with the dish, remove the pork from the marinade, discard the marinade, and pat the pork dry with paper towels.

3. Heat the olive oil and 2 tablespoons of the butter in a large sauté pan over medium heat. Season the pork with salt and pepper and dredge in the flour, patting to remove any excess. Place in the pan and sauté on each side for about 2½ minutes until golden brown. Remove the pork to a serving platter and cover loosely with foil to keep warm while finishing the dish.

4. Melt the remaining 1 tablespoon of butter in the sauté pan over medium heat, toss in the chanterelles, chives, basil, and thyme, and sauté until lightly browned and softened, about 5 to 6 minutes. Add the shallots, onion, garlic, and bacon, and sauté until lightly browned, about 1½ minutes more. Stir in the demi-glace and cook for another 2 minutes.

5. To serve, arrange the pork medallions on a serving platter and spoon the mushrooms and sauce overtop. Garnish with parsley.

HERE IS ANOTHER DISH IN WHICH LAGER—A LIGHT, REFRESHING, GOLDEN BEER—PLAYS A FLAVORFUL ROLE. IN HOME, GASTHAUS, AND HOTEL KITCHENS, WE OFTEN EMPLOY MARINADES TO TENDERIZE POULTRY, MEAT, AND GAME AND INFUSE THEM WITH MORE FLAVOR. LAGER AND OTHER KINDS OF BEER ARE SO PLENTIFUL THAT WE OFTEN ADD THEM TO MARINADES. LIKE WINE, THEY ARE NATURAL TENDERIZERS.

THIS DISH IS EASY TO PREPARE AND COMES TOGETHER QUICKLY ONCE THE MEAT HAS MARINATED FOR SEVERAL HOURS. IN THE BLACK FOREST, WE USUALLY USE THE WHOLE PORK TENDERLOIN, BUT I HAVE MADE THE COOKING PROCESS SIMPLER BY SUGGESTING YOU USE PORK MEDALLIONS INSTEAD. I ALSO CALL FOR USING CHANTERELLE MUSHROOMS HERE, BUT ANY VARIETY WILL DO. IF YOU CHOOSE PARTICULARLY LARGE CHANTERELLES, CHOP THEM ROUGHLY SO THAT THEY COOK MORE QUICKLY.

Serves 6

4 pounds pork tenderloin, fat trimmed, sliver skin removed, and sliced into ¼-inch-thick medallions

4 cups lager

1 teaspoon salt

1 teaspoon freshly ground black pepper

1 sprig fresh thyme

2 tablespoons olive oil

3 tablespoons unsalted butter

1 cup all-purpose flour, for dredging

1 pound chanterelle mushrooms

1 tablespoon chopped fresh chives

1 tablespoon chopped fresh basil

1 tablespoon chopped fresh thyme

4 medium shallots, peeled and finely chopped

½ medium onion, peeled and finely chopped

2 cloves garlic, peeled and finely chopped

3 slices bacon, very finely chopped

2 cups Demi-Glace (page 312) or prepared brown sauce

3 tablespoons chopped fresh parsley

Pork Roast à la Dijonnaise

GEBRATENER SCHWEINERÜCKEN MIT SENFSOßE

T HIS ROAST WAS, OF COURSE, INSPIRED BY THE FRENCH TOWN OF DIJON, WHERE MUSTARD IS CELEBRATED AND USED FREQUENTLY IN COOKING AND FOR SAUCES. THE RED WINE MARINADE INFUSES THE PORK WITH INTENSE FLAVOR, AND THE MUSTARD, MUSHROOMS, DEMI-GLACE, AND CREAM LEND A FLAVORFUL ELEGANCE TO THE FINAL DISH.

SINCE THIS RECIPE SERVES QUITE A FEW PEOPLE, I RECOMMEND MAKING IT FOR A HOLIDAY OR SPECIAL OCCASION, AS THE LEFTOVERS WILL NOT FREEZE WELL.

Serves 8 to 10

6 to 8 pounds boneless pork loin roast

4 cups full-bodied red wine, such as Burgundy

7 medium onions, peeled and thinly sliced

8 cloves garlic, peeled and chopped

1 dried bay leaf

1 sprig fresh thyme

3 tablespoons Dijon mustard

Salt

Freshly ground black pepper

About 1½ pounds white button mushrooms, sliced (about 7½ cups)

2 cups Demi-Glace (page 312) or prepared brown sauce

1 cup heavy cream

Chopped scallions (green parts only), for garnish

1. The day before serving the dish, set the roast in a large casserole dish, pour in 2 cups of the wine, and arrange the onions, garlic, bay leaf, and thyme around the roast. Cover with plastic wrap and set in the refrigerator to marinate for at least 4 hours or overnight, turning the roast several times to marinate evenly.

2. The next day or when you are ready to proceed with the dish, preheat the oven to 375°F.

3. Remove the roast from the marinade, reserving the marinade, and set the roast in a medium roasting pan. Coat the roast with mustard, season with salt and pepper, and roast until a meat thermometer registers 155°F. when inserted into the pork, about 2 hours.

4. Meanwhile, pour the reserved marinade into a small saucepan and bring to a boil over high heat, boiling until reduced to about ¼ cup, about 10 minutes. Remove from the heat, discard the bay leaf and thyme, and set aside.

5. Transfer the roast to a cutting board, cover loosely with foil, and set aside to rest for about 15 minutes before carving. (The temperature will rise about 5 degrees during this time.)

6. Discard any excess fat in the roasting pan and heat over medium heat. Add the mushrooms and sauté until softened, about 2½ minutes. Add the remaining 2 cups of wine to deglaze, stirring with a wooden spoon to loosen any browned bits on the bottom of the pan. Stir in the reduced marinade and simmer until reduced by half, about 10 minutes.

7. Stir in the demi-glace and cream and reduce the heat to medium low. Simmer the sauce gently, about 5 minutes, and season with salt and pepper.

8. To serve, slice the roast into ¼-inch-thick pieces and arrange on a serving platter. Drizzle a little sauce overtop, garnish with scallions, and serve the sauce in a gravy boat on the side.

Beef Stroganov

FILETGULASCH STROGANOV

Serves 6 to 8

THIS WELL-KNOWN DISH, NAMED AFTER THE NINETEENTH-CENTURY RUSSIAN DIPLOMAT COUNT PAUL STROGANOV, WAS ALWAYS A FAVORITE IN BLACK FOREST HOTEL RESTAURANTS. IT COMES TOGETHER SO QUICKLY, IN FACT, THAT WE ALWAYS PREPARED IT TO ORDER.

THIS RECIPE REMAINS ESSENTIALLY TRUE TO THE CLASSIC VERSION. THE BLACK FOREST CHARACTER UNDENIABLY PEEKS THROUGH, HOWEVER, WITH THE DELIGHTFULLY TANGY ADDITION OF PICKLES.

BEEF STROGANOV IS DELICIOUS ON ITS OWN, BUT IT IS EVEN MORE SATISFYING SERVED WITH POTATOES, NOODLES, OR SPÄTZLE. TO PRESENT IT IN A PARTICULARLY ELEGANT MANNER, AS WE DID AT THE HOTELS, SPOON THE BEEF INTO GOLDEN INDIVIDUAL **VOLS-AU-VENT** (PUFF PASTRY SHELLS, PAGE 80).

---

1. Melt the butter in a large sauté pan over medium-high heat, add the shallots, and sauté until golden brown, about 2 minutes. Add the mushrooms and sauté until slightly softened, about 2 minutes. Season the tenderloin strips with salt and pepper, raise the heat to high, and add to the pan, sautéing until they are lightly browned.

2. Stir in the demi-glace and mustard, reduce the heat to medium, and simmer until the tenderloin strips are cooked to your desired doneness and the sauce is slightly reduced, about 2 to 3 minutes.

3. To serve, incorporate the pickles and Cognac, pour the stroganov onto a serving platter, and garnish with dollops of sour cream, chives, and small spoonfuls of caviar.

Serves 6 to 8

2 tablespoons unsalted butter

About 4 shallots, peeled and finely chopped (about 1/2 cup)

About 8 white button mushrooms, cut into strips about 2 inches long and 1/8 inch thick (about 1 cup)

3 pounds beef tenderloin tips, cut into strips 2 inches long and 1 inch thick

Salt

Freshly ground black pepper

2 cups Demi-Glace (page 312) or prepared brown sauce

3 tablespoons Dijon mustard

6 large kosher pickles, peeled and cut into strips about 2 inches long and 1/8 inch thick

1 1/2 tablespoons Cognac or other brandy

Sour cream, for garnish

Chopped fresh chives, for garnish

Caviar, for garnish (optional)

When the weather turned cold, hotel patrons ordered this rich warming dish frequently for lunch. True to French culinary tradition, the beef is marinated for several hours to flavor and tenderize it, and then it is simmered slowly with aromatics, vegetables, and bacon to produce a rich saucy stew.

Although beef burgundy is delicious enough to enjoy on its own, it pairs particularly well with egg noodles or spätzle, as we traditionally served it in the Black Forest.

Since this recipe serves quite a few people, I recommend making it for a Sunday brunch or special occasion, as the leftovers will not freeze well.

Beef Burgundy

BURGUNDER RINDER RAGOÛT

Serves 8 to 10

5 pounds boneless beef chuck, cut into 2-inch cubes

6 cups full-bodied red wine, such as Burgundy

5 medium onions, 1 peeled and quartered, 4 peeled and chopped

3 tablespoons olive oil

2 dried bay leaves

1 teaspoon coarsely ground black pepper

1 sprig fresh thyme

9 slices lean bacon, finely chopped

3 cloves garlic, peeled and chopped

2 tablespoons all-purpose flour

3 large carrots, peeled and cut into about ½-inch pieces

20 pearl onions, peeled, or 2 cups frozen and thawed

1 teaspoon ground allspice

2 tablespoons unsalted butter

8 ounces white button mushrooms, sliced (about 2½ cups)

Salt

Freshly ground black pepper

1 cup Herbed Croutons (page 31), for garnish

Chopped fresh parsley, for garnish

1. The day before serving the dish, toss together the beef, wine, the quartered onion, 1 tablespoon of the olive oil, bay leaves, pepper, and thyme in a large bowl, cover with plastic wrap, and set in the refrigerator to marinate overnight.

2. The next day or when you are ready to proceed with the dish, remove the beef from the marinade and pat dry with paper towels. Strain the marinade through a fine mesh strainer or cheesecloth into a large saucepan and reserve.

3. Heat the remaining 2 tablespoons of oil over high heat in a large Dutch oven or heavy-bottomed saucepan, add the bacon, and sauté until crisp, about 2 minutes. Remove the bacon from the pan and set aside.

4. Add the beef to the hot pan and cook until browned, about 10 minutes. Stir in the chopped onions and garlic and sauté until golden, about 3 minutes. Sprinkle in the flour, stirring to incorporate, remove from the heat, and set aside momentarily.

5. Bring the reserved saucepan of marinade to a boil over high heat. Pour 3 cups of the marinade over the flour-coated beef and bring to a boil over high heat. Reduce the heat to medium and simmer, stirring frequently, until the sauce thickens, about 30 minutes.

6. Stir the carrots, pearl onions, allspice, reserved bacon, and remaining 3 cups of marinade into the simmering beef, raise the heat to high, and cook for 3 minutes. Reduce the heat to low, cover, and simmer until the beef and vegetables are tender, about 1 hour.

7. Melt the butter in a large sauté pan over medium heat, add the mushrooms, and sauté until browned and softened, about 5 minutes.

8. Stir the mushrooms into the beef burgundy, simmer for an additional 5 minutes, and season with salt and pepper.

9. To serve, pour the beef burgundy into a large serving bowl or platter and garnish with herbed croutons and parsley.

New York Strip Steak à la Café de Paris

RUMPSTEAK MIT CAFÉ DE PARIS BUTTER

Serves 6

REDUCTION:

1 tablespoon unsalted butter

About 4 large shallots,
  peeled and roughly chopped (about 1 cup)

1½ teaspoons anchovy paste, or 4 whole anchovy fillets

¼ teaspoon dried tarragon

¼ teaspoon dried sage

¼ teaspoon dried thyme

1 small bunch fresh parsley, stemmed and roughly chopped

½ cup dry white wine, such as Sauvignon Blanc

2 cups Au Jus (*see Sources, page 320*)

COMPOUND BUTTER:

1 pound unsalted butter, softened

3 tablespoons Dijon mustard

⅛ teaspoon powdered mustard

1 teaspoon Hungarian paprika

1½ teaspoons curry powder

Juice of 2 lemons

1 teaspoon Worcestershire sauce

½ teaspoon hot pepper sauce

½ teaspoon freshly ground white pepper

2 tablespoons Reduction

ASSEMBLY:

4 New York strip steaks or sirloin steaks (16 ounces each)

Salt

Freshly ground black pepper

1. To make the reduction, melt the butter in a large saucepan over medium heat, add the shallots, and sauté until softened and translucent, about 1 minute. Stir in the anchovy paste and herbs and cook for about 20 seconds. Add the wine to deglaze, stirring with a wooden spoon to loosen any browned bits on the bottom of the pan, and simmer until just about all of the liquid has evaporated. Pour in the Au Jus and simmer until most of the liquid has evaporated once again, leaving about ¼ cup of thick reduction. Set aside to cool completely.

2. Transfer the reduction to a small blender or food processor fitted with the blade attachment and purée until smooth. Scrape into a small bowl and set aside at room temperature.

3. To make the compound butter, place the butter in the bowl of an electric mixer fitted with the paddle attachment and beat on medium speed until smooth and light, about 2 minutes. Add the remaining ingredients and mix on medium speed until incorporated.

4. Scrape the butter onto a sheet of parchment or plastic wrap, shaping it roughly into a log about 1½ inches in diameter. Tightly roll into a log and set in the refrigerator to chill. (This butter also freezes well.)

5. To assemble the steaks, preheat the broiler and heat a large skillet or heavy-bottomed sauté pan over high heat. Season the steaks with salt and pepper, place in the pan, and brown on each side for about 5 minutes, or until cooked to medium-rare.

6. Transfer the steaks to a baking sheet and top each one with 1 tablespoon of the compound butter. Place under the broiler and cook, watching carefully, until the butter melts, browns, and glazes the steaks. Serve immediately.

WHEN I GRADUATED FROM THE HOTEL POST, THE HOTEL'S CHEF DE CUISINE, WHO WAS ALSO MY TEACHER, MARKED THE OCCASION BY GIVING ME THIS CLASSIC RECIPE. HE HAD ACQUIRED IT WHILE WORKING AT THE ILLUSTRIOUS CAFÉ DE PARIS ON BOULEVARD HAUSSMAN NEAR THE OPÉRA DE PARIS. EVEN AS A YOUNG CHEF, I APPRECIATED THE MAGNITUDE OF THIS OFFERING. THIS STEAK HAD BECOME THE CAFÉ'S SIGNATURE DISH, AND, IN KEEPING WITH THE COMPETITIVE CULINARY SPIRIT, THE RECIPE REMAINED CLOSELY GUARDED THROUGH THE YEARS. IN FACT, ALTHOUGH I GLADLY SHARE THIS RECIPE IN REMEMBRANCE OF MY HOTEL DAYS, I ADMIT I HAVE FAILED TO FULLY DISCLOSE ITS CONTENTS. IN HONOR OF MY CULINARY FRATERNITY, I HAVE LEFT OUT AN INGREDIENT HERE AND THERE TO PRESERVE THE SECRET OF THE DISH'S TRUE IDENTITY.

THE REDUCTION AND COMPOUND BUTTER REQUIRE A BIT OF ADVANCE PREPARATION, BUT ONCE THEY ARE COMPLETE THE STEAKS COME TOGETHER IN MINUTES. YOU WILL PROBABLY HAVE SOME REDUCTION AND BUTTER LEFT OVER, BUT THEY BOTH STORE WELL AND ARE FLAVORFUL ADDITIONS TO A VARIETY OF SAUTÉED AND ROASTED MEAT AND POULTRY DISHES.

Veal is a popular item in restaurants throughout the Black Forest. In fact, it is common for a menu to list three or four veal dishes at one time. This is a classic recipe that comes together quickly and relies on a limited number of flavorful ingredients. We prepared it often when I worked in Gstaad, Switzerland, at the Aga Khan's famous restaurant, The Chessery. There, we prepared this dish À LA MINUTE (to order) and actually did so tableside on a moveable table called a GUÉRIDON. One night at The Chessery, I was fortunate enough to cook these veal medallions for the famous actress Brigitte Bardot. But that's another story. I think you will find that veal medallions are as well suited to a quiet supper as they are to a more formal dinner party.

Veal Medallions in Mushroom Cream Sauce

KALBSMEDALLIONS IN CHAMPIGNON RAHMSOßE

Serves 4

1 veal tenderloin (about 2 to 3 pounds),
    sliced into 1/2-inch medallions

5 tablespoons unsalted butter

1 cup plus 3 tablespoons all-purpose flour

Salt

Freshly ground white pepper

3 shallots, peeled and finely chopped

12 white button mushrooms

Juice of 1/2 lemon (about 1 tablespoon)

3 tablespoons brandy

1 cup dry white wine, such as Sauvignon Blanc

1 cup heavy cream

1/2 cup Demi-Glace (page 312) or prepared brown sauce

2 tablespoons chopped fresh parsley

Chopped fresh parsley, for garnish

CHEF'S NOTE: Flambéing is a wonderful way to add flavor and intensity to a dish, but it must be done with care. First, pour the amount of liquor required into a separate measuring cup or container. Next, remove the pan from the heat and stir in the liquor. Finally, return the pan to the heat and carefully set flame to it, allowing the fire to naturally extinguish or covering the pan to do so.

1. Place each piece of veal between two sheets of parchment or wax paper and pound into 1/4-inch-thick medallions.

2. Melt 2 tablespoons of the butter in a large sauté pan over medium heat. Place 1 cup of the flour in a shallow dish. Season the medallions with salt and white pepper, dredge in the flour, patting to remove any excess, and place several pieces at a time in the pan, cooking on each side for about 2 minutes or until golden brown. Remove the browned medallions from the heat and cover loosely with foil to keep warm while finishing the rest.

3. When all the medallions are browned, continue to heat the sauté pan over medium heat and add the shallots, sautéing until softened and translucent, about 1 minute. Slice the mushrooms and toss together with the lemon juice in a medium bowl. Add the mushrooms to the pan and sauté until any liquid they release has evaporated, about 4 minutes.

4. Stir in the brandy and simmer for about 1 minute, flambéing it, if desired. Add the wine to deglaze, stirring with a wooden spoon to loosen any browned bits on the bottom of the pan. Stir in the cream and bring the sauce to a boil over medium-high heat.

5. Place the remaining 3 tablespoons of butter in a small bowl and knead in the remaining 3 tablespoons of flour a bit at a time to form a beurre manié. Stir the beurre manié into the sauce a little at a time until incorporated. Add the demi-glace, stirring for about 1 minute until the sauce thickens. Toss in the parsley and season with additional salt and white pepper.

6. To serve, arrange several medallions on each plate, spoon some of the sauce overtop, and garnish with parsley.

Veal Liver with Calvados, Apples & Caramelized Onions

KALBSLEBER MIT CALVADOS, APFEL & ZWIEBEL

1. Melt 2 tablespoons of the butter in a large sauté pan over medium heat, add the apples, and sauté until slightly softened and golden brown, about 7 to 10 minutes. Remove from the heat and set aside momentarily to keep warm.

2. Melt another 2 tablespoons of the butter in another large sauté pan over medium heat, add the onions, and sauté, stirring frequently, until golden brown and caramelized, about 10 minutes. Remove from the heat and set aside momentarily to keep warm.

3. Melt the remaining 2 tablespoons of butter in another large sauté pan over medium-high heat. Lightly dredge the liver slices in flour, patting off the excess, place in the pan, and brown on each side for about 1 minute. Remove the slices from the pan and set aside momentarily to keep warm.

4. Pour about 1 tablespoon of butter out of the pan in which the liver was sautéed, add the shallots to the pan, and sauté until golden brown, about 2 minutes. Pour in the Calvados and bring to a simmer over medium heat, flaming with a match (flambéing) if desired. Stir in the demi-glace and simmer for about 2 minutes more. Remove from heat and whisk in the mustard.

5. To serve, arrange two slices of liver on each plate and spoon some of the sauce overtop. Place some apple slices and caramelized onions over the liver and garnish with watercress.

THIS IS SUCH AN IMPRESSIVE DISH THAT IT IS OFTEN SURPRISING THAT IT COMES TOGETHER IN LESS THAN FIFTEEN MINUTES. WE PREPARED VEAL LIVER IN THIS MANNER AT HOME ALMOST AS MUCH AS WE DID IN FANCY HOTEL RESTAURANTS, FOR IT RELIES ON BASIC INGREDIENTS. AT HOME, WE USED HOMEMADE APPLE EAU DE VIE RATHER THAN THE MORE ELEGANT CALVADOS, BUT REALLY ANY APPLE BRANDY WILL DO.

THE SAUCE HERE IS ALREADY QUITE RICH AND CREAMY, BUT IF YOU WISH IT TO BE EVEN MORE VELVETY, WHISK IN TWO MORE TABLESPOONS OF BUTTER AT THE END ALONG WITH THE MUSTARD.

Serves 4

6 tablespoons unsalted butter

4 Granny Smith apples, peeled, cored, and sliced

2 onions, peeled and finely sliced

8 slices veal liver (2 to 3 ounces each)

All-purpose flour, for dredging

3 shallots, peeled and finely chopped (about ½ cup)

⅓ cup Calvados (dry aged apple brandy)

1½ cups Demi-Glace (page 312) or prepared brown sauce

1 to 2 tablespoons Dijon mustard (optional)

Watercress, for garnish

Breaded Veal Cutlets

WIENER SCHNITZEL

Just about everyone has heard of this dish, but many are in a quandary about what it actually is. WIENER SCHNITZEL is German for "Viennese cutlet" and, adding to the confusion, it originated in France. To make matters worse, in America especially, diners often don't know whether the cutlet is pork or veal, as both are commonly used nowadays. Traditionally, however, the dish is always prepared with veal. In fact, in the Black Forest, if a chef uses pork, the menu will almost always read, "pork schnitzel in the Wiener style."

Home cooks and café, Gasthaus, and hotel chefs alike regularly prepare Wiener schnitzel, although home cooks usually forego the fancy garnishes. It is definitely one of the region's classic dishes and it is served in a variety of ways. JAGERSCHNITZEL, for example, is served with mushrooms; PAPRIKASCHNITZEL is prepared with paprika; RAHMSCHNITZEL is served with a creamy demi-glace sauce; and ZIGEUNERSCHNITZEL is served with a sauce flavored with slivered tongue, bacon, onion, and pickles.

Serves 4

CUTLETS:

4 veal cutlets (6 to 8 ounces each)

Salt

Freshly ground white pepper

4 tablespoons unsalted butter

½ cup all-purpose flour, for dredging

2 eggs, lightly beaten

1½ cups dry bread crumbs

Lemon Garnish:

4 anchovy fillets

4 thin round lemon slices

1 teaspoon nonpareil (small) capers

4 sprigs fresh curly-leaf parsley, for garnish

1. To make the cutlets, pound the veal cutlets to about ⅛ inch thick using a mallet or heavy-bottomed pan and season both sides with salt and pepper.

2. Melt the butter in a large sauté pan over medium-high heat. Place the flour, eggs, and bread crumbs in separate shallow dishes. Dredge the cutlets first with flour, then with egg, and finally with bread crumbs. Place them in the pan and sauté on each side for about 2 minutes until golden brown.

3. Meanwhile, to make the lemon garnish, roll each anchovy fillet into a loose scroll, set on top of a lemon slice, and fill with capers.

4. To serve, place the cutlets on individual plates, drizzle with the butter from the pan, and top with a lemon garnish and parsley sprig.

Veal Sweetbreads with Sautéed Fennel

KALBSBRIESLE MIT FENCHEL

1. Bring a large saucepan of lightly salted water to a boil over high heat, reduce the heat to low, and maintain at a gentle simmer. Pierce the onion with the bay leaf and cloves. Drop the onion and sweetbreads into the water and poach until just cooked, about 35 to 40 minutes. Remove the saucepan from the heat and leave the sweetbreads to cool completely in the poaching liquid.

2. Remove the cooled sweetbreads from the liquid, remove any excess fat, and slice into 1-inch pieces.

3. Melt the butter in a large sauté pan over medium heat. Place the flour and eggs in separate shallow dishes. Pat the sweetbread slices dry and season with salt and pepper. Dredge the sweetbreads first with flour, patting to remove any excess, and coat with egg. Place in the pan and sauté on each side for about 4 to 5 minutes until golden brown.

4. Fold together the truffles and hollandaise sauce in a small bowl.

5. To serve, place the sautéed fennel in the center of a serving platter, arrange the sweetbreads overtop, and drizzle with truffle-hollandaise sauce.

THIS IS ANOTHER DISH THAT WAS EXCLUSIVE TO HOTEL RESTAURANTS AND WAS RARELY, IF EVER, PREPARED AT HOME. SWEETBREADS ARE CONSIDERED QUITE A DELICACY IN THE BLACK FOREST, AND WE OFTEN SERVED THEM AT THE SOMMERBERG HOTEL IN BAD WILDBAD.

DIPPED IN FLOUR AND EGG, THE SWEETBREADS DEVELOP A WONDERFULLY CRUNCHY CRUST THAT CONTRASTS MARVELOUSLY WITH TENDER SAUTÉED FENNEL.

Serves 6

1 medium yellow onion, peeled

1 dried bay leaf

3 whole cloves

4 pounds veal sweetbreads

4 tablespoons unsalted butter

1 cup all-purpose flour, for dredging

2 eggs, beaten with 1 tablespoon water

Salt

Freshly ground white pepper

1 tablespoon chopped black truffles

1 cup Hollandaise Sauce (page 311)

2 cups Sautéed Fennel (page 254)

Filet of Veal with Foie Gras

KALBSFILET MIT GÄNSELEBER

1. Make a small slit at one end of each tenderloin using a paring knife. Using the handle of a wooden spoon or other similarly shaped object, carefully press the implement through the length of each tenderloin to create a narrow opening. (Do not pierce through to the opposite end.)

2. Slice the pâté into thin strips, carefully stuff into each tenderloin, and set aside in the refrigerator for about 2 hours.

3. Meanwhile, set the caul fat in cold water to soak for 1 hour.

4. Preheat the oven to 350°F.

5. Melt 2 tablespoons of the butter in a large sauté pan over medium heat. Set each tenderloin in the pan slit side down to sear it closed and prevent the pâté from escaping during cooking. Continue browning the tenderloins on all sides and remove from the pan. Drain the caul fat and wrap pieces of it around each tenderloin, completely encasing each one. Return the tenderloins to the pan and roast to medium-rare, about 15 minutes. Remove the tenderloins from the pan, cover loosely with foil, and set aside to rest for about 5 minutes while finishing the dish.

6. Add the remaining 2 tablespoons of butter to the sauté pan, melt over medium heat, and add the shallots, sautéing until softened and translucent, about 1½ minutes. Add the Cognac to deglaze, stirring with a wooden spoon to loosen any browned bits on the bottom of the pan. Stir in the demi-glace and simmer until reduced by half. Stir in the cream and reduce by about one-quarter. Add the truffles and simmer the sauce for about 1 minute more.

8. To serve, arrange the tenderloins on a platter, drizzle some of the sauce around them, and serve the remaining sauce in a gravy boat on the side.

In good faith, I feel I must offer a disclaimer at the outset and declare that this elegant dish is labor intensive, expensive, and never prepared at home in the Black Forest. That being said, the filet is really rather straightforward to prepare, and I encourage you to try it for a special occasion. When I was an apprentice, we prepared the dish to order as the meat course of elegant multi-course dinners. The truffles and foie gras make this an expensive entrée, so we only showcased it on the menu occasionally.

If you do try this dish, I suggest you use the caul fat (a thin, fatty membrane that lines the stomach), as it helps maintain the shape of the filets and prevents the foie gras from escaping during cooking. If your butcher doesn't keep it in stock, he should be able to get it for you.

Serves 6

3 butt-end veal tenderloins (10 ounces each), silver skin removed

8 ounces foie gras pâté, chilled

Caul fat, as needed (optional)

4 tablespoons unsalted butter

5 shallots, peeled and finely chopped (about 1 cup)

¼ cup Cognac

2 cups Demi-Glace (page 312) or prepared brown sauce

1 cup heavy cream

2 tablespoons chopped black truffles

Chicken with Riesling Cream Sauce

HÜHNER FRICASÉE MIT RIESLING RAHMSOßE

THIS DISH PAYS TRIBUTE TO THE CLASSIC FRENCH COQ AU VIN, TRA-
DITIONALLY PREPARED WITH BURGUNDY WINE. IN THE BLACK FOR-
EST, HOWEVER, WE ARE MORE LIKELY TO TAKE A CULINARY CUE
FROM OUR ALSATIAN NEIGHBORS AND USE OUR BELOVED DELICATE, FRUITY
RIESLING WINE. ALTHOUGH THIS RICH, CREAMY CHICKEN DISH IS A BIT TIME
CONSUMING TO PREPARE, IT IS REALLY RATHER A STRAIGHTFORWARD TASK.
THE MOST IMPORTANT PART OF YOUR PREPARATION IS TO PURCHASE THE
RIGHT KIND OF CHICKEN—ONE THAT HAS A SUFFICIENT AMOUNT OF FAT
AND FLAVOR. IN FRANCE, SUCH CHICKENS ARE CALLED POULARDES. WE
KNOW THEM AS "ROASTERS," AND THEY RANGE BETWEEN TWO AND A HALF
AND FIVE POUNDS AND CAN BE AS MUCH AS EIGHT MONTHS OLD. COQ AU
RIESLING WAS ALWAYS A FAVORITE IN ELEGANT BLACK FOREST HOTELS,
BUT IT IS SO DELICIOUS AND SATISFYING THAT I RECOMMEND IT FOR
SWANKY AND MODEST GATHERINGS ALIKE.

Serves 4 to 6

2 whole chickens (2½ to 3 pounds each),
   legs tied together with kitchen twine

1 onion

6 whole cloves

5 tablespoons unsalted butter

2 shallots, peeled and finely chopped (about 3 tablespoons)

½ small white onion, peeled and finely chopped (about 3 tablespoons)

3 tablespoons all-purpose flour

3 cups Riesling, or other delicate fruity white wine

1 cup pearl onions, peeled

2 cups quartered white button mushrooms

Salt

Freshly ground black pepper

1 cup heavy cream

Chopped fresh parsley, for garnish

1. Place the chickens in a large saucepan or casserole and cover with cold water. Pierce the onion with the cloves and place in the pot. Bring to a boil over high heat, reduce the heat to low, and gently simmer until the chickens are fully cooked, about 25 to 30 minutes.

2. Discard the onion, remove the chickens from the pan, and set aside, covered. Bring the broth to a boil over high heat and reduce by about three-quarters. (Make sure you end up with at least 3 cups of reduced broth.) Strain and set aside.

3. Melt 3 tablespoons of butter in a large saucepan over medium-high heat, add the shallots and onion, and sauté until translucent and softened, about 2 minutes. Whisk in the flour to make a roux, add the Riesling and 3 cups of the reduced broth, and bring to a boil. Reduce the heat to medium low and simmer the sauce until is thickened, stirring occasionally, about 3 to 5 minutes.

4. Meanwhile, melt the remaining 2 tablespoons of but-ter in a large sauté pan over medium-high heat, add the pearl onions and mushrooms, and sauté until the onions are slightly translucent and the mushrooms are slightly softened.

5. Remove the kitchen twine from the chickens and carve them, removing the breast meat, separating the legs and thighs, and reserving the wings for another use. Arrange the chicken pieces on a serving platter, sprinkle with salt and pepper, and spoon the pearl onions and mushrooms overtop.

6. To finish the sauce, stir the heavy cream into the thickened sauce and season with salt and pepper.

7. To serve, pour the sauce over the chicken and gar-nish with parsley. Serve with spätzle or egg noodles.

Venison Medallions with Cognac Cream Sauce

REHMEDALLIONS MIT COGNAC RAHMSOßE

1. At least 8 hours or the day before serving the dish, place the venison medallions in a medium casserole dish and add the wine, rosemary, sage, garlic, and about two-thirds of the chopped shallots, turning the medallions to coat on all sides. Cover with plastic wrap and set aside in the refrigerator to marinate for at least 8 hours or overnight.

2. The next day or when you are ready to proceed with the dish, remove the venison from the marinade, discarding the marinade, and pat the venison dry with paper towels.

3. Melt the butter in a large sauté pan over medium-high heat, add the venison medallions, and sauté for about 3 minutes on each side until browned and cooked to medium-rare, or to desired doneness. Remove the medallions from the pan, cover loosely with foil, and set aside to keep warm while finishing the dish.

4. Place the sauté pan over medium heat, add the remaining chopped shallots, and sauté until softened and translucent, about 1 minute. Stir in the leek and mushrooms and sauté until softened, about 2 to 3 more minutes.

5. Add the Cognac to deglaze, stirring with a wooden spoon to loosen any browned bits on the bottom of the pan. Stir in the demi-glace, reduce the heat to medium low, and simmer for about 3 minutes. Remove from the heat, stir in the sour cream, and season the sauce with salt and pepper.

6. To serve, arrange the venison medallions on a serving platter and spoon the sauce overtop.

ALL RESTAURANTS IN THE BLACK FOREST SERVE A VARIETY OF GAME DISHES. IN ADDITION TO VENISON, GAME SUCH AS WILD BOAR, RABBIT, AND PHEASANT ARE PLENTIFUL AND MUCH LOVED FOR THEIR FLAVORFUL MEAT.

I LEARNED TO PREPARE THIS DISH AT THE SOMMER-BERG HOTEL IN BAD WILDBAD, AND IT IS ONE OF MY FAVORITE WAYS TO SERVE VENISON. THERE IS REALLY NOTHING COMPLICATED HERE, AND THE RECIPE COMES TOGETHER QUICKLY ONCE THE VENISON MEDALLIONS ARE MARINATED. JUST REMEMBER TO USE A GOOD-QUALITY COGNAC OR BRANDY HERE. THE SAUCE IS SO SIMPLE THAT IT DEPENDS ON A RICH, ROUND COGNAC TO GIVE IT PER-SONALITY AND DEPTH.

Serves 4 to 6

$1\frac{1}{2}$ pounds venison tenderloin, fat trimmed, silver skin removed, and sliced into $\frac{1}{4}$-inch-thick medallions (see Sources, page 320)

2 cups full-bodied red wine, such as Burgundy

1 sprig fresh rosemary

$\frac{1}{8}$ teaspoon dried rubbed sage

2 cloves garlic, peeled and finely chopped

3 medium shallots, peeled and finely chopped

1 teaspoon unsalted butter

1 medium leek (white part only), trimmed and sliced into strips about 2 inches long and $\frac{1}{16}$ inch wide

About 6 white button mushrooms, sliced (about $1\frac{1}{2}$ cups)

$\frac{1}{2}$ cup Cognac

2 cups Demi-Glace (page 312) or prepared brown sauce

2 tablespoons sour cream

Salt

Freshly ground black pepper

Venison Ragoût with Bacon & Mushrooms

REH RAGOÛT JÄGER ART

1. Combine the olive oil and butter in a medium casserole or heavy-bottomed saucepan over high heat, add the venison, and sauté, stirring occasionally, until the pieces are well browned, about 5 minutes.

2. Reduce the heat to medium, toss in the onions, bacon, garlic, and mushrooms, and sauté, stirring frequently, about 10 minutes more, until the vegetables and bacon have begun to brown lightly and any liquid they release has reduced.

3. Remove the venison, vegetables, and bacon from the casserole with a slotted spoon to a bowl, drain the fat from the pan, and return it to medium heat. Pour in 2¾ cups of the wine to deglaze, stirring with a wooden spoon to loosen any browned bits on the bottom of the pan.

4. Return the venison, vegetables, and bacon to the casserole, add the sage, paprika, thyme, and bay leaves, and bring to a boil over high heat. Reduce the heat to low, cover, and simmer for about 1 hour, or until the venison is fully cooked and tender and the juices have reduced and thickened slightly.

5. Whisk together the remaining ¼ cup of wine with and the arrowroot or cornstarch in a small bowl until velvety smooth. Remove the thyme sprigs and bay leaves from the casserole and stir the wine mixture into the ragoût in a steady stream. Simmer about 5 minutes more until the ragoût has thickened and season with salt and pepper.

6. To serve, ladle the ragoût into a deep serving platter or bowl and garnish with chives.

VENISON IS PLENTIFUL IN THE BLACK FOREST, SO IT IS HARDLY SURPRISING THAT WE OFTEN SERVED IT IN HOTEL RESTAURANTS. THIS RECIPE IS BASED ON THOSE I USED DURING MY YEARS AS AN APPRENTICE WITH ONE MAIN EXCEPTION: WE BUTCHERED DEER INTO LARGE RACKS OF VENISON IN THE RESTAURANTS, AND I AM SUGGESTING YOU PURCHASE SOME VENISON SHOULDER HERE. YOU MIGHT BE ABLE TO FIND THIS MEAT IN A HIGH QUALITY MARKET, BUT IF YOU CANNOT, YOU CAN ORDER IT THROUGH THE MAIL (SEE SOURCES, PAGE 320) THIS RAGOÛT IS BASED ON THE CLASSIC FRENCH À LA FORESTIÈRE PREPARATION, WHICH TRANSLATES AS "OF THE FOREST" AND CALLS FOR SUCH INGREDIENTS AS MUSHROOMS, BACON, AND HERBS. THIS RICH, FLAVORFUL DISH IS ALSO TRADITIONALLY PAIRED WITH POTATOES, BUT FOR AN AUTHENTICALLY BLACK FOREST PRESENTATION, I SUGGEST SERVING IT WITH SPÄTZLE.

Serves 8

3 tablespoons olive oil

2 tablespoons unsalted butter

5 pounds venison shoulder, cut into 2-inch cubes

5 large white onions, peeled and chopped

9 slices lean bacon, chopped

3 cloves garlic, peeled and finely chopped

½ cup sliced porcini mushrooms

½ cup sliced portobello mushrooms

½ cup sliced white button mushrooms

3 cups full-bodied red wine, such as Burgundy

1 teaspoon dried sage

1 teaspoon Hungarian paprika

2 sprigs fresh thyme

2 dried bay leaves

1 tablespoon arrowroot, or 2¼ teaspoons cornstarch

Salt

Freshly ground black pepper

Chopped fresh chives, for garnish

Stuffed Quail

GEFÜLLTE WACHTEL

HERE IS YET ANOTHER GAME DISH MUCH LOVED IN THE BLACK FOREST. UNLIKE AMERICAN QUAIL THAT PREFER WALKING TO FLYING, THE EUROPEAN GAME BIRD IS MIGRATORY. QUAIL ARE PLENTIFUL IN THE REGION, AND THEIR ROBUST FLAVOR PAIRS WELL WITH A VARIETY OF EQUALLY STURDY INGREDIENTS.

QUAIL ARE SERVED IN MANY WAYS AND WITH NUMEROUS STUFFINGS. IN THIS RECIPE, A STUFFING OF SWEET PEARS, PLUMP RAISINS, CRUNCHY WALNUTS, TENDER MUSHROOMS, RICH FOIE GRAS, AND FIRM BREAD, ALL PERFUMED WITH POIRE WILLIAMS, PERFECTLY COMPLEMENTS THE HEARTY BIRD. THE TANGY RED WINE SAUCE WITH SOUR CREAM ADDS YET ANOTHER LAYER OF PERSONALITY, AND THE SAUERKRAUT SERVED BENEATH THE QUAIL CONTRIBUTES AN EVEN GREATER DEPTH OF FLAVOR.

AS THE INGREDIENTS SUGGEST, THIS STUFFED QUAIL IS PARTICULARLY SUITED TO FALL AND WINTER MENUS.

Serves 8

FOIE GRAS STUFFING:

1 tablespoon unsalted butter

1 onion, peeled and finely chopped

6 white button mushrooms, finely chopped

2 Bartlett pears, peeled, cored, and finely chopped

1 tablespoon Poire Williams (pear-flavored eau de vie)

1 loaf stale French bread, cut into small cubes

2 tablespoons chopped fresh parsley

4 ounces foie gras pâté, cubed

½ cup chopped walnuts

½ cup raisins, chopped

1 cup Chicken Stock (page 308), warmed

ASSEMBLY:

16 quail (see Sources, page 320)

Salt

Freshly ground white pepper

2 teaspoons dried thyme

2 teaspoons dried sage

2 teaspoons dried marjoram

2 tablespoons vegetable oil

1 medium carrot, peeled and roughly chopped

1 rib celery, roughly chopped

½ yellow onion, peeled and roughly chopped

SAUCE:

1½ cups full-bodied red wine, such as Burgundy

1½ cups Demi-Glace (page 312) or prepared brown sauce

3 tablespoons sour cream

2 tablespoons Poire Williams

3 tablespoons unsalted butter, at room temperature

4 cups Riesling Sauerkraut (page 261), for serving

1. To make the stuffing, melt the butter in a large sauté pan over medium heat, add the onion, and sauté until softened and translucent, about 1 minute. Add the mushrooms and sauté until softened and any liquid they release has evaporated, about 3 minutes. Toss in the pears and sauté until slightly softened and fragrant, about 1 to 2 minutes. Remove from the heat and stir in the Poire Williams.

2. Combine the sautéed vegetables and pears with the bread cubes, parsley, pâté, walnuts, and raisins in a large bowl, tossing gently to mix well. Stir in the stock a little at a time until the stuffing is moist enough to hold together. Set aside momentarily.

3. Preheat the oven to 450°F.

4. To assemble the quail, rinse the quail in cold water and pat dry. Season the cavities of the quail with salt, white pepper, and half of the dried herbs, then fill with the stuffing. Tie the legs together with kitchen twine and brush each quail all over with oil. Season the outsides with additional salt, white pepper, and the remaining herbs, place in a large roasting pan breast sides up, and roast for 8 to 10 minutes until lightly browned. Reduce the oven temperature to 375°F., toss the carrot, celery, and onion in the pan around the quail, and roast, basting frequently, until a meat thermometer inserted in the thighs registers 185°F., about 15 to 20 minutes.

5. Remove the quail from the pan and set aside, covered loosely with foil, to rest while preparing the sauce.

6. To make the sauce, place the roasting pan over medium-high heat, add the wine to deglaze, stirring with a wooden spoon to loosen any browned bits on the bottom of the pan, and simmer until reduced by about two-thirds. Stir in the demi-glace and simmer until reduced by about half. Remove from heat, incorporate the sour cream, and strain through a wire mesh strainer into a small saucepan. While off the heat, stir in the Poire Williams and whisk in the butter.

7. To serve, spoon some sauerkraut on each plate, arrange two quail on top, and drizzle with sauce.

Pheasant à la Souvarov

FASAN NACH DER ART
VON PRINZ SOUVAROV

Sometimes the mere name of a dish elicits grand visions of elegant feasts, glistening centuries-old dining rooms, and menus designed to represent a chef's culinary prowess as much as the elite status of the diners who passionately consumed them. Such is the case with this dish. It was named for a particular Prince Souvarov, a descendant of the governor of the Crimea who dined often in Paris.

"Souvarov" refers to the preparation of pheasant as well as other game birds, including quail, partridge, and woodcock. Occasionally, it is also prepared with chicken. The traditional French recipe calls for stuffing the whole bird with foie gras and truffles, searing it, and roasting it in a decorative covered terrine, which is sealed with pastry or salt dough (a stiff, salty paste made with water, salt, and flour). The covered casserole is then ceremoniously presented to the table.

My version takes its cues from the original recipe, but I prefer using pheasant thighs to the whole bird as they cook more evenly and remain moist. I also think covering the entire dish with puff pastry is a tasty and elegant alternative to using the lid of a casserole dish. Like many dishes from Black Forest hotels, this one is a bit time consuming, but it is truly a show stopper and marvelous for entertaining. I'm sure that when you try it, you, too, will get a taste of cooking and eating in the grand European tradition.

Serves 4

PHEASANT:

12 boneless pheasant thighs (*see* Sources, page 320)

$4\frac{1}{3}$ cups full-bodied red wine, such as Burgundy

1 sprig fresh rosemary

1 sprig fresh thyme

1 teaspoon whole peppercorns

2 tablespoons olive oil

2 tablespoons unsalted butter

1 cup all-purpose flour, for dredging

Salt

Freshly ground white pepper

SAUCE:

1 tablespoon unsalted butter

3 medium shallots, peeled and finely chopped

3 tablespoons Cognac

$\frac{1}{2}$ cup full-bodied red wine, such as Burgundy

3 cups Demi-Glace (page 312) or prepared brown sauce

$\frac{1}{4}$ cup heavy cream

2 tablespoons sour cream

Salt

Freshly ground white pepper

ASSEMBLY:

8 ounces foie gras pâté, cut into small cubes

1 fresh black truffle, chopped

8 ounces prepared puff pastry, rolled to $\frac{1}{8}$ inch thick

Egg wash, prepared with 1 egg and 1 tablespoon water

249

1. At least 4 hours or the day before serving the dish, place the pheasant thighs in a shallow baking dish and pour in 4 cups of the wine, or enough to cover. Toss in the rosemary and thyme sprigs and the peppercorns, cover with plastic wrap, and set in the refrigerator to marinate for at least 4 hours or overnight.

2. The next day or when you are ready to proceed with the dish, preheat the oven to 375°F.

3. Heat the olive oil and butter in a large sauté pan over medium-high heat. Place the flour in a shallow dish. Remove the pheasant thighs from the marinade, discarding the marinade, and pat the thighs dry. Season with salt and white pepper, dredge in the flour, patting to remove the excess, and place skin sides down in the pan, sautéing until well browned, about 2½ minutes. Turn and brown for about 2½ minutes more.

4. Remove the pheasant thighs to a baking sheet, drizzle with the remaining ⅓ cup of wine, and roast until fully cooked but tender, about 15 to 20 minutes.

5. Meanwhile, to make the sauce, pour the oil, browned butter, and rendered fat out of the sauté pan, add the butter, and melt over medium heat. Add the shallots and sauté until softened and translucent, about 1 minute. Add the Cognac to deglaze, stirring with a wooden spoon to loosen any browned bits on the bottom of the pan. Stir in the wine and demi-glace and simmer until reduced by about one-third. Pour in the cream and simmer until slightly thickened. Remove the sauce from the heat, stir in the sour cream, and season with salt and white pepper.

6. To assemble the dish, arrange the roasted pheasant thighs in a 2-quart casserole dish and pour the sauce overtop. Sprinkle with pâté and truffles and set aside or in the refrigerator to cool to nearly room temperature. Trim the puff pastry to the size of the casserole dish, set on top of the pheasant, and brush with egg wash. Reduce the oven temperature to 350°F. and bake until the pastry is puffed and golden, about 7 to 8 minutes.

SALT DOUGH

Combine ¹/2 cup salt and ¹/2 cup flour, then add enough water to form a stiff dough. Roll into a ball. Measure the circumference of the pot with a piece of kitchen twine, then roll the dough into a rope the length of the twine. Place the lid on the pot, then seal the outside rim with the salt dough.

c

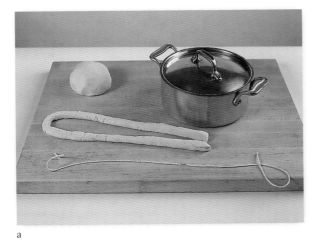

a

d

b

Brussels Sprouts Braised with Bacon & Fennel

ROSENKOHL MIT SPECK & FENCHEL

Serves 6

1½ pounds fresh Brussels sprouts,
  tough outer leaves removed and stem end trimmed

2 slices lean bacon, finely chopped

1 teaspoon olive oil

1 medium yellow onion, peeled and finely chopped

¾ cup Chicken Stock (page 308)

1 teaspoon fennel seeds, lightly crushed in a mortar
  and pestle or with the bottom of a heavy pan

Salt

Freshly ground pepper

BRUSSELS SPROUTS ARE A FAVORITE IN THE BLACK FOREST. WE ENJOYED THEM EVEN INTO THE COLD MONTHS, FOR, LIKE LEEKS, WE LEFT THEM IN THE GARDEN, WHERE THEY FROZE DURING THE WINTER, AND PICKED THEM AS NEEDED. IT WAS A COLD BUSINESS, AND I WAS USUALLY THE ONE ASSIGNED THE TASK.

THIS DISH IS PARTICULARLY RICH AND FLAVORFUL, AS IT COMBINES THE STRONG, SLIGHTLY BITTER CHARACTER OF THE BRUSSELS SPROUTS WITH CRISP SALTY BACON AND THE LICORICE PERFUME OF FENNEL SEED. THESE TENDER BRAISED BRUSSELS SPROUTS PAIR PARTICULARLY WELL WITH ROASTED BEEF, PORK, AND GAME.

1. Using a paring knife, cut a small ⅛-inch-deep cross in the stem end of each Brussels sprout. Bring a large saucepan of salted water to a boil over high heat, add the Brussels sprouts, and cook until just tender, about 6 to 8 minutes.

2. Drain the Brussels sprouts in a colander and set aside in a bowl of cold water to quickly stop the cooking, about 5 minutes. Drain again and set aside momentarily.

3. Heat a large sauté pan over medium heat, add the bacon, and cook until crisp, about 5 minutes. Remove the bacon and set aside to drain on paper towels.

4. Remove most of the bacon fat from the pan, wiping out the pan with paper towels if you wish, add the olive oil, and heat over medium heat. Add the onion and sauté until softened and very lightly browned, about 5 minutes. Add the stock, fennel seeds, Brussels sprouts, and bacon and simmer, stirring frequently, until the liquid is reduced, about 3 minutes.

5. To serve, season with salt and pepper and pour onto a large serving platter.

Sautéed Fennel

FENCHEL SAUTÉ

1. Trim the fennel bulbs of the long stalks, reserving the fronds. Core the fennel bulbs and slice as thinly as possible. Place the fennel in a bowl, toss with salt, and set aside at room temperature for 1 hour. Transfer the fennel to a clean kitchen towel and squeeze out as much water as possible.

2. Melt the butter in a large sauté pan over medium heat, add the garlic and shallot, and sauté until softened and translucent, about 1½ minutes. Stir in the anise seed and fennel and season with pepper and additional salt if necessary, sautéing until the fennel is heated, about 2 minutes more.

3. Serve the fennel in a serving bowl garnished with reserved fennel fronds.

FRESH FENNEL BESPEAKS THE SOUTH OF FRANCE, BUT WE ARE FORTUNATE THAT IT ALSO GROWS EFFORTLESSLY IN THE BLACK FOREST. WITH ITS DELICATE ANISE FLAVOR AND CRISP TEXTURE, THIS VEGETABLE IS AS DELICIOUS SERVED RAW IN SALADS AS IT IS SAUTÉED, BRAISED, ROASTED, OR IN BOUILLABAISSE.

THIS RECIPE HAILS FROM THE SOMMERBERG HOTEL IN BAD WILDBAD, WHERE IT WAS QUITE POPULAR WITH DINERS. IT REQUIRES A BIT OF ADVANCED PREPARATION, AS THE FENNEL SITS FOR A TIME IN SALT TO ADD FLAVOR AND EXTRACT EXCESS LIQUID BEFORE IT IS SAUTÉED. AS A RESULT, THE DISH DEVELOPS A CONCENTRATED YET DELICATE CHARACTER THAT PAIRS WELL WITH ROBUST MEAT AND GAME.

Serves 4

3 large bulbs fennel

2 tablespoons salt

1 tablespoon unsalted butter

1 clove garlic, peeled and finely chopped

1 medium shallot, peeled and finely chopped

⅛ teaspoon whole anise seed

Freshly ground white pepper

Creamed Spinach with Anisette

RAHMSPINAT MIT ANIS

Creamed spinach pairs deliciously with just about any entrée, and the addition of anisette gives a particular nod to the Black Forest. For an especially elegant presentation, serve it in tomato halves or individual VOLS-AU-VENT (puff pastry shells, page 80).

Serves 4

1 pound spinach, cleaned and stems removed

1 teaspoon salt

1 cup Béchamel Sauce (page 313)

½ cup heavy cream

¼ teaspoon freshly grated nutmeg

2 tablespoons anisette (anise-flavored liquor)

2 tablespoons unsalted butter

Salt

Freshly ground black pepper

1. Heat a large saucepan over low heat, add the spinach and salt, and cook, stirring occasionally, until the spinach is wilted, about 5 minutes. Remove the spinach to a bowl, cool for 3 to 5 minutes, and reserve the saucepan.

2. Squeeze out as much liquid as possible from the spinach, chop finely, and set aside momentarily.

3. Combine the béchamel, cream, nutmeg, and anisette in the reserved saucepan and bring to a simmer over medium heat. Stir in the spinach and butter, season with salt and pepper, and spoon into a serving bowl.

Herb Crêpes

KRÄUTER PFANNKUCHEN

1. Combine all of the ingredients in a large bowl, mixing until smooth.

2. Heat a large nonstick sauté pan over medium heat. Pour in just enough batter to thinly and evenly coat the pan (about ⅓ to ½ cup). Cook for about 30 seconds, flip the crêpe with a spatula, and cook on the second side for another 30 seconds. Turn the crêpe out onto a plate, cover loosely with a towel to keep warm, and continue with the remaining batter.

3. To serve, fold each crêpe into a square and arrange on a large serving platter.

CHEF'S NOTE: Clarified butter (also called drawn butter or *ghee*) is easy to prepare. Because it is free of milk solids, it has a higher smoking point than regular butter (meaning it doesn't burn as quickly), has a longer shelf life, and a lighter flavor. To prepare it, slowly melt unsalted butter in a saucepan and gently simmer until the white milk solids have sunk to the bottom of the pan and the clear, clarified butter remains on top. Skim any foam that rises to the surface, carefully pour the clarified butter into a jar, and store in the refrigerator.

THESE CRÊPES COULD NOT BE EASIER TO PREPARE AND THEY ARE A DELICIOUS ADDITION TO MANY DISHES. IN THE HOTELS, WE SERVED THEM MOST FREQUENTLY WITH ASPARAGUS DURING **SPARGELZEIT**, THE SPRING CELEBRATION SURROUNDING THE ASPARAGUS HARVEST. WE ALSO OCCASIONALLY USED THESE CRÊPES IN **FLÄDLESSUPPE**—A SIMPLE BUT FLAVORFUL SOUP PREPARED BY SLICING THE CRÊPES IN STRIPS AND STIRRING THEM INTO THE FLAVORFUL BOUILLON FROM THE BEEF SALAD (PAGE 129).

Makes 16 Crêpes

4½ cups all-purpose flour

6 eggs, beaten

4½ cups whole milk

3 tablespoons clarified butter or olive oil (*see Chef's Note*)

2 tablespoons finely chopped fresh basil

2 tablespoons finely chopped fresh parsley

2 tablespoons stemmed and finely chopped fresh thyme

2 tablespoons finely chopped fresh chives

⅛ teaspoon freshly grated nutmeg

⅛ teaspoon salt

⅛ teaspoon freshly ground white pepper

Mushroom Risotto

PILZ RISOTTO

IF YOU ARE THINKING THAT THIS RISOTTO SEEMS OUT OF CHARACTER IN THE BLACK FOREST, YOU ARE CORRECT. AS AN APPRENTICE AT THE SOMMERBERG HOTEL IN BAD WILDBAD, HOWEVER, I WAS FORTUNATE TO COOK UNDER A CHEF WHO WAS KEEN ON FINE ITALIAN CUISINE. SO MUCH SO, IN FACT, THAT IN ADDITION TO PREPARING THIS WONDERFUL DISH EVERY SO OFTEN, HE ALSO OCCASIONALLY IMPORTED ITALIAN TRUFFLES.

LIKE ALL RISOTTOS, THIS RECIPE REQUIRES A BIT OF PATIENCE. ARBORIO RICE SIMPLY REFUSES TO BE RUSHED AND LIKES TO BE PAMPERED WITH INCREMENTAL ADDITIONS OF STOCK AND LOTS OF STIRRING. IT IS REALLY QUITE A SIMPLE DISH, THOUGH, AND, DESPITE THE TIME IT REQUIRES, I AM SURE IT WILL SEDUCE YOU TO MAKE IT AS OFTEN AS POSSIBLE.

Serves 6 to 8

1 quart Chicken Stock (page 308)

2 tablespoons unsalted butter

1 medium shallot, peeled and finely chopped

1 cup sliced porcini mushrooms or other variety

¼ cup dry white wine, such as Sauvignon Blanc

2 cups Arborio rice

¼ cup grated Parmesan cheese

---

1. Bring the stock to a simmer over medium-low heat.

2. Melt 1 tablespoon of the butter in a medium risotto pan or saucepan over medium heat, add the shallot, and sauté until softened and translucent, about 1 minute. Add the mushrooms and sauté until softened and any liquid they release has evaporated, about 3 minutes. Stir in the wine and simmer until the pan is nearly dry.

3. Stir in the rice and cook until the grains are translucent and coated with butter, about 2 minutes.

4. Begin gradually ladling the simmering stock into the pan, adding about ½ cup at a time and stirring constantly until completely absorbed. The process should take about 15 to 20 minutes. The final risotto should be thick and creamy and the rice should be slightly firm but tender.

5. Stir in the Parmesan cheese and remaining 1 tablespoon of butter and pour into a large serving bowl.

Risotto with Escargots

SCHNECKEN RISOTTO

1. Bring the stock to a simmer in a medium saucepan over medium-low heat.

2. Melt 2 tablespoons of the butter in a medium saucepan over medium heat, add the shallots and garlic, and sauté until softened and translucent, about 2 to 3 minutes. Add the escargots, thyme, and mushrooms and sauté about 3 minutes. Stir in the wine and simmer until the pan is nearly dry. Remove the escargots and mushroom mixture and set aside.

3. Return the pan to medium heat and add another tablespoon of butter. Add the rice and cook until the grains are translucent and coated with butter, about 2 minutes.

4. Begin gradually adding the simmering stock to the pan, about ½ cup at a time, and stirring constantly until completely absorbed. The process should take about 15 to 20 minutes. The final risotto should be thick and creamy and the rice should be slightly firm but tender.

5. Heat the remaining 1 tablespoon of butter in a small sauté pan over medium heat and toss in the escargots mixture, cooking for 2 to 3 minutes until heated.

6. Stir the parsley into the risotto, divide among individual bowls, and top with escargots.

RISOTTO WAS A POPULAR DISH IN THE HOTELS WHERE I APPRENTICED, AND WE IN THE KITCHEN ENJOYED DEVELOPING FLAVORFUL VARIATIONS FOR OUR DISCERNING CLIENTELE. MUSHROOMS, VEGETABLES, SEAFOOD, POULTRY, AND ALL SORTS OF MEATS ARE FLAVORFUL ADDITIONS TO THE DISH, BUT, FOR ME, INCORPORATING ESCARGOTS (SNAILS) MAKES FOR A PARTICULARLY SPECIAL RISOTTO.

ESCARGOTS ARE MUCH LOVED THROUGHOUT THE BLACK FOREST, WHERE THEY ARE MOSTLY SERVED BUBBLING WITH HERB BUTTER AS ESCARGOTS BOURGUIGNONS. BEYOND THEIR FLAVORFUL CULINARY APPLICATIONS, THESE DELICIOUS MORSELS ELICIT JOYFUL MEMORIES OF MY CHILDHOOD. THEY REMIND ME OF THE MANY AFTERNOONS I (AND SOMETIMES MY BROTHER) SPENT WITH MY GRANDFATHER SEARCHING FOR HIBERNATING SNAILS. DURING THOSE OUTINGS, WE SPENT HOURS TRAIPSING THROUGH VINEYARDS AND OVER HILLS IN SEARCH OF THE DELICATE COILED SHELLS IN WHICH THEY WERE SLEEPING. MY GRANDFATHER INSTRUCTED US TO PICK ONLY SHELLS THAT WERE TIGHTLY CLOSED, AND WE PACKED THEM IN BURLAP BAGS IN PREPARATION FOR SELLING THEM TO WHOLESALERS.

TODAY, FEW FOLKS, EVEN IN THE BLACK FOREST, COOK WITH FRESH SNAILS, AS CLEANING AND PREPARING THEM IS A VERY LABOR-INTENSIVE ENDEAVOR. FORTUNATELY, THERE ARE MANY GOOD QUALITY, FLAVORFUL CANNED VARIETIES AVAILABLE. EVEN IF YOU ARE UNCERTAIN ABOUT YOUR PRESENT AFFECTION FOR ESCARGOTS, I'M SURE THIS RISOTTO WILL TRANSFORM YOU INTO A FAN IN NO TIME.

Serves 6 to 8

1 quart Chicken Stock (page 308)

4 tablespoons unsalted butter

2 medium shallots, peeled and finely chopped

6 cloves garlic, peeled and chopped

24 extra large escargots (see Sources, page 320)

¼ cup stemmed and chopped fresh thyme

1 cup sliced porcini mushrooms or other firm flavorful variety

½ cup dry white wine, such as Sauvignon Blanc

2 cups Arborio rice

¼ cup chopped fresh parsley

Red Beans and Burgundy

ROTE BOHNEN IN BURGUNDERWEIN

1. At least 8 hours before serving the dish, pour the beans into a colander and rinse thoroughly, removing any stones or hard bits. Remove the beans to a large bowl, add water until the beans are covered by about 1 inch, and set aside at room temperature for 8 hours or overnight.

2. The next day or when ready to prepare the dish, drain and rinse the beans and place them in a large saucepan. Add water to cover the beans by about 1 inch, toss in the bouquet garni, salt, and pepper, and bring to a boil over high heat. Reduce the heat to medium low and simmer until the beans are tender, about 1½ to 2 hours. Remove the bouquet garni, drain the beans in a colander, and set aside.

3. Place the saucepan over high heat, add the bacon, and sauté until crisp, about 3 minutes. Remove the bacon, drain on paper towels, and set aside.

4. Reduce the heat to medium, add the onions and garlic to the bacon drippings, and sauté until golden brown, about 3 minutes. Toss in the carrots and sauté until softened, about 5 minutes.

5. Return the beans and bacon to the pan, stir in the wine and sage, and bring to a boil over high heat. Reduce the heat to medium, simmer until the wine is reduced to a medium gravy consistency, about 10 minutes, and season with additional salt and pepper as needed.

6. To serve, spoon the beans into individual ramekins or small bowls.

THIS IS A VERY BASIC DISH THAT PAIRS WONDERFULLY IN THE COLD MONTHS WITH MEAT, POULTRY, OR PORK. WHEN I COOKED AT THE HOTEL POST IN NAGOLD, WE SERVED IT FREQUENTLY WITH ROAST PORK (PAGE 43). DESPITE THEIR INHERENT HUMILITY, WE TRANSFORMED THESE BEANS INTO QUITE AN ELEGANT LITTLE SIDE DISH, SERVING THEM IN A RAMEKIN BESIDE A LOVELY SLICE OF PORK.

Serves 4 to 6

¾ pound dried red beans or kidney beans

1 Bouquet Garni (page 80)

1½ teaspoons salt

½ teaspoon freshly ground black pepper

2 slices lean bacon

1 medium yellow onion, peeled and chopped

1 clove garlic, peeled and chopped

1 large carrot, peeled and finely chopped

2 cups full-bodied red wine, such as Burgundy

½ teaspoon dried rubbed sage

Riesling Sauerkraut

SAUERKRAUT MIT RIESLING

W E HAVE NUMEROUS RECIPES FOR SAUERKRAUT IN THE BLACK FOREST, AND HERE IS YET ANOTHER TASTY VERSION. THE COMBINATION OF BACON, CARAWAY SEEDS, AND RIESLING WINE MAKE THIS DISH AT ONCE RICH, ROBUST, AND EARTHY AS WELL AS EVER SO SLIGHTLY FRUITY AND DELICATE. GIVEN THESE LAYERS OF FLAVOR, THIS SAUERKRAUT PAIRS WONDERFULLY WITH GAME DISHES.

Serves 6

3 tablespoons unsalted butter

9 slices lean bacon, finely chopped

2 medium onions, peeled and chopped

1 clove garlic, peeled and chopped

4 cups prepared sauerkraut, rinsed and drained (bagged and refrigerated is best)

1 (750ml) bottle Riesling or other fruity white wine

½ teaspoon caraway seeds

Salt

Freshly ground white pepper

1. Melt the butter in a large saucepan over medium heat, add the bacon, and sauté until crisp, about 3 minutes. Stir in the onions and garlic and sauté until golden brown, about 5 minutes.

2. Stir in the sauerkraut, wine, and caraway seeds and bring to a boil over high heat. Reduce the heat to medium low and simmer until the liquid is reduced by about three-quarters, about 30 minutes.

3. Season with salt and white pepper and serve hot.

CHEF'S NOTE: If you like your sauerkraut on the slightly sweet side, you can make *Ananaskraut* by adding pineapple. Omit the caraway seeds and add about 2 cups of pineapple juice and 1½ cups of chopped pineapple in Step 2.

Rice Pilaf

REIS PILAW

R ICE PILAF IS A STAPLE IN EVERY BLACK FOREST RESTAURANT. IT COMES TOGETHER IN NO TIME, AND ONCE THE INGREDIENTS ARE COMBINED, THE OVEN DOES THE REST OF THE WORK. THE FOLLOWING RECIPE IS TRADITIONAL AND LENDS ITSELF TO A VARIETY OF ADDITIONAL INGREDIENTS. STIR IN SOME PAPRIKA, HERBS, OR PINE NUTS, FOR EXAMPLE. THIS BASIC PILAF PAIRS BEAUTIFULLY WITH JUST ABOUT ANY MEAT OR POULTRY DISH. I PARTICULARLY LIKE IT WITH VEAL FRICASSÉE (PAGE 149).

Serves 6 to 8

2 tablespoons unsalted butter

1 medium onion, peeled and finely chopped

2 ribs celery, finely chopped

1 carrot, peeled and finely chopped

4 white button mushrooms, sliced

2 cups long-grain white rice

1 quart Chicken Stock (page 308)

1 dried bay leaf

1 tablespoon chopped fresh parsley

Salt

Freshly ground white pepper

1. Preheat the oven to 400°F.

2. Melt 1 tablespoon of the butter in a large ovenproof saucepan over medium heat, add the onion, celery, carrot, and mushrooms, and sauté until softened, about 3 to 5 minutes.

3. Stir the rice, stock, bay leaf, parsley, and remaining 1 tablespoon of butter into the sautéed vegetables and season with salt and white pepper. Cover and bake for 40 minutes. Serve hot.

Twice-Cooked Polenta

ZWEIMAL GEBACKENE MAISSCHNITTE

THIS DISH REVEALS THE INFLUENCE OF ITALIAN CUISINE IN BLACK FOREST RESTAURANTS. THIS RECIPE IS A DELICIOUS ADDITION TO ANY STEW OR BRAISED MEAT SERVED WITH LOTS OF DELICIOUS SAUCE. WE EVEN SERVED THIS POLENTA AS A GARNISH FOR GOULASH.

POLENTA COOKED IN THIS MANNER REQUIRES A BIT OF ADVANCED PLANNING, AS IT NEEDS TO CHILL FOR SEVERAL HOURS AND BECOME FIRM BEFORE IT IS CUT INTO SHAPES. I HAVE SUGGESTED FINISHING THE CUT POLENTA IN A SAUTÉ PAN, BUT IF YOU WISH, YOU CAN MAKE THE TASK EVEN EASIER BY BRUSHING THE PIECES WITH BUTTER AND BROWNING THEM IN A HOT OVEN.

Serves 6 to 8

½ cup milk

1 cup Chicken Stock (page 308)

1 tablespoon olive oil

5 tablespoons unsalted butter

2 cups coarse yellow cornmeal

2 tablespoons chopped fresh parsley

½ teaspoon salt

½ teaspoon freshly ground white pepper

---

1. Butter an 11 x 17-inch baking sheet.

2. Combine the milk, stock, oil, and 3 tablespoons of the butter in a medium saucepan and bring to a boil over medium heat. Gradually incorporate the cornmeal, pouring in a steady stream and whisking constantly, and stir in the parsley, salt, and white pepper. Pour the polenta onto the prepared baking sheet, spreading it evenly, and set aside to cool slightly. Cover with plastic wrap and set in the refrigerator to chill and become firm, about 3 to 4 hours.

3. Cut the chilled polenta into desired shapes (cookie cutters are great for this). Melt the remaining 2 tablespoons of butter in a large sauté pan over medium heat, place the polenta pieces in the pan, and cook for about 4 minutes on each side until golden brown.

Salsify Gratin

ÜBERBACKENE SCHWARZWURZEL

SALSIFY IS QUITE POPULAR IN THE BLACK FOREST. THIS ROOT VEG-
ETABLE IS ADMITTEDLY STRANGE LOOKING WITH ITS LONG, SLENDER,
BRANCH-LIKE FORM AND GRAY OR BLACK OUTER SKIN. IT IS CELE-
BRATED FOR ITS DELICATE, SOME SAY OYSTER-LIKE FLAVOR, HOWEVER,
AND IT STORES WELL IN HOME AND RESTAURANT ROOT CELLARS.

THIS CREAMY AND WARMING GRATIN IS TRADITIONALLY PAIRED WITH
SEAFOOD AND VEAL DISHES. LIKE THE VEGETABLE ITSELF, THIS RECIPE IS
DELICATELY FLAVORED. FOR MORE PIZZAZZ, TRY STIRRING IN A BIT IF SAF-
FRON, PAPRIKA, OR DRIED RED PEPPER FLAKES.

---

1. To make the salsify, prepare a steamer. Butter a 9-inch gratin dish or six to eight 6-ounce ramekins.

2. Toss together the salsify and lemon juice in a large bowl, place the salsify in the steamer, and cook until just tender, about 3 minutes. Set aside while preparing the sauce.

3. To make the sauce, melt the butter in a large saucepan over medium heat, add the shallots, and sauté until softened and translucent, about 1 minute. Whisk in the flour to form a roux, stir in the wine and cream, and simmer until the sauce is thickened and slightly reduced, about 3 to 5 minutes. Stir in the nutmeg and season with salt and white pepper.

4. To assemble the dish, preheat the broiler. Add the salsify to the sauce, gently mixing to coat, and pour into the prepared gratin dish or indi-vidual ramekins. Sprinkle with Parmesan cheese, set under the broiler until golden and bubbly, and serve hot.

Serves 6 to 8

SALSIFY:

2½ pounds salsify, stemmed, peeled,
   and cut on the diagonal into 2-inch pieces

Juice of 1 lemon

SAUCE:

3 tablespoons unsalted butter

3 medium shallots, peeled and finely chopped

3 heaping tablespoons all-purpose flour

1 cup dry white wine, such as Sauvignon Blanc

1 cup heavy cream

⅛ teaspoon freshly grated nutmeg

Salt

Freshly ground white pepper

ASSEMBLY:

½ cup grated Parmesan cheese

Macaire Potatoes

MACAIRE KARTOFFEL

Here is yet another of the many potato side dishes I served in hotel restaurants. This version is based on the classic French recipe rich with egg yolks and lightly seasoned with nutmeg.

We usually served these potato cakes with the special of the day, but they are delicious with virtually any entrée.

1. Preheat the oven to 350°F.

2. Place the potatoes in a large saucepan filled with lightly salted water, bring to a boil over high heat, and boil until the potatoes are just tender, about 15 minutes. Drain the potatoes, place on a baking sheet, and set in the oven to dry further, about 5 minutes. Set the potatoes aside to cool slightly.

3. Push the potatoes through a potato ricer or food mill into a large bowl, add the egg yolks, salt, pepper, nutmeg, bacon, and chives, and mix thoroughly to combine.

4. Using slightly wet hands, shape the potatoes into cakes about 3 inches in diameter and $1/2$ inch thick. Arrange the cakes on a parchment-lined baking sheet coated with vegetable spray and bake until golden brown, about 15 minutes.

Serves 8

8 large Yukon gold potatoes, peeled

4 egg yolks

1 teaspoon salt

$1/2$ teaspoon freshly ground white pepper

$1/8$ teaspoon freshly grated nutmeg

4 slices bacon, cooked and finely chopped

1 tablespoon finely chopped chives

Ratatouille

GEMÜSE KASSEROLLE

RATATOUILLE IS YET ANOTHER SIDE DISH INSPIRED BY THE INGREDIENTS AND COOKING TECHNIQUES OF PROVENCE. EGGPLANT AND SQUASH ARE INTEGRAL TO THE RECIPE, BUT COOKS PERSONALIZE THE DISH BY ADDING A VARIETY OF OTHER VEGETABLES. TOMATOES AND BELL PEPPERS ARE FLAVORFUL ADDITIONS, AS ARE BLACK OLIVES, ESPECIALLY IF YOU WOULD LIKE TO GIVE THE RATATOUILLE A PARTICULARLY NIÇOISE CHARACTER.

1. Heat the oil in a large sauté pan over medium heat, add the garlic, and sauté until lightly browned, about 1½ minutes. Stir in the onion and peppers and sauté until softened, about 1½ minutes.

2. Toss in the eggplant and squash and stir in the tomato paste. Raise the heat to high, bring to a boil, and boil for about 5 to 8 minutes, stirring frequently.

3. Add the tomatoes, cook for 1 minute more, and season with salt and white pepper.

Serves 6 to 8

¼ cup olive oil

3 cloves garlic, peeled and finely chopped

1 onion, peeled and chopped

2 red bell peppers, cored, seeded, and chopped

1 large eggplant, trimmed and chopped

1 yellow squash, trimmed and chopped

1 cup tomato paste

2 tomatoes, cored, seeded, and chopped

Salt

Freshly ground white pepper

CHEF'S NOTE: This ratatouille is also delicious served chilled as a salad. To add a bit of extra flavor, dress it with a vinaigrette prepared with ½ cup olive oil and ¼ cup balsamic vinegar. Serve this salad with a bit of crunchy Black Forest Cracker Bread (page 182) on the side.

Plum Tart

ZWETSCHGENKUCHEN

THIS TART IS ONE OF THE MOST TRADITIONAL AND LOVED IN THE BLACK FOREST. WE ALWAYS PREPARE IT WITH **ZWETSCHGE** PLUMS—A FIRM, DARK-PURPLE-SKINNED VARIETY WITH GOLDEN YELLOW FLESH. THEY HAVE A LONG GROWING SEASON, WHICH EXTENDS FROM THE SPRING THROUGH THE FALL, BUT THOSE AVAILABLE IN LATE SEPTEMBER, AT THE END OF THE SEASON, ARE MOST HIGHLY PRIZED. AT THAT TIME, WHEN THE AIR BECOMES CRISP AND COOL, HOME COOKS AND RESTAURANT CHEFS ALIKE GLADLY BAKE MANY OF THESE SWEET AND PRETTY TARTS.

THIS RECIPE IS STRAIGHTFORWARD AND DELICIOUS. THE ONLY DIFFICULTY YOU MIGHT ENCOUNTER IS FINDING ZWETSCHGE PLUMS, ALSO KNOWN AS QUETSCH PLUMS. IF THIS IS THE CASE, I SUGGEST YOU USE A FIRM PLUM LIKE SANTA ROSA, OR, IF YOU FIND THE PLUMS AVAILABLE TO YOU TO BE QUITE JUICY, SIMPLY INCREASE THE AMOUNT OF BREAD OR CAKE CRUMBS TO SOAK UP SOME OF THE JUICE.

FOLKS IN THE BLACK FOREST COMMONLY ORDER THIS TART WITH A WARMING BOWL OF SOUP. IT IS DELICIOUS AS A SNACK OR DESSERT AND PAIRS WONDERFULLY WITH A DOLLOP OF WHIPPED CREAM.

Makes one 11 x 17-inch Tart

1 pound Pâte Sucrée (page 315)

2 cups dry bread or cake crumbs

3 pounds ripe plums, pitted and quartered lengthwise

½ cup sugar

3 tablespoons ground cinnamon

1 cup slivered almonds

1. Preheat the oven to 375°F. and butter an 11 x 17-inch baking sheet.

2. Lightly flour a work surface and roll the pâte sucrée into a rectangle about ¼ inch thick and about 1½ inches longer and wider than the baking sheet. Place the pastry on the baking sheet, gently pressing into the sides, fold over the edges, and crimp decoratively.

3. Sprinkle the bread crumbs evenly over the pastry and arrange the plum quarters in rows, standing upright, on top.

4. Stir together the sugar and cinnamon in a small bowl and sprinkle evenly over the plums. Sprinkle with almonds and bake until the pastry is golden brown and the plums are softened and caramelized, about 20 to 30 minutes. Set on a rack to cool before serving.

Vacherin Glacé

WILDBADER MERINGEN

Serves 8

MERINGUES:

4 large egg whites

1 tablespoon cream of tartar

¾ cup granulated sugar

1 cup confectioners' sugar, sifted

Zest of 1 orange, finely chopped

ASSEMBLY:

About 4 cups vanilla ice cream

2 cups heavy cream

¼ cup sugar

About 1 cup chopped hazelnuts

1. At least 8 hours or the day before serving the meringues, pre-heat the oven to 150°F. and line a large baking sheet with parchment paper.

2. To make the meringues, combine the egg whites and cream of tartar in the bowl of an electric mixer fitted with the whisk attachment and whip on high speed to soft peaks. Reduce the mixing speed to medium, slowly incorporate the granulated sugar, and continue whipping the meringue to stiff peaks.

3. Remove the meringue from the mixer and, using a spatula, gently fold in the confectioners' sugar and orange zest.

4. Fit a large pastry bag with a #16 straight tip, fill about half full with meringue, and pipe into 2-inch circles onto the prepared baking sheet (images a–f). Bake the meringues for about 8 hours or overnight. (It is best if the meringues remain white, although they easily color, even in a low oven.)

5. Remove the meringues from the oven and set them aside to cool to room temperature.

6. To assemble the meringues, begin by spooning about ½ cup of ice cream onto one meringue circle (image g). Place another meringue circle on top (image h). Repeat the process to create eight meringue sandwiches, set them on a baking sheet, and freeze until firm, about 30 minutes. (You might want to set each finished sandwich directly in the freezer while you complete the rest.)

7. Combine the cream and sugar in the bowl of an electric mixer fitted with the whisk attachment and whip on medium-high speed to firm peaks. Transfer the whipped cream to a pastry bag fitted with a straight tip. (Fill the bag about half full and refill as needed.)

8. Pipe the whipped cream around the edge of each sandwich, smooth the edge with a knife or flat spatula (image i), and roll in the chopped hazelnuts (images j–k). Serve immediately.

VACHERINS (BASICALLY MERINGUE "CONTAINERS") TAKE MANY FORMS, AND THIS IS ONE WE SERVED OFTEN AT THE SOMMERBERG HOTEL. SOMETIMES WE FILLED THE MERINGUES WITH STRAWBERRY ICE CREAM, BUT VANILLA, WHICH I SUGGEST HERE, WAS QUITE POPULAR, TOO. ROLLING THE EDGES OF THE VACHERINS IN HAZELNUTS CREATES A LOVELY PRESENTATION AND ADDS GREAT FLAVOR. HOWEVER, IT IS PERFECTLY RESPECTABLE TO TAKE A SIMPLER APPROACH, AND OMIT THEM.

VACHERIN GLACÉ

To make the meringues, trace 2-inch circles onto parchment paper, then fill in with meringue piping with a #16 straight tip. Once the meringues are baked and cooled, assemble them into ice cream sandwiches. Fill in the sides with whipped cream and dip in hazelnuts.

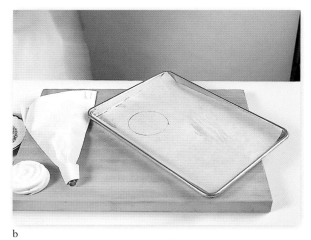

a

c

b

d

e

f

i

g

j

h

k

273

Poached Pears

POCHIERTE BIRNEN

1. Stir together the wine, sugar, cinnamon sticks, cloves, and vanilla bean in a large saucepan and bring to a boil over medium-high heat. Reduce the heat to low and maintain the poaching liquid at a gentle simmer.

2. Drop the pears into the poaching liquid, place a plate or piece of cheesecloth overtop to keep them submerged, and simmer until a paring knife easily pierces the bases (the thickest part) of the pears, about 15 to 20 minutes. (Be careful not to overcook the pears or they will become mushy.)

3. Prepare a large bowl with ice water. Remove the pears from the poaching liquid using a slotted spoon and place immediately in the ice water to cool. Drain the cooled pears and set aside to warm to room temperature.

4. To make the sabayon, prepare a double boiler, making sure the water doesn't touch the top portion, and maintain at a simmer. Whisk together the egg yolks, sugar, and Port in the top portion and continue to whisk vigorously until thickened and foamy, about 5 minutes. (To prevent the eggs from scrambling, constantly whisk the sabayon and remove the top portion of the double boiler once or twice if it appears to be cooking too quickly.)

5. To serve, stand each pear in the center of a dessert plate, trimming the bases, if necessary. Drizzle with sabayon and garnish with a cinnamon stick.

THIS CLASSIC DESSERT IS TRULY ELEGANT IN ITS SIMPLICITY. IN ADDITION TO PEARS, WE LIKE TO POACH A VARIETY OF FRUIT IN THE BLACK FOREST, INCLUDING APPLES AND PLUMS. I HAVE CHOSEN TO ACCOMPANY THE PEARS WITH SABAYON—A FRENCH TERM FOR THE CLASSIC ITALIAN DESSERT KNOWN AS ZABAGLIONE. THIS FROTHY WHIPPED CUSTARD OF EGG YOLKS AND SUGAR IS TRADITIONALLY FLAVORED WITH MARSALA, BUT I HAVE SUBSTITUTED PORT IN THIS RECIPE. THIS RICH, DARK FORTIFIED WINE ADDS A SMOKY SWEETNESS TO THE SABAYON AND WONDERFULLY COMPLEMENTS THE SPICY, RED WINE-INFUSED PEARS.

Serves 4

PEARS:

3 cups full-bodied red wine, such as Burgundy

¾ cup sugar

2 sticks cinnamon

1 tablespoon whole cloves

1 vanilla bean

4 firm Bosc pears, peeled and stems on

PORT SABAYON:

8 egg yolks

¼ cup sugar

⅓ cup Port

4 sticks cinnamon, for garnish

Crème Brûlée

1. Place the cream in a large saucepan. Carefully scrape the seeds from the vanilla bean using a paring knife, add the bean and seeds to the milk, and bring to a boil over medium-high heat.

2. Meanwhile, whisk together the sugar, egg yolks, and egg in a medium bowl.

3. Lift the vanilla bean out of the boiling cream, remove from the heat, and gradually whisk the cream into the eggs and sugar, about $1/3$ cup at a time. Strain through a fine mesh strainer and set in a large bowl of ice water to cool quickly. Place the custard in the refrigerator and chill for at least 2 hours.

3. Preheat the oven to 300°F.

4. Gently stir the custard to evenly distribute the vanilla seeds. Pour the custard into eight 8-ounce ramekins and arrange in a medium roasting pan. Fill the pan with hot water (creating a water bath) so that the water reaches about halfway up the sides of the ramekins. Carefully transfer the pan to the oven and bake until the custard is just set, about 25 minutes. Set the roasting pan on a rack and leave the custards in the water bath to cool completely. Remove the ramekins to the refrigerator and chill for 1 hour.

5. To assemble, preheat the broiler or ready a blowtorch. Sprinkle the custards with sugar, moving and shaking the ramekins to evenly coat. Place under the broiler or use the blowtorch to caramelize the sugar until golden brown and bubbly. (The sugar will brown and burn easily, so keep a watchful eye.)

6. Serve the crèmes brûlées immediately, garnished with berries, if desired.

CRÈME BRÛLÉE IS A CLASSIC FRENCH DESSERT THAT REQUIRES LITTLE INTRODUCTION. THIS RECIPE IS SIMPLE AND TRADITIONAL AND RELIES ON ONLY SEVERAL INGREDIENTS, FRESH CREAM, EGGS, VANILLA, AND SUGAR, WHICH WHEN COOKED GENTLY TOGETHER CREATE A VELVETY CUSTARD. THE CRISP, CARAMELIZED SUGAR ON TOP IS THE PERFECT FINISH TO THIS PERFECT DESSERT.

Serves 8

$1\frac{1}{2}$ quarts heavy cream

1 vanilla bean, split lengthwise

1 cup sugar

10 large egg yolks

1 large egg

Assembly:

$1/4$ sugar

Assorted berries, for garnish (optional)

Grand Marnier
Chocolate Mousse Cake

SCHOKOLADE & GRAND MARNIER TORTE

CHOCOLATE IN EVERY FORM IS POPULAR IN THE BLACK FOREST. FROM MOUSSE, TO CAKE, TO GANACHE, TO SAUCE, CHOCOLATE DESSERTS RANK QUITE HIGH ON RESTAURANT DESSERT MENUS. THIS RICH CAKE IS NOT ONLY DELICIOUS, BUT ALSO SATISFYING DUE TO ITS TEXTURAL VARIETY. IN ADDITION, THE GRAND MARNIER IN THE MOUSSE ADDS A DELIGHTFUL HINT OF SPICY ORANGE—A NATURAL COMPLEMENT TO CHOCOLATE. IN THE BLACK FOREST, WE ASSEMBLE THIS CAKE IN A VARIETY OF SHAPES AND SIZES. IT MAKES A LOVELY LARGE CAKE, AS I SUGGEST HERE, AS WELL AS SMALL INDIVIDUAL CAKES AND NAPOLEONS.

Makes two 9-inch cakes

CAKE:

5 cups cake flour

$\frac{1}{4}$ cup unsweetened Dutch-processed cocoa powder

2 teaspoons baking soda

$\frac{1}{2}$ teaspoon salt

$\frac{1}{2}$ pound (2 sticks) unsalted butter, at room temperature

2 cups sugar

4 large eggs

1 cup whole milk

MOUSSE:

4 ounces semisweet chocolate, chopped

4 large eggs, separated

$\frac{1}{2}$ cup heavy cream

3 tablespoons Grand Marnier

GANACHE:

2 cups heavy cream

24 ounces semisweet chocolate, chopped

Candied flowers or chopped nuts, for garnish (optional)

1. Preheat the oven to 350°F. Butter two 9-inch round cake pans and line the bottoms with 9-inch parchment-paper circles.

2. To make the cake, sift together the flour, cocoa powder, baking soda, and salt into a large bowl.

3. Place the butter in the bowl of an electric mixer fitted with the paddle attachment and begin mixing on medium-high speed. Gradually add the sugar and continue mixing until light and fluffy, stopping occasionally to scrape the sides of the bowl. Incorporate the eggs one at a time, stopping again to scrape the sides of the bowl. Reduce the mixing speed to low and alternately incorporate the sifted dry ingredients and the milk, beginning and ending with the dry ingredients. Mix until just combined, stopping several times to scrape the sides of the bowl.

4. Divide the batter between the two pans and bake until a skewer inserted in the centers comes out clean, about 30 to 35 minutes. Place the cakes on wire racks to cool for about 10 minutes. Turn the cakes out of the pans and cool completely.

5. To make the mousse, prepare a double boiler, making sure the water doesn't touch the top portion, and maintain at a simmer. Place the chocolate in the top portion of the double boiler and stir occasionally until melted and smooth. Remove the chocolate from heat and set aside for several minutes to cool slightly. Whisk in the egg yolks and set aside to cool to room temperature.

6. Place the cream in the bowl of an electric mixer fitted with the whisk attachment and whip on medium speed to soft peaks. Set aside momentarily.

7. Place the egg whites in the bowl of an electric mixer fitted with the whisk attachment and whip on medium speed to soft peaks.

8. Gently fold the whipped cream into the cooled chocolate until just incorporated. Add the egg whites and Grand Marnier, again folding gently until just combined. Cover the mousse with plastic wrap and set in the refrigerator for at least 1 hour.

9. To make the ganache, bring the cream to a boil in a medium saucepan over medium-high heat. Remove from the heat and add the chocolate, whisking gently until melted and smooth. Set aside to cool to room temperature, cover with plastic wrap, and refrigerate for about 30 minutes.

10. To assemble the cake, place the cooled ganache in the bowl of an electric mixer fitted with the paddle attachment and beat on medium-high speed until smooth and creamy. (If the ganache is very cold and firm, warm it to room temperature before beating in the mixer.) Slice each cake in half horizontally using a serrated knife. Place one of the rounds on a cake plate, spread with one-third of the mousse, and top with another slice of cake. Continue layering two more times, finishing with a round of cake. Frost the cake with ganache and refrigerate until ready to serve.

11. Serve garnished with sugared flowers or chopped nuts, if desired.

Coconut Macaroons

KOKOSNUß GEBÄCK

1. Preheat the oven to 425°F. Line two baking sheets with parchment paper and fit a pastry bag with a #16 star tip.

2. Stir together the honey, lime juice, and zest in a small bowl.

3. Place the egg whites in the bowl of an electric mixer fitted with the whisk attachment and whip on medium speed until foamy. Gradually incorporate the sugar, increase the mixing speed to high, and whip the meringue to medium-stiff peaks. Reduce the mixing speed again to medium and incorporate the lime honey. Increase the mixing speed to high and whip to stiff peaks.

4. Remove the meringue from the mixer and fold in the toasted coconut. Fill the prepared pastry bag half-full with the coconut meringue and pipe 1-inch-round rosettes about 2 inches apart onto the prepared baking sheets. (You can also drop spoonfuls of the meringue onto the baking sheet.)

5. Place the baking sheet in the oven and immediately reduce the temperature to 350°F. Bake until the macaroons are light golden brown, about 7 to 10 minutes. Set on wire racks and cool the macaroons completely on the baking sheets before removing and storing in air-tight containers.

THESE MACAROONS ARE POPULAR THROUGHOUT THE BLACK FOREST. A LOVELY COMBINATION OF HONEY, LIME, AND COCONUT, THEY ARE DELICATELY SWEET, SLIGHTLY CHEWY, AND PERFECT WITH A CUP OF AFTERNOON TEA OR SERVED AS PART OF AN ELEGANT PETIT FOUR OR COOKIE DISPLAY, AS ON PAGE 289.

Makes 2 dozen macaroons

2 tablespoons honey

Juice and finely chopped zest of 2 limes

6 large egg whites, at room temperature

⅛ teaspoon salt

1 cup sugar

2 cups grated unsweetened coconut, toasted (*see Chef's Note*, page 72)

Chocolate Soufflé

SCHOKOLADE SOUFFLÉ

Serves 6

CHOCOLATE BASE:

2 cups half-and-half

6 ounces semisweet chocolate, chopped

4 egg yolks, divided

2 eggs

¼ cup all-purpose flour

¼ cup cornstarch

¼ cup granulated sugar

MERINGUE:

4 egg whites

4 tablespoons sugar

⅛ teaspoon cream of tartar

2 tablespoons cornstarch

Crème Anglaise (recipe follows), for serving

1. Preheat oven to 375°F.

2. To make the chocolate base, bring the half-and-half to a boil over medium heat in a large saucepan. Remove from the heat, whisk in the chocolate and 2 egg yolks (image a), and set aside to cool to room temperature.

3. Beat the eggs and remaining 2 egg yolks in a medium bowl (image b). Whisk in the flour, cornstarch, and sugar, mixing until smooth (image c). Remove the cream from the heat, and drizzle about ⅓ cup of the hot half-and-half into the egg mixture, whisking constantly. Gradually pour the cream and egg mixture back into the saucepan of half-and-half, stirring constantly. Set over medium-low heat, stirring constantly (image d), and cook until thickened. Set aside to cool to room temperature.

4. To make the meringue, place the egg whites in the bowl of an electric mixer fitted with the whisk attachment, and whip on high speed until frothy. Gradually add the sugar and cream of tartar, and whip to soft peaks. Sprinkle in the cornstarch, and whip for about 20 seconds more until just incorporated (image e).

5 To assemble the soufflés, butter and sugar six 4½-ounce ramekins, tapping to remove any excess, and arrange on a baking sheet. Add about one-quarter of the meringue to the chocolate base and mix to combine. Add the remaining meringue, this time folding carefully until just incorporated (image f). Divide among the ramekins, filling to about ½ inch from the rim (image g), and bake until puffed, about 20 minutes.

6. Serve immediately with Crème Anglaise (recipe follows).

Chocolate soufflé is another favorite in the Black Forest thanks to the culinary influence of France. Soufflés can be intimidating, but I highly recommend you try this recipe. I have used it again and again and have found it to be very reliable. The sugar, cream of tartar, and cornstarch in the meringue make the batter a bit sturdier, thus ensuring that these charming individual soufflés will remain puffed and gorgeous as you transport them from the oven to the table.

CHOCOLATE SOUFFLÉ

Whisk chocolate into hot half-and-half. Separately beat eggs and remaining egg yolks, then whisk in flour, cornstarch, and sugar. Temper eggs with half-and-half, then pour cream and egg mixture back into saucepan of half-and-half, stirring constantly. Cook until thickened, then cool to room temperature. For meringue, whip egg whites on high speed until frothy. Add sugar and cream of tartar and whip to soft peaks. Sprinkle in cornstarch and whip until just incorporated. Add meringue to chocolate base and mix to combine. Fill ramekins and bake until puffed.

b

c

a

d

e

f

g

Crème Anglaise

Makes 1½ cups

2 cups milk

1 vanilla bean, split

¼ cup sugar

4 large egg yolks

2 tablespoons brandy or Cognac

1. Place the milk in a medium saucepan. Carefully scrape the seeds from vanilla bean using a paring knife, add the bean and seeds to the milk, and bring to a boil over medium-high heat.

2. Meanwhile, whisk together the sugar, egg yolks, and brandy in a medium bowl.

3. Lift the vanilla bean out of the boiling milk, remove from the heat, and gradually whisk the milk into the eggs and sugar, about ⅓ cup at a time. Strain through a fine mesh strainer and set in a large bowl of ice water to cool quickly. (The crème anglaise will keep fresh sealed in an airtight container and stored in the refrigerator for up to 5 days.)

RICE DESSERTS ARE VERY POPULAR IN THE BLACK FOREST. THERE ARE MANY VARIETIES, RANGING FROM MODEST, COMFORTING PUD-DINGS TO ELEGANT, MOLDED PRESENTATIONS COMPOSED OF FRENCH CUSTARDS AND FRUIT.

THIS RECIPE IS A DELICIOUS COMBINATION OF TRADITIONAL, CREAMY RICE PUDDING AND LIGHT, SLIGHTLY CARAMELIZED MERINGUE. ENJOYED WARM RIGHT OUT OF THE OVEN, AT ROOM TEMPERATURE, OR CHILLED, THIS DESSERT IS AT ONCE COMFORTING AND ELEGANT.

Rice Pudding with Meringue

SÜßER REISBERG

Serves 6

RICE PUDDING:

2 cups water

¾ cup uncooked long-grain white rice

2½ cups whole milk

½ cup sugar

3 large eggs

1½ tablespoons unsalted butter, melted

2 teaspoons vanilla extract

1½ teaspoons ground cinnamon

MERINGUE:

4 large egg whites

1 tablespoon cream of tartar

¾ cup granulated sugar

1 cup confectioners' sugar, sifted

1. Preheat oven to 325°F. and butter a 1½-quart casserole dish.

2. To make the rice pudding, bring the water to a boil in a medium saucepan over high heat and stir in the rice. Reduce the heat to low, cover the pan, and simmer until the liquid is reduced by about two-thirds and the rice is cooked to al dente, about 10 minutes. Remove from the heat and let stand, covered, for about 5 minutes.

3. In another medium saucepan, bring the milk to a boil over high heat. Stir in the rice and any residual cooking water, reduce the heat to medium, and simmer until the rice is fully cooked, about 10 minutes.

4. Meanwhile, whisk together the sugar, eggs, butter, vanilla, and cinnamon in a large bowl.

5. Gradually stir the cooked rice into the egg mixture and pour the pudding into the prepared casserole, spreading it evenly. Set the casserole in a large roasting pan or casserole and make a water bath by pouring boiling water into the larger pan so that it comes about halfway up the sides of the pudding. Cover the pudding with foil and carefully transfer the pans to the oven, baking for 20 to 30 minutes, or until a knife inserted in the center comes out clean.

6. To make the meringue, combine the egg whites and cream of tartar in the bowl of an electric mixer fitted with the whisk attachment and whip on high speed to form soft peaks. Reduce the mixing speed to medium, gradually add the granulated sugar, and whip to form stiff peaks. Remove the meringue from the mixer and, using a spatula, gradually fold in the confectioners' sugar.

7. Carefully lift the finished rice pudding out of the water bath and remove the foil. Spread the meringue evenly over the top of the pudding, return the casserole to the oven (without the water bath), and bake until the meringue is golden brown, about 15 to 25 minutes.

8. Serve the pudding warm, at room temperature, or chilled.

Financiers

COOKS WHO LEAVE THE BLACK FOREST TO APPRENTICE IN FRANCE OFTEN RETURN HOME WITH AN EXTENSIVE REPERTOIRE OF FRENCH RECIPES. INCLUDED IN THEIR PASTRY NOTES IS ALMOST ALWAYS AT LEAST ONE RECIPE FOR FINANCIERS—LITTLE SPONGE CAKES PREPARED WITH GROUND ALMONDS AND SERVED PLAIN OR DECORATED AS PETITS FOURS. THIS VERSION IS BASED ON A CLASSIC RECIPE, BUT I HAVE INCLUDED SOME ORANGE ZEST, ORANGE LIQUEUR, AND NUTMEG TO ADD A BIT OF SPICE TO THE MILD ALMOND CAKE.

TRADITIONAL OVAL AND RECTANGULAR FINANCIER PANS ARE AVAILABLE IN SPECIALTY KITCHEN AND BAKING STORES, BUT YOU CAN ALSO SIMPLY SUBSTITUTE MINI-MUFFIN PANS, WHICH WORK JUST AS WELL.

Makes 2 dozen financiers

6 tablespoons unsalted butter, cubed

2 tablespoons vanilla extract

2 tablespoons orange liqueur, such as Cointreau or Triple Sec

1 cup sliced almonds, toasted (*see Chef's Note*, page 165)

1 cup all-purpose flour

1⅔ cups sugar

Zest of 1 orange

⅛ teaspoon freshly grated nutmeg

5 large egg whites

⅛ teaspoon salt

1. Prepare an ice bath. Melt the butter in a small saucepan over medium-low heat, cooking until dark golden brown. Remove from the heat and set the pan directly in the ice bath to cool quickly and stop the cooking. Cool for about 1 minute and stir in the vanilla and orange liqueur. Continue to chill the browned butter in the ice bath, stirring occasionally, remove from the ice bath, and set aside at room temperature.

2. Combine the almonds, flour, 1 cup of the sugar, orange zest, and nutmeg in the bowl of a food processor fitted with the blade attachment and process until the almonds are finely ground and the mixture is powdery. Remove to a medium bowl and set aside.

3. Place the egg whites and salt in the bowl of an electric mixer fitted with the whisk attachment and whip on medium speed until foamy. Gradually incorporate the remaining ⅔ cup sugar, increase the mixing speed to high, and whip the meringue to medium-stiff peaks. Remove the meringue to a large bowl.

4. To assemble the financiers, fold about one-quarter of the almond flour into the meringue, followed by about one-third of the cooled browned butter. Continue this process until the batter is smooth. Set in the refrigerator for about 2 hours.

5. Meanwhile, butter and flour a 24-cup mini-muffin or financier pan and refrigerate until the butter is firm.

6. Preheat the oven to 425°F.

7. Fill each cup of the prepared mini-muffin or financier pan half-full with the chilled batter, place in the oven, and immediately reduce the temperature to 375°F. Bake until the financiers are golden, about 7 minutes. Set on wire racks to cool the financiers for several minutes in the pan and turn out to cool completely.

COCONUT MACAROONS (PAGE 281), FINANCIERS, AND PISTACHIO CRESCENTS (PAGE 290)
MAKE A BEAUTIFUL AND DELECTABLE COOKIE TRAY.

Pistachio Crescents

HALBMOND GEBÄCK MIT PISTAZIENNUß

I LEARNED TO MAKE THESE COOKIES AS AN APPRENTICE AT THE HOTEL POST IN NAGOLD. ENRICHED AND FLAVORED WITH PISTACHIOS, THESE BUTTERY, DELICATE CRESCENTS GIVE A NOD TO ITALIANS' FONDNESS FOR THE MEATY GREEN NUT.

THIS RECIPE COMES TOGETHER VERY EASILY. JUST KEEP IN MIND THAT THE DOUGH IS QUITE SOFT AND NEEDS TO BE CHILLED FOR AT LEAST A COUPLE HOURS BEFORE SHAPING THE CRESCENTS. IF, AS YOU ARE WORKING WITH IT, IT BECOMES TOO WARM AND SOFT, SIMPLY RETURN IT TO THE REFRIGERATOR TO CHILL FOR A FEW MINUTES.

Makes 32 crescents

½ cup shelled pistachio nuts, toasted (*see Chef's Note*, page 165)

1¾ cup plus 2 tablespoons all-purpose flour

1 vanilla bean, split lengthwise

4 cups confectioners' sugar

½ pound (2 sticks) unsalted butter, at room temperature

3 large egg yolks

1. Combine the pistachios and 2 tablespoons of the flour in the bowl of a food processor fitted with the blade attachment and process until the nuts are finely ground. Remove to a small bowl.

2. Carefully scrape the seeds from vanilla bean using a paring knife. Stir together the seeds and ¾ cup of the confectioners' sugar in a small bowl.

3. Combine the butter and vanilla sugar in the bowl of an electric mixer fitted with the paddle attachment and mix on medium speed until smooth, stopping to scrape the sides of the bowl. Incorporate the egg yolks one at a time, stopping again once or twice to scrape the sides of the bowl. Reduce the mixing speed to low and gradually incorporate the remaining 1¾ cup flour and ground pistachios, mixing until just combined.

5. Remove the dough to a lightly floured work surface and knead several times until smooth. Roll the dough into three logs about 1 inch wide and 12 inches long, wrap in plastic wrap, and set in the refrigerator to chill for 2 hours.

6. Meanwhile, line two baking sheets with parchment paper.

7. Place the chilled dough on a lightly floured work surface and slice into 2-inch pieces. Roll each piece into a cylinder, tapering the ends, and curve into a half-moon shape (crescent). (If the dough becomes too soft, set in the refrigerator for several minutes to firm slightly. Avoid using too much flour when rolling the dough to prevent the cookies from becoming tough and dry.) Arrange the crescents about 1 inch apart on the prepared baking sheets and set in the refrigerator to chill for about 30 minutes.

8. Preheat the oven to 350°F.

9. Bake the chilled crescents until light golden brown, about 8 minutes. Set on wire racks to cool on the baking sheets for about 2 minutes.

10. Place the remaining confectioners' sugar in a medium bowl. While still warm, toss the crescents one or two at a time in the sugar, coating them well. Set on wire racks to cool completely and toss again in sugar before serving or storing in airtight containers.

BLACK FOREST
FOREST
A CELEBRATIONS

Carnival

FASTNACHT

To this day, when I think about Faschingszeit, or the days of carnival, one memory rises above the rest—the aroma of hot oil and fresh beignets, just out of the frying pan. My mother prepared great piles of these yeast-dough pastries on the days leading towards Faschingsdienstag (Shrove Tuesday), and we ate them in abundance sprinkled with powdery confectioner's

Chimney Sweeps
A Burgeoning Chef

sugar, coated with spicy cinnamon sugar, or filled with homemade jam. Beignets are similar to donuts. The risen dough is cut into rounds or diamonds and then fried in vegetable oil or lard, creating a dark crust and tender inner crumb.

Beignets are traditional *Fastnacht* (Shrovetide) confections and for good reason. Like Mardi Gras, Faschingsdienstag represents the last day of feasting on the Christian calendar before Lent begins on Ash Wednesday the next day. Rich, delicious beignets are perfect for this festive time of year when *Fastnachtspielen* (Shrovetide plays) and *Fastnachtsumzugen* (Shrove Tuesday processions) abound in Black Forest towns. Although food played a significant role at these events, we kept things fairly simple at home. My mother was busy with a variety of preparations, and she always spent a lot of time making the costumes my brother, sister, and I wore to carnival festivities. **I STILL REMEMBER BEING FOUR YEARS OLD AND TELLING HER I WANTED TO DRESS UP LIKE A CHEF. I WAS THRILLED ON CARNIVAL DAY TO WEAR MY LITTLE CHEF'S JACKET AND HAT. MY MOTHER EVEN ALLOWED ME TO CARRY MY GREAT GRANDMOTHER'S QUARTER-LITER MEASURING CUP FOR ADDED EFFECT.** Amidst the fun and excitement, it was easy to grab a beignet or two (or three!) as we rushed out the door to a party or parade.

Of course, my mother prepared other dishes as well, but kept them simple due to the hectic holiday schedule. She often served Knockwurst with Potato Salad during these busy days. When I grew a little older, I remember she prepared other easy one-pot-meals such as Puszta Stew and Goulash Stew—dishes that required little attention and happily simmered away on the stove while we were running about.

Whether you wait to make beignets for Shrovetide, or prepare them whenever you have a hankering for a delicious homemade pastry, I hope you will try this recipe. When I smell freshly fried beignets, many wonderful memories come flooding back to me. If you're lucky, maybe they will become part of your traditions and future food memories, too.

292

Beignets

FASTNACHTSKÜCHLE

1. Whisk together the yeast, sugar, milk, and salt in the bowl of an electric mixer. Fit the mixer with the dough hook attachment and begin mixing on low speed. Add 2½ cups of the flour, increase the speed to medium, and continue to mix until combined, about 2 minutes. Remove the bowl from the mixer, cover with a kitchen towel, and set aside in a warm area for about 30 minutes.

2. Return the bowl of dough to the electric mixer again fitted with the dough hook attachment. Mixing on low speed, add the remaining flour, mixing until incorporated. Add the eggs and butter, increase the speed to medium, and mix until smooth, about 3 minutes. (The dough will appear quite wet.)

3. Turn the dough out onto a floured work surface. Roll to ⅛ inch thick and cut into 2½-inch rounds or diamonds, using a floured cookie cutter or knife.

4. Heat the oil in a large saucepan over medium heat to 375°F., or until it appears to shimmer on the surface. Carefully drop 4 to 5 pieces of the dough one at a time into the oil and fry until puffed and golden brown, about 5 to 7 minutes. Remove the beignets with a skimmer or slotted spoon and set on paper towels to drain.

5. Liberally sprinkle the beignets while still warm with cinnamon sugar and serve immediately.

Makes 30

1 tablespoon active dry yeast

¼ cup sugar

1 cup milk

1 teaspoon salt

3¾ cups all-purpose flour

2 eggs

5 tablespoons unsalted butter, melted

1 quart vegetable oil, for frying

Cinnamon sugar, for serving

Spargelzeit

ASPARAGUS FESTIVAL

I N THE BLACK FOREST, FOOD NOT ONLY PLAYS A SIGNIFICANT ROLE IN CELEBRATIONS, BUT IN MANY CASES, FESTIVITIES EXIST SPECIFICALLY TO PAY HOMAGE TO CERTAIN FOODS. *SPARGELZEIT*, THE ANNUAL SPRING asparagus fest, is one such event. Every year, Germans eagerly anticipate this celebration showcasing the country's "king of vegetables." Not all asparagus is featured here—just the tender white variety. It is attentively grown under the sandy soil to shield it from the sun and prevent it from turning green, and the growing conditions in the Black Forest are considered the best in Germany for cultivating the lily-white stalks.

Spargelzeit begins in mid-April, after the first crop of asparagus is harvested, and continues until the Feast of John the Baptist on June 24. For these two months, all of Germany turns its attention to the vegetable. It is in the Black Forest, though, where most of the festive events take place. So much asparagus is grown in the region that the top producing towns of Schwetzingen, Reilingen, Karlsruhe, and Rastatt are connected by what is known as "Asparagus Road." During

Spargelmenu

APPETIZER

SMOKED TROUT & ASPARAGUS SALAD

ENTRÉE

POACHED WHITE ASPARAGUS
Hollandaise Sauce, Sauce Malta, Drawn Butter

BOILED NEW POTATOES

BLACK FOREST HAM

MEDALLIONS OF BEEF À LA
CAFÉ DE PARIS

POACHED SALMON WITH DILL CREAM SAUCE

Smoked Trout & Asparagus Salad (page 180); Poached White Asparagus; Hollandaise Sauce (page 311); Sauce Malta—Hollandaise Sauce with the juice of 1 blood orange added at the end (page 311); Drawn Butter (page 256); Boiled New Potatoes; Black Forest Ham; Medallions of Beef à la Café de Paris— substitute medallions for New York Strip (page 229); Poached Salmon with Tomatoes and Dill Cream Sauce—omit the tomatoes (page 206)

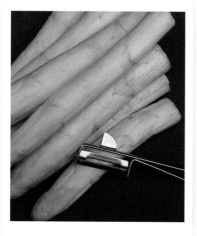

White Asparagus

Peeling Asparagus

Spargelzeit, this route hosts numerous festivals and peeling contests. Schwetzingen's celebrations are among the largest in the Black Forest. This "Asparagus Capital of the World" hosts many eagerly awaited events, the grandest of which is the naming of the annual asparagus king or queen.

GERMANS ARE SO FOND OF ASPARAGUS THAT THEY CONSUME ABOUT 72,000 TONS OF THE VEGETABLE EACH YEAR. During Spargelzeit, they take advantage of the country's abundant crops and are known to enjoy asparagus at least once a day. Restaurants take an active role in the festivities and literally feed this culinary enthusiasm by offering asparagus in almost every way imaginable. Some restaurants refashion their menus completely to accommodate traditional and innovative asparagus dishes. When I was an apprentice at the Hotel Post, and later a young chef at the Sommerberg Hotel, the kitchens remained virtual whirlwinds of activity during the two months of the festival. Not only were we challenging ourselves with new dishes, but we were also constantly busy driving to growers all over the region in an attempt to purchase the freshest and whitest stalks.

The enthusiasm for Spargelzeit is as great today in the Black Forest as when I was a boy and young apprentice. The same excited frenzy continues in restaurants as well, and patrons continue to clamor for asparagus in dishes of all kinds. Some perennial favorites include *Spargel mit Butter* (Asparagus with Butter), *Spargel mit Holländischesoße* (Asparagus with Hollandaise Sauce), and *Spargel mit Schinken* (Asparagus with Ham).

The array of dishes presented below displays a sampling of favorites commonly served during Spargelzeit. Sometimes, as in Smoked Trout and Asparagus Salad, the vegetable is incorporated into the dish. Often, however, the asparagus takes center stage simply poached and served in a beautiful bundle. Other dishes, such as Medallions of Beef à la Café de Paris or Poached Salmon, are also presented to the table on large platters to round out the meal. These entrées are always elegant and beautifully prepared, but it is the perfectly cooked white asparagus that receives the most attention. Prepared with white or green asparagus, these dishes are delicious any time of year, but I hope you will try them especially in the spring when the most tender and flavorful crops are available.

Christmas

WEIHNACHTEN

CHRISTMAS IN THE BLACK FOREST IS SIMPLY MAGICAL. BLANKETS OF SNOW COVER THE REGION, CHRISTMAS LIGHTS SPARKLE AMIDST THE COLD, DARK NIGHTS, PINE DECORATIONS PERFUME THE HOUSES, and families gather around tables laden with lovingly prepared dishes. In typical European fashion, we always celebrated three days of Christmas, beginning on Christmas Eve and ending on the 26th, which we call the second Christmas Day.

When I was a boy, the early days of December were filled with the anticipation of presents, church celebrations, and special foods. My family waited until December 24th to trim the tree and, having accomplished that task, we exchanged gifts as well. The night was one of joy and laughter, but we were always mindful of those who were no longer with us to share such special family time. Honoring and remembering them played a significant role in our Christmas Eve

Weihnachtsfest

APERITIFS

WASSAIL

❧

CHRISTMAS DINNER

CHRISTMAS GOOSE WITH HERBED STUFFING

BRAISED RED CABBAGE

BRUSSELS SPROUTS WITH BACON & FENNEL

POTATO DUMPLINGS

SPÄTZLE

POACHED PEARS

SCHWARZWÄLDER STOLLEN

EGGNOG

Wassail (page 301); Christmas Goose with Herbed Stuffing (page 300); Braised Red Cabbage (page 159); Brussels Sprouts with Bacon & Fennel (page 253); Potato Dumplings (page 162); Spätzle (page 161); Poached Pears (page 275); Schwarzwälder Stollen (page 302); Eggnog (page 303)

celebrations. The activities of that night always included a trip to the cemetery, where we placed little Christmas trees on loved ones' graves. We usually enjoyed a light meal to accommodate these evening events and also to save our energy and appetites for the following day.

Christmas Day was one of great celebration and it centered on two distinct activities: attending church and feasting. Upon returning from morning services, the cooking, eating, and drinking began in earnest. The joyful spirit followed us from church right into the house, where we passed around mugs of eggnog and hot spiced *Glühwein* (wassail). Having refreshed and warmed ourselves, dinner preparation began. It is traditional in the Black Forest to serve either a large venison roast or stuffed goose on Christmas Day. As the menu below reflects, my mother almost always prepared a goose, as she preferred it to venison. Roasted with homemade stuffing, this glistening golden centerpiece was unmistakably the star of the show. Bowls filled with steaming sweet and sour cabbage and spätzle played supporting roles, but they were always beautifully presented and perfect accompaniments to the rich goose. Of course, we finished the meal with my mother's Christmas *Stollen*—a rich, dense cake bejeweled with dried fruit and coated with confectioners' sugar or a glossy sugar glaze.

The festivities continued on second Christmas Day with more gifts and feasting. My mother usually prepared a stuffed veal breast or beef *Rouladen*, and we spent the day with family and friends, drinking, nibbling, and enjoying the Christmas spirit. The reason you make something big is because family members and relatives stop in constantly.

I encourage you to try the recipes above for your holiday celebrations. The Christmas Goose and Stollen take a bit of extra time to prepare, but during the holidays, I always find that extra time in the kitchen with family and friends adds to the joy of the season.

Christmas Goose
with Herbed Stuffing

WEIHNACHTS GANS

Serves 6

HERBED BREAD STUFFING:

1 cup milk

2 medium 1- to 2-day-old baguettes, cut into ¼-inch cubes

1½ pounds bacon, chopped

2 tablespoons unsalted butter

2 medium onions, peeled and finely chopped

2 bunches fresh parsley, stemmed and finely chopped

1 cup chopped chestnuts

4 whole eggs

4 egg yolks

½ cup chopped fresh herbs, such as sage,
    tarragon, thyme, and chives

¼ teaspoon freshly grated nutmeg

Salt

Freshly ground black pepper

ASSEMBLY:

1 goose (about 10 pounds), neck and gizzard discarded

Salt

Freshly ground black pepper

SAUCE:

1 medium onion, peeled and finely chopped (about 1 cup)

½ medium celery root, peeled and finely chopped (about 1 cup)

3 medium carrots, peeled and finely chopped (about 1 cup)

¼ cup all-purpose flour

1 cup red wine, such as Burgundy

2 cups Chicken Stock (page 308)

½ cup heavy cream

Salt

Freshly ground black pepper

1. To make the stuffing, bring the milk to a simmer in a small saucepan over high heat. Place the bread cubes in a large bowl and pour enough of the milk over the bread to moisten it, tossing to coat. (Depending on the dryness of the bread, you might not need all of the milk.) Set aside while preparing the remaining ingredients.

2. Heat a medium sauté pan over medium-high heat, add the bacon, and sauté until crisp and golden. Remove the bacon to paper towels to drain.

3. Melt the butter in a large sauté pan over medium-high heat, add the onions, and sauté until translucent and slightly softened, about 1½ minutes. Stir in the parsley and sauté for 1 minute more. Remove from the heat and set aside to cool.

4. Add the drained bacon, sautéed onion and parsley, chestnuts, eggs, egg yolks, chopped herbs, and nutmeg to the moistened bread, tossing gently to combine. Season with salt and pepper and set aside for about 30 minutes.

5. Preheat the oven to 425°F.

6. To assemble the goose, set a rack in a large roasting pan. Rinse the goose inside and out with cold water and pat completely dry. Season the cavity with salt and pepper and fill loosely with the stuffing. (If there is any stuffing left over, place

it in a buttered casserole dish and bake until golden along with the goose.) Tie the legs together with kitchen twine and place breast side up on the rack.

7. Roast uncovered until the skin is golden brown, basting frequently, about 20 minutes. Reduce the oven temperature to 350°F., cover the goose with foil, and continue to roast for 1½ hours, basting frequently. Remove the foil and roast until a meat thermometer inserted in the thigh registers 185°F., about another 10 minutes. Remove the goose from the pan and cover loosely with foil to keep warm and rest while preparing the sauce.

8. To make the sauce, discard all but about ¼ cup of drippings from the roasting pan and set the pan over medium heat. Add the onion, celery root, and carrots and sauté until the vegetables are softened, about 5 minutes. Sprinkle the flour over the vegetables, stirring to incorporate. Pour in the wine to deglaze, stirring with a wooden spoon to loosen any browned bits on the bottom of the pan. Stir in the chicken stock, bring to a simmer, and cook, stirring frequently, until thickened, about 3 minutes. Strain the sauce through a fine mesh strainer, stir in the cream, and season with salt and pepper.

9. To serve, present the goose on a platter and serve the sauce in a gravy boat.

Wassail

GLÜHWEIN

Makes 8 cups

Zest of 1 medium orange

Zest of 1 medium lemon

10 whole cloves

5 sticks cinnamon

2 (750ml) bottles red wine, such as Burgundy

½ cup dark brown sugar

⅛ teaspoon freshly grated nutmeg

1. Place the orange and lemon rinds, cloves, and cinnamon sticks on a square (about 6 x 6-inch) piece of cotton cheesecloth and tie in a bundle with kitchen twine to make a sachet.

2. Heat the wine in a large saucepan over low heat. Stir in the sugar, add the sachet, and gently simmer (do not boil) until the sugar is melted and the wassail is fragrant, about 10 minutes.

3. Remove and discard the sachet and serve in a heatproof punch bowl.

Schwarzwälder Stollen

Makes four 1-pound loaves

¼ cup chopped glacé cherries

½ cup chopped Candied Citrus Peel (page 316)

¼ cup chopped dried apricots

⅓ cup chopped dried figs

½ cup golden raisins

½ cup dark raisins

½ cup chopped almonds

½ cup chopped walnuts

⅓ cup chopped chestnuts

½ cup dark rum

Zest of 1 lemon

2 tablespoons active dry yeast

¾ cup milk, warmed

1½ teaspoons salt

1 tablespoon honey

3 tablespoons sugar

2 eggs

¼ teaspoon ground cloves

1½ teaspoons ground cardamom

1 teaspoon freshly ground cinnamon

½ teaspoon freshly ground allspice

¼ teaspoon freshly grated nutmeg

2¾ cups bread flour

½ pound plus 2 tablespoons (2¼ sticks)
   unsalted butter, softened

½ cup almond paste

GLAZE:

4 cups confectioners' sugar, sifted

3 tablespoons milk

1. At least 24 hours before baking the stollen, combine the dried fruit and nuts in a large bowl. Stir in the rum and lemon zest, cover the bowl with plastic wrap, and set aside to macerate at room temperature for at least 24 hours, stirring occasionally.

2. The next day or when you are ready to proceed with the recipe, stir together the yeast and milk in a large bowl. Add the salt, honey, sugar, eggs, and spices, whisking to combine. Mix in about 1½ cups of the bread flour, stirring until incorporated. Add the butter and remaining flour and again stir until incorporated.

3. Turn the dough out onto a floured work surface and knead until the dough is smooth and elastic. Place the dough in a lightly oiled large bowl, cover with a kitchen towel, and set aside in a warm area until it has doubled in volume, about 1 hour.

4. Turn the risen dough onto a floured work surface and knead in the macerated fruit mixture and almond paste by hand. Place the dough again in a large oiled bowl, again cover with a kitchen towel, and set aside in a warm area until it has once again doubled in volume, about 45 minutes.

5. Turn the dough out again onto a lightly floured work surface, press it to expel any air, and divide it into 4 equal portions. Shape the pieces into oval loaves about 8 inches long and 2 inches wide, reincorporating any fruit that might have escaped, and rolling each loaf to slightly taper the ends.

6. Arrange the loaves on heavy-bottomed parchment-lined sheet pans and set aside in a warm area until they have risen to one and one-half times their original size.

7. Preheat the oven to 350°F.

8. Bake the stollen until golden brown, about 45 minutes. Place the loaves on a wire rack and cool completely before glazing.

9. To make the glaze, stir together the confectioners' sugar and milk in a large bowl until smooth. Spread liberally over the stollen and set aside to dry for about 10 minutes before serving.

Eggnog
EIER LIKÖR

Makes about 6 cups

7 large egg yolks

¾ cup sugar

2 cups heavy cream

1 cup milk

¾ cup bourbon

¾ cup rum

¼ cup brandy

Freshly grated nutmeg, for garnish

1. Combine the egg yolks and sugar in the bowl of an electric mixer fitted with the whip attachment. Beat on high speed until thickened and pale yellow, about 5 minutes.

2. Reduce the mixing speed to medium and gradually add the cream, milk, bourbon, rum, and brandy, mixing just until incorporated. Cover and refrigerate until completely chilled.

3. Serve the eggnog in a punch bowl or in individual cups and garnish with nutmeg.

Saint Sylvester Night

HEILIGE SILVESTERNACHT

OF ALL THE HOLIDAYS IN THE BLACK FOREST, *SILVESTER*—OUR NEW YEAR'S EVE—IS THE LARGEST AND GRANDEST OF THE YEAR. THROUGHOUT GERMANY, IN FACT, THIS MAGICAL NIGHT IS FILLED with an array of festive events. Although most have come to celebrate Silvester (also called *Silvesternacht* and *Silvesterabend*) with swanky concerts and elegant dinners, the holiday is about more than simply parties and noisemakers.

Silvester actually takes its name from the Catholic Feast of Saint Sylvester, which is also celebrated on December 31st. Before Sylvester was canonized, he was first elected Pope Sylvester I, his pontificate lasting from the year 314 until his death in 335. He is most recognized for his participation in the Council of Nicea, baptizing the Emperor Constantine, and leading the Church in its triumph over Roman paganism.

In the Black Forest, as in the rest of Germany, the Feast of Saint Sylvester and his namesake New Year's celebrations have merged into a single festive holiday defined by elegance, grand

Fête de
Saint Sylvestre

♦

FIRST COURSE

SMOKED TROUT & ASPARAGUS SALAD

♦

SECOND COURSE

VOL-AU-VENT WITH SWEET BREADS
EN MINIATURE

♦

SOUP COURSE

MUSHROOM BISQUE

♦

FISH COURSE

PAUPIETTE OF TROUT

♦

ENTRÉE

FILET OF VEAL WITH FOIE GRAS
Macaire Potatoes

♦

DESSERT

CHOCOLATE SOUFFLÉ

Smoked Trout & Asparagus Salad (page 180); Vol-au-Vent with Sweet Breads en Miniature (page 188); Mushroom Bisque (page 197); Paupiette of Trout (page 212); Filet of Veal with Foie Gras (page 239); Macaire Potatoes (page 265); Chocolate Soufflé (page 282) affairs, and opulent food. Most events begin in the evening and extend into the early hours of morning. Some revelers enjoy a light meal around five o'clock, but usually it isn't until after at least nine o'clock that the *Silvesterfeiern* (New Year's Eve parties) begin. Many of these late nights commence at

the opera or theater and continue at elaborate masquerade balls, for which guests plan costumes and attire months in advance.

Partygoers look forward to festive food and drink at every affair. If there is one night to splurge on culinary finery, this is the one. To celebrate in high style, many patrons reserve tables at restaurants featuring formal multi-course dinners. Hotel restaurants in particular go to great lengths to elegantly outfit their dining rooms for such extravagant events. With great care and attention to detail, wait staff set tables with special china, shining silver, sparkling crystal, and shimmering damask linens, reserved especially for this night. Silvester menus, of course, complement the fashionable settings and feature a variety of special dishes, each gorgeously presented and prepared with expensive del-

icacies. Shark-fin soup, poached carp, beef Wellington, quail eggs decorated with gold leaf, and caviar are among the traditional favorites. Others, represented in the above menu, include Vol-au-Vent with Sweetbreads, Paupiette of Trout, and Filet of Veal with Foie Gras. Each restaurant pairs these dishes with its best wines and Champagnes, virtually ensuring that guests will welcome the New Year in the most spirited fashion.

Although pork infrequently appears on Silvester menus, pigs are considered good luck for the New Year and are theatrically showcased in the dining room. The performance is most often assigned to a culinary apprentice, or *commis*. Inspiring much revelry and cheer, he walks through the dining room holding a piglet, which the patrons are invited to pet for good luck. Even pastry chefs take part in this popular folklore. They spend hours sculpting little marzipan piglets, each with a brand new good luck penny in its mouth, for the evening's artfully arranged petit four trays.

The Black Forest is filled with traditions of all sorts, and Silvester represents the most elaborate of them all. The menu I have compiled is quite an elegant one, each dish requiring a fair amount of preparation time. I guarantee that you will dazzle your guests with this array of dishes, but you can certainly impress them by simply serving one or two. Regardless of the other festivities that may occupy your New Year's Eve, dining on such elegant dishes is sure to make the holiday particularly joyful and delicious.

THE
BLACK FOREST
PANTRY

Chicken Stock

GEFLÜGELFOND

Chicken stock is essential to so many dishes that in restaurant kitchens we make and keep on hand literally gallons of the golden liquid, preparing it fresh many times a week. Once you make homemade stock you will never go back to the canned variety. It freezes so well, after one afternoon's worth of work, you can keep it on hand for several weeks at a time.

---

1. Rinse the chicken in cold running water and trim off any excess fat. Place the chicken in a 12-quart stockpot and pour in the water. Add the remaining ingredients and bring to a boil over medium-high heat. Reduce heat to medium and simmer gently until fully cooked, occasionally removing any foam that rises to the surface, about 30 minutes. Remove the chicken and reserve for use in another dish.

2. Continue to simmer the stock until it is reduced to about 5 quarts, about 1½ hours more.

3. Line a large colander or fine mesh strainer with two layers of cheesecloth, set in a large bowl, and strain the stock.

4. Return the stock to the pan and bring to a boil over medium heat. Reduce the heat to low and simmer until reduced by half to 2½ quarts, about 4 hours.

5. Cool the stock in an ice bath and pour into jars or plastic containers. Refrigerate for up to 1 week.

Makes 2½ quarts

1 stewing chicken or hen (about 4½ pounds), whole or cut into eight pieces (see Chef's Note)

2½ gallons water

½ celery root, skin on, coarsely chopped

2 carrots, peeled and coarsely chopped

2 medium onions, peeled and coarsely chopped

1 leek, trimmed, cut in half lengthwise and rinsed thoroughly

1 dried bay leaf

4 sprigs fresh thyme

½ bunch fresh parsley

12 whole black peppercorns, crushed

CHEF'S NOTE: Stewing chickens (also called hens, boiling fowl, or simply fowl) are usually between 10 and 18 months old and weigh between three and six pounds. Because they are older and larger than roasting chickens, they are more flavorful but also less tender. These qualities thus make them particularly good candidates for stewing and making rich golden stock. There is an alternative, though, to cooking a whole chicken. Simply use chicken necks and backs, which are certainly inexpensive and full of flavor.

Marinade for Beef, Pork, Game, or Chicken

BEIZE FÜR RIND, SCHWEIN, WILD ODER GEFLÜGEL

THIS FLAVORFUL MARINADE ADDS INTENSITY AND CHARACTER TO ANY BEEF, PORK, RABBIT, OR CHICKEN RECIPE. SIMPLY COMBINE THE INGREDIENTS AND FOLLOW THE MARINATING INSTRUCTIONS FOR THE PARTICULAR RECIPE YOU ARE PREPARING.

Makes 1 quart

1 medium onion, peeled and thinly sliced

1 clove garlic, peeled and crushed

1 small carrot, peeled and thinly sliced

1 rib celery, chopped

2 tablespoons chopped fresh parsley

3 whole black peppercorns

1 dried bay leaf

1 sprig fresh thyme

2 cups full-bodied red wine, such as Burgundy

½ cup red wine vinegar

½ cup brandy or Cognac

1 tablespoon vegetable oil

1 teaspoon salt

½ teaspoon freshly ground black pepper

Combine all of the ingredients in a large container or saucepan and use to marinate beef, pork, rabbit, or chicken as the recipe advises.

CHEF'S NOTE: When marinating game, add rosemary and/or sage for a fuller, more robust flavor.

Beef Bouillon

RINDER KRAFTBRÜHE

Makes 3 quarts

4 pounds meaty beef or veal bones, such as neck bones, shank pieces, short ribs, knuckles, or leg bones with marrow

9 quarts water

2 garlic cloves, peeled and lightly crushed

1 leek, trimmed, cut in half lengthwise, and rinsed thoroughly

1 celery root, skin on, coarsely chopped

3 carrots, peeled and coarsely chopped

2 tomatoes, seeded and coarsely chopped

½ bunch fresh parsley

1 dried bay leaf

2 sprigs fresh thyme

2 whole cloves

2 tablespoons salt

1 teaspoon cracked black pepper

1. Combine all ingredients in a 12-quart stockpot and bring to a boil over high heat. Reduce the heat to low and simmer for 1½ hours, occasionally removing any foam that rises to the surface.

2. Line a large colander or fine mesh strainer with two layers of cheesecloth, set in a large bowl, and strain the bouillon.

3. Return the bouillon to the pot and simmer until reduced to 3 quarts.

4. Cool the bouillon in an ice bath and pour into jars or plastic containers. Refrigerate for up to 1 week.

Beef Stock

RINDER FOND

BEEF STOCK IS A STAPLE IN EVERY RESTAURANT KITCHEN. WITH A LITTLE PREPARATION AND TIME IT IS ALSO EASY TO MAKE AT HOME. FREEZE THIS STOCK AND KEEP IT ON HAND FOR ROASTS, STEWS, AND SAUCES.

---

1. Preheat the oven to 350°F.

2. Place the bones in a large roasting pan and roast, turning the bones once, until the meat and bones are well browned, about 1 to 1½ hours.

3. Drain the fat from the roasting pan, add the wine to deglaze, stirring with a wooden spoon to loosen any browned bits on the bottom of the pan.

4. Increase the oven temperature to 375°F. Add the celery, carrots, onion, and garlic to the pan, place back in the oven, and roast for 15 minutes.

5. Remove the pan from the oven, pour in the water, and bring to a boil over medium-high heat. Stir in the tomato paste, leek, bay leaves, parsley, thyme, peppercorns, and browned meat and bones, and return to a boil. Reduce the heat to low and simmer, occasionally removing any foam that rises to the surface, until the stock is reduced to 2 quarts, about 4 hours.

5. Line a large colander or fine mesh strainer with two layers of cheesecloth, set in a large bowl, and strain the stock.

6. Cool the stock in an ice bath and pour into jars or plastic containers. Refrigerate for up to 1 week.

Makes 3 quarts

3 pounds meaty beef or veal bones, such as neck bones, shank pieces, short ribs, knuckles, or leg bones with marrow

3 cups full-bodied red wine, such as Burgundy

1 celery root, skin on, coarsely chopped

2 carrots, peeled and coarsely chopped

1 large white onion, peeled and coarsely chopped

6 garlic cloves, peeled and lightly crushed

2 gallons water, chilled

1 (6-ounce) can tomato paste

1 leek, trimmed, cut in half lengthwise, and rinsed thoroughly

3 dried bay leaves

1 small bunch fresh parsley

4 sprigs fresh thyme

12 white peppercorns

Vegetable Stock

GEMÜSE FOND

THIS STOCK IS A FLAVORFUL ALTERNATIVE TO CHICKEN OR BEEF STOCK. IT COMES TOGETHER EASILY AND STORES WELL.

Makes 2 quarts

1 gallon water

1 celery root, skin on, coarsely chopped

3 carrots, peeled and coarsely chopped

2 medium white onions, peeled and coarsely chopped

2 large ripe tomatoes

1 leek, trimmed, cut in half lengthwise, and rinsed thoroughly

3 dried bay leaves

6 garlic cloves, peeled and lightly crushed

1 small bunch fresh parsley

4 sprigs fresh thyme

12 white peppercorns

1. Combine all of the ingredients in a large (at least 2-gallon) stockpot and bring to a boil over medium-high heat. Reduce the heat to low and simmer until the stock is reduced to 2 quarts, about 4 hours.

2. Line a large colander or fine mesh strainer with two layers of cheesecloth, set in a large bowl, and strain the stock.

3. Cool the stock in an ice bath and pour into jars or plastic containers. Refrigerate for up to 1 week.

Hollandaise Sauce

HOLLÄNDISCHESOßE

REGARDLESS OF ITS REPUTATION, THERE IS SIMPLY NO NEED FOR HOLLANDAISE SAUCE TO BE INTIMIDATING. THIS RECIPE REQUIRES JUST A BIT OF TIME AND ATTENTION, BUT IT COMES TOGETHER EASILY, AND THE RICH FLAVOR AND VELVETY TEXTURE ARE WELL WORTH THE EFFORT EVERY TIME.

Makes 1½ cups

4 large egg yolks

Juice of 1 large lemon (about 3 tablespoons)

1 tablespoon dry white wine, such as Sauvignon Blanc

About ⅛ teaspoon cayenne pepper

1 cup clarified butter (see Chef's Note, page 254)

Salt

Freshly ground white pepper

1. Prepare a double boiler and maintain at a simmer over low heat. Whisk together the egg yolks, lemon juice, and wine in the top portion until light yellow and thick, removing the pan occasionally to prevent overheating and scrambling the eggs.

2. Add the cayenne pepper and, in a slow, steady stream, add the clarified butter, whisking until the sauce is emulsified. (Add a few drops of wine if the sauce is too thick.)

3. Season with salt and white pepper and set aside to keep warm or serve immediately.

Demi-Glace

BRAUNE KRAFTSOßE

Makes 7 cups

½ pound (2 sticks) unsalted butter

½ cup chopped shallots

1 cup sliced white button mushrooms

3 Roma tomatoes, coarsely chopped

3 tablespoons tomato paste

3 cups full-bodied red wine, such as Burgundy

7 cups Beef Stock (page 310)

½ cup chopped leek

2 sprigs fresh thyme (or 1 teaspoon dried thyme)

6 tablespoons all-purpose flour

DEMI-GLACE IS ANOTHER FRENCH SAUCE THAT EVERY SELF-RESPECTING RESTAURANT KEEPS ON HAND. AS AN APPRENTICE, I PREPARED IT THOUSANDS OF TIMES FOR USE IN A VARIETY OF OTHER SAUCES AND DISHES.

ALSO CALLED BROWN SAUCE, DEMI-GLACE IS TRADITIONALLY PREPARED WITH WHAT THE FRENCH REFER TO AS ESPAGNOLE SAUCE (A MIXTURE OF BROWN STOCK, VEGETABLES, BROWN ROUX, AND TOMATOES), BROWN STOCK, AND MADEIRA OR SHERRY. I HAVE SIMPLIFIED THIS METHOD TO CREATE A FLAVORFUL SAUCE YOU CAN KEEP ON HAND TO ADD INTENSE FLAVOR TO A NUMBER OF DISHES.

CHEF'S NOTE: When reheating, add a bit of red wine to the demi-glace and bring to a boil over medium heat. Remove from heat and whisk in 1 tablespoon of room temperature butter per cup of demi-glace before serving to ensure proper consistency and flavor.

1. Melt 4 tablespoons of the butter in a large saucepan over medium heat, add the shallots, and sauté until translucent, about 2 to 3 minutes. Toss in the mushrooms and tomatoes and sauté until any liquid they release has evaporated.

2. Stir in the tomato paste, then add 1 cup of the wine to deglaze, stirring with a wooden spoon to loosen any browned bits on the bottom of the pan. Simmer until almost dry, then deglaze with 1 more cup of the wine. Simmer until almost dry again.

3. Add the remaining cup of wine, stock, tomato, leek and thyme, and bring to a boil. Reduce the heat to low and simmer for about 15 to 20 minutes.

4. In a medium bowl, knead together the flour and remaining butter to form a paste (beurre manié). Whisk this paste into the demi-glace and simmer for about 15 to 20 minutes, or until the sauce is smooth and velvety.

5. Strain through a fine mesh sieve and cool the demi-glace in an ice bath. Pour into a jar or plastic container and refrigerate for up to 1 week.

Béchamel Sauce

WEIßE GRUND SOßE

As a young apprentice, béchamel was one of the four French "mother sauces" I learned to master. This thick, rich, milk-based sauce is often used on its own, draped over fish or poultry, or as an integral creamy component of a variety of stews, casseroles, and baked pasta dishes, such as lasagna.

Makes about 1½ cups

1½ cups milk

2 tablespoons unsalted butter

1 small onion, peeled and finely chopped

2 tablespoons all-purpose flour

1 teaspoon salt

1 whole clove

1 dried bay leaf

⅛ teaspoon freshly grated nutmeg

Salt

Freshly ground white pepper

1. Bring the milk to a boil in a small saucepan over high heat. Remove from the heat and set aside to keep warm.

2. Melt the butter in a medium saucepan over medium heat, add the onion, and sauté until softened and translucent, about 3 minutes. Gradually stir in the flour to form a roux, and cook, stirring frequently, until well combined, about 1 minute.

3. Gradually whisk in the reserved warm milk, bring the mixture to a boil, and add the salt, clove, bay leaf, and nutmeg. Reduce the heat to low and simmer until thickened to the consistency of medium gravy, about 20 minutes.

4. Season with salt and pepper and strain through a fine mesh strainer. Set aside to keep warm for serving, or pour into a jar or plastic container and store in the refrigerator for up to 1 week.

Mayonnaise

Fresh, homemade mayonnaise is always preferable to the store-bought variety. This recipe is so easy and delicious that you might decide to permanently cross this jarred item off your shopping list.

Makes about 1½ cups

3 large egg yolks

1 teaspoon lemon juice

1 tablespoon white wine vinegar

1 teaspoon sugar

1½ cups vegetable oil

Salt

Freshly ground white pepper

1. Combine the egg yolks, lemon juice, vinegar, and sugar in a blender or in the bowl of a food processor fitted with the blade attachment. Begin blending on high speed and whip until thick and light yellow in color. Pouring in a slow, steady stream, add the oil, continuing to blend until thickened and emulsified.

2. Season with salt and white pepper and transfer the mayonnaise to a storage or serving bowl. Cover and store in the refrigerator for up to 3 days.

Pickles

GEWÜRZGURKEN

Dill pickles are prepared often at home and in restaurants in the Black Forest. This is an easy, tasty recipe that just might wean you from the store-bought varieties.

Makes 2 pounds

2 pounds whole gherkin cucumbers

3 quarts white vinegar

1 quart water

¾ cup salt

¼ cup whole peppercorns

8 whole garlic cloves, peeled

3 whole cloves

3 dried bay leaves

1½ tablespoons sugar

½ cup dried dill

1. Wash the cucumbers thoroughly in salt water and place in a large heatproof container, crock, or saucepan.

2. Combine the remaining ingredients in a large saucepan and bring to a boil over high heat. Remove from heat and pour over the cucumbers, immersing them completely. Cover and set aside in the refrigerator or in a cool area to cure for at least 3 days before serving.

Pâte Brisée

PÂTE BRISÉE IS REALLY JUST THE FRENCH TERM FOR SHORT PASTRY, OR PIE DOUGH. MIXING TOGETHER BUTTER AND SHORTENING GIVES THIS PASTRY A DELICATE FLAVOR AND A FLAKY TEXTURE THAT ARE WELL SUITED TO NEARLY ALL TYPES OF FRUIT OR CREAM PIE.

Makes 12 ounces,
or enough for one 9-inch pie crust

1⅓ cups all-purpose flour, sifted
¼ teaspoon salt
4 tablespoons unsalted butter, chilled and cubed
4 tablespoons vegetable shortening, chilled
4 to 5 tablespoons ice water

1. Stir together the flour and salt in a medium bowl. Add the butter and shortening and, using a pastry cutter or two knives, incorporate into the flour until the mixture resembles coarse crumbs.

2. Add the water, 1 tablespoon at a time, tossing the dough together with a fork, until it starts to come together. (The dough will be a little sticky.)

3. Form the dough into a disk and wrap in plastic wrap. Chill in the refrigerator for at least 30 minutes before using, or store in the freezer for up to 2 months.

Pâte Sucrée

THIS PASTRY IS RICHER AND SWEETER THAN REGULAR SHORT PASTRY, OR PÂTE BRISÉE. IN ADDITION TO PIES AND TARTS, IT IS ALSO WELL SUITED TO FILLED COOKIES.

Makes 2 pounds,
or enough for one 9-inch double crust pie

3 cups all-purpose flour, sifted
¼ cup sugar
½ pound (2 sticks) unsalted butter, chilled and cubed
2 large eggs

1. Combine the flour and sugar in the bowl of a food processor fitted with the blade attachment and pulse to combine. Add the butter and pulse until the mixture is crumbly.

2. With the processor running, add the eggs, stopping once to scrape the sides of the bowl. Continue processing just until the dough comes together.

3. Form the dough into a disk and wrap in plastic wrap. Chill in the refrigerator for at least 1 hour before using, or store in the freezer for up to 2 months.

Candied Citrus Peel

ORANGEADE & CITRONADE

1. Using a paring knife, carefully remove the rind from the oranges (or lemons) and slice into strips about 2½ inches long and ¼ inch wide. (Try to leave as little of the bitter white pith on the slices as possible and scrape it off of the slices if necessary.)

2. Bring a large saucepan of water to a boil. Carefully place a few of the orange peel slices in the water, blanching them for about 20 seconds. Strain the slices and repeat the process with the remaining slices.

3. Return the orange peel to the pan and add 4 cups of water and 6 cups of sugar. Bring to a boil over medium-high heat, reduce the heat to low, and simmer until the slices are translucent and softened and the sugar water is syrupy, about 10 to 20 minutes. Remove from the heat, cover when cool, and set aside at room temperature for at least 8 hours or overnight.

4. The next day or when you are ready to finish the peel, place the remaining 4 cups of sugar in a shallow dish, strain the orange slices from the syrup, and toss in the sugar, coating the slices generously. Arrange the slices on a wire rack and set aside for at least 8 hours, or until the sugar coating is firm and the slices are no longer sticky. Store the candied peel in an airtight container at room temperature for up to 3 weeks.

CANDYING ORANGE AND LEMON PEEL HAS ALWAYS BEEN A TASTY WAY TO USE EVERY BIT OF WINTER CITRUS FRUIT. THIS WAS ESPECIALLY IMPORTANT CENTURIES AGO, WHEN CITRUS WAS QUITE COSTLY AND RARE. TODAY, OF COURSE, ORANGES AND LEMONS ARE AVAILABLE YEAR-ROUND AND WE CAN PREPARE CANDIED PEEL ANYTIME.

THESE DELICATE STRIPS OF SUGARY CITRUS ARE DELICIOUS ON THEIR OWN, AS WELL AS STIRRED INTO A VARIETY OF BAKED GOODS FOR A BIT OF ZESTY SWEETNESS.

Makes 4 cups

8 oranges, or 12 lemons

4 cups water

10 cups sugar

Candied Ginger

GLACIERTE INGWER

1. Place the ginger in a medium saucepan, add enough water to cover, and bring to a boil over medium-high heat. Immediately remove from heat, strain, and set aside to cool to room temperature.

2. Slice the cooled ginger into ¼-inch-thick slices and bring a large saucepan of water to a boil. Carefully place some of the ginger slices in the water, blanching them for about 20 seconds. Strain the slices and repeat the process with the remaining slices.

3. Return the ginger to the pan and add the 4 cups water and 6 cups of the sugar. Bring to a boil over medium-high heat, reduce the heat to low, and simmer until the ginger slices are translucent and softened and the sugar water is syrupy, about 10 to 20 minutes. Remove from the heat, cover when cool, and set aside at room temperature for at least 8 hours or overnight.

4. The next day or when you are ready to finish the ginger, place the remaining 4 cups of sugar in a shallow dish, strain the ginger slices from the syrup, and toss in the sugar, coating the slices generously. Arrange the slices on a wire rack and set aside for at least 8 hours, or until the sugar coating is firm and the slices are no longer sticky. Store the candied ginger in an airtight container at room temperature for up to 3 weeks.

CANDIED GINGER IS DELICIOUS SERVED AS A SWEET SNACK WITH TEA, AS PART OF A PRETTY PETITS FOURS TRAY, OR MIXED INTO A VARIETY OF CAKES AND PASTRIES.

Makes 4 cups

1 pound fresh ginger, peeled

4 cups water

10 cups granulated sugar

Pear or Apple Preserves

APFEL ODER BIRNEN MARMELADE

1. Place the pears in a large saucepan and cook over medium heat, stirring occasionally until the fruit is slightly softened, about 2 minutes.

2. Stir in the lemon zest, ginger, cinnamon stick, and sugar and cook, stirring occasionally until the sugar is dissolved, about 3 minutes. Reduce the heat to low and simmer, skimming any foam that rises to the surface and stirring occasionally, until the preserves reach a setting point, about 30 minutes. They are set when a candy thermometer placed in the simmering preserves reads 220°F., or when a spoonful of preserves placed on a cold plate begins to set within about 15 seconds.

3. Remove the preserves from the heat and, lift out the cinnamon stick. Immediately spoon the preserves into sterilized jars and seal. Set on wire racks to cool completely and store in the refrigerator.

In the Black Forest, we preserve pears and apples (and many other fruits) in a variety of ways. The most beautiful apples and pears, for example, are preserved whole in sugar syrup and stored in large jars. Other less attractive but equally delicious specimens are used to make eau de vie (Schnaps) or thick preserves, which we enjoy as spreads or sweet additions to piping hot bowls of cream of wheat. Yet another way we preserve fruit is by drying it in the sun on big linen sheets and hanging it, wrapped in burlap, in the larder. This dried fruit is then reconstituted and used in baked goods, or again stirred into hot cereal where it becomes plump and tender.

These preserves are a delicious way to enjoy flavorful fall pears and/or apples. The lemon zest brightens these sweet preserves, and the ginger and cinnamon (if you choose to use them) lend a delicate spiciness that beautifully complements the fruit.

I suggest spooning the preserves into sterilized jars, but, unless you choose to finish the preserving process by boiling the jars in a water bath, you will still need to refrigerate them.

Makes 3 to 4 cups

4 pears or apples, peeled, cored,
   and chopped (about 6 cups)

1 teaspoon finely chopped lemon zest

2 tablespoons finely chopped ginger (optional)

1 stick cinnamon (optional)

5 cups sugar

Summer Berry Preserves

FRÜCHTE MARMELADE

Threa is a great way to preserve summer berries, although out-of-season frozen berries work just as well. This recipe requires a bit of time and patience, and I recommend giving the preserves your entire attention as they cook to prevent them from burning or boiling too rapidly. The result is well worth the effort, though. The preserves are richly colored and filled with tender pieces of sweet fruit that are as delicious on toast as they are swirled into hot cream of wheat, as my mother used to prepare.

As with all homemade preserves, I suggest spooning these preserves into sterilized jars, but, unless you choose to finish the preserving process by boiling the jars in a water bath, you will still need to refrigerate them.

Makes about 3 cups

16 ounces mixed berries (about 3 cups),
    such as blackberries, raspberries, strawberries,
    gooseberries, or blueberries
½ cup water
1 tablespoon freshly squeezed lemon juice
2½ cups sugar

---

1. Combine the berries and water in a medium saucepan. Bring to a simmer over medium heat, cooking until the berries are soft and juicy, about 7 minutes.

2. Stir in the lemon juice and sugar and cook, stirring occasionally until the sugar is dissolved, about 3 minutes. Reduce the heat to low and simmer, skimming any foam that rises to the surface and stirring occasionally, until the preserves reach a setting point, about 30 to 40 minutes. They are set when a candy thermometer placed in the simmering preserves reads 220°F., or when a small spoonful of preserves placed on a cold plate begins to set within about 15 seconds.

3. Remove the preserves from the heat, immediately spoon into sterilized jars, and seal. Set on wire racks to cool completely and store in the refrigerator.

Sources

D'Artagnan
800-327-8246
www.dartagnan.com
Fresh, exotic selection of game and fowl,
including venison, pheasant and rabbit,
and fresh and dried exotic mushrooms.
National delivery available.

Dietz and Watson
800-333-1974
www.dietzandwatson.com
Purveyor of the world's best meat delicacies
and artisan cheeses. Available at the finest
supermarkets and neighborhood delis.

More Than Gourmet
800-860-9385
www.morethangourmet.com
Purveyor of chef-quality classic French stocks
and sauces, such as Chicken Stock, Demi-Glace,
or Au Jus, sold in small portions for home use.
National delivery available.

Caviar Assouline
800-521-4492
www.icaviar.com
Purveyor of gourmet foods from all over the
world, including caviar, truffles, truffle oil, foie
gras, and escargots. National delivery available.

JB Prince
800-473-0577
www.jbprince.com
Purveyor of the world's finest chef tools,
including specialty cookware and bakeware,
cutters, pastry bags, spätzle presses, spritz
cookie presses, etc. National delivery available.

Index

Guten Appetit!